FERNIE AT WAR

Caitlin Press Inc.

8100 Alderwood Road, Halfmoon Bay, BC V0N 1Y1
www.caitlin-press.com

Text design and cover design by Vici Johnstone
Maps by Mader & Associates
Edited by Susan Mayse
Printed in Canada

Caitlin Press Inc. acknowledges financial support from the Government of Canada and the Canada Council for the Arts, and the Province of British Columbia
through the British Columbia Arts Council and the Book Publisher's Tax Credit.

Library and Archives Canada Cataloguing in Publication

Norton, Wayne, 1948-, author
        Fernie at war : 1914-1919 / Wayne Norton.

ISBN 978-1-987915-49-5 (softcover) \
        1. Fernie (B.C.)—History—20th century. 2. Fernie (B.C.)—
Social conditions—20th century. 3. World War, 1914-1918—British
Columbia—Fernie. 4. World War, 1914-1918—Social aspects—
British Columbia—Fernie. 5. Canada—History—1914-1918. I. Title.

FC3849.F475N67 2017   971.1'6503   C2017-904595-4

FERNIE AT WAR
1914–1919

BY WAYNE NORTON

CAITLIN PRESS

CONTENTS

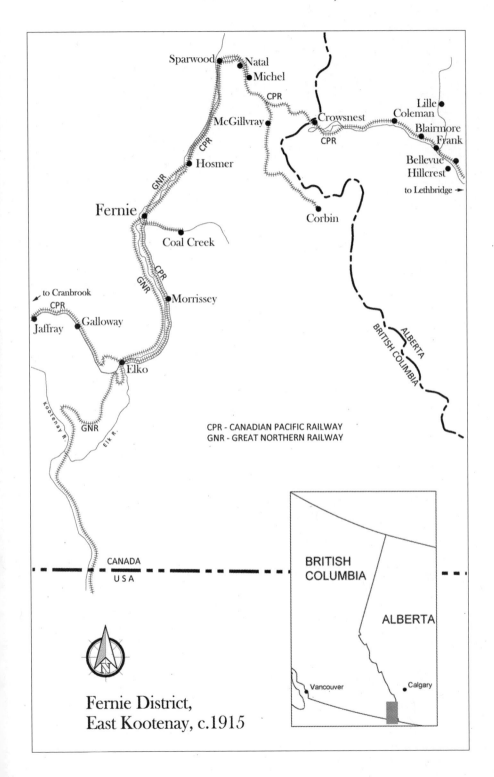

Fernie District,
East Kootenay, c.1915

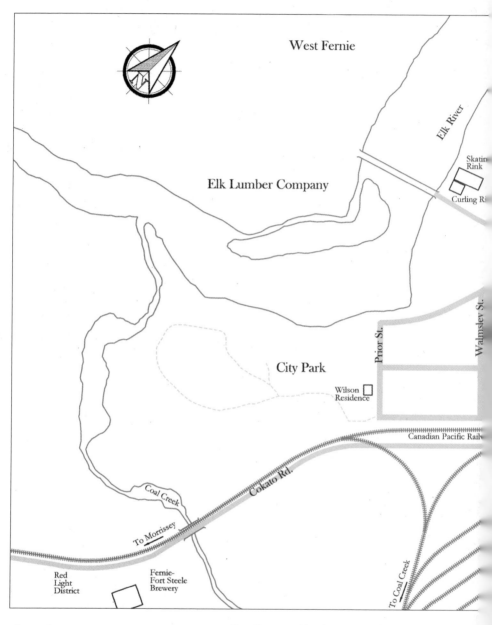

West Fernie

Elk River

Elk Lumber Company

Skating Rink

Curling Ri

Walmsley St.

Prior St.

City Park

Wilson Residence

Canadian Pacific Rail

Coal Creek

Cokato Rd.

To Morrissey

To Coal Creek

Red Light District

Fernie- Fort Steele Brewery

Legend

1. Presbyterian Church
2. Central Hotel
3. Miners' Hall (Grand Theatre)
4. Victoria Hall
5. Fernie Free Press Office
6. King's Hotel
7. Napanee Hotel
8. Socialist Hall
9. District Ledger Office and U.M.W.A. District 18 Headquarters
10. Recruiting Office of 54th Kootenay Battalion
11. Hotel Fernie
12. Trites – Wood Store

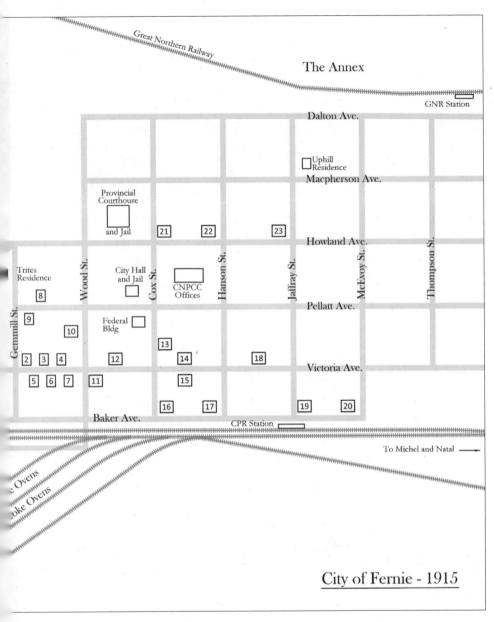

City of Fernie - 1915

13. Salvation Army Hall
14. Northern Hotel
15. Waldorf Hotel
16. Royal Hotel
17. Imperial Hotel
18. 41 Market Company Store
19. Roma Hotel
20. Queen's Hotel

21. Church of England
22. Catholic Church
23. Baptist Church

Maps by Mader & Associates.

MARCH AND TWO-STEP

I'm Only a Khaki-clad Soldier And I Hail from Old B.C.

Words by
HARRY L. SHAW

Music by
GEORGE W. CHALMERS

WESTERN SPECIALTY LIMITED, MUSIC PRINTERS, VANCOUVER, B.C.

Courtesy of the author.

FOREWORD

by Stephen Hume

Throughout the sun-burnished late summer and fall of 1914 and on into 1915, troop trains chugged tirelessly through British Columbia's tawny interior. All through the boundary country, the Crowsnest Pass, the Kootenays, from mining towns like Fernie and Coal Creek to the grasslands around Ashcroft, from the Okanagan's leafy green orchards to the dusty valleys of the Monashee and Selkirk mountains, young men flocked to enlist with regiments bearing nicknames like the Kootenay Borderers, the Rocky Mountain Rangers, Tuxford's Dandies and Tobin's Tigers. They were cowboys and coal miners, company clerks and farm hands, surveyors and trappers. They came in on horseback from Kettle Valley ranches and mustered in civilian clothes at the corner of Nanaimo and Martin streets in Penticton. Many were infused with an intoxicating mix of patriotism, youthful dreams of glory and romantic notions of imperialistic adventure fuelled by tales from *Boy's Own Magazine* and the writing of H. Rider Haggard and Rudyard Kipling.

One of those trains, jammed with volunteers who included men from Fernie and the Kootenays, finally arrived at Penticton en route to France and The Great War. The sweltering journey had been delayed twice by washouts on the recently completed Kettle Valley Railway, which connected Midway to the South Okanagan Valley. As the train pulled into the station, the excited recruits were greeted by the girls and women of the lake city. Faces glowing, the women stepped out to the railway cars wearing long, white dresses and big summer hats. The cherry crop was in harvest. The *Penticton Herald* reported that the equally excited women reached up to hand the troops bags of fat, sweet Bing cherries, a quarter of a ton of the dark, succulent fruit favoured by orchardists a century ago.

The laughing, khaki-clad soldiers transferred to a sternwheeler for their trip down Okanagan Lake to connect with the Canadian Pacific Railway at Vernon's army camp. As the ship glided down the glassy lake reflecting the blue sky, fluffy white clouds, green orchards and golden grasslands flanking rugged hills, the men ate their cherries and spat their pits over the rail. Soon the gleaming white paint of the ship's sides was streaked with long, crimson stains of cherry juice.

The image makes for a striking metaphor. Few of those young men or the mothers, sisters, sweethearts and families they were leaving behind could yet imagine the horrors of industrialized carnage—a new kind of war for the factory age—that awaited them. By the end of 1915, those schoolboy dreams of glory had devolved into a nightmare of muck, corpse-fed rats, flooded craters oozing gas that would flay a man's skin and brutal night raids with clubs, axes and bayonets. A constant threat from snipers and incessant artillery bombardments—the French alone were firing 230,000 rounds a day—addled brains and buried men whole, then churned them up again as putrefying body parts. By 1916, an estimated 40 percent of the casualties in the front lines were shell-shock cases.

Of the 43,000 spirited young British Columbia men who enlisted—about 17 percent of the province's male population aged fifteen to fifty and 10 percent of the total population—almost 20,000 would be killed or wounded. Eighteen months after that festive cherry harvest, casualty lists for the British Expeditionary Force in France were averaging 35,000 names a month. In total some million and a half men would be disabled and mutilated over the 1,566 days of fighting. The human cost of battles was tallied in the hundreds of thousands for a few metres gained here or lost there. A battalion mustered 1,100 men and officers. Two battles might use up an entire battalion. Some units lost more than 75 percent of their men in a single day.

As the trickle of returning wounded became a torrent, the fathers of teenagers like Joe Brown of Fernie begged their sons not to volunteer but instead to go down the dangerous coal mines. Almost four hundred men had perished down Crowsnest pits in the blackdamp, firedamp, afterdamp, blasts, bumps and blowouts over the decade before the war, yet now the mines were safer than the trenches. The war was more than 7,000 kilometres away yet its bony finger reached into the valleys, homesteads and streets of Fernie, transforming its families and workplaces.

The Great War was fought not only in Europe but in the cities and hinterlands of BC, where it worked changes that altered the province immensely and forever. In *Fernie at War: 1914–1919*, Wayne Norton charts one town's journey from sunny optimism to grief. He unravels the complicated tensions that arose from rapid change and from differing visions of the war and drove the community to dramatic conflicts between its best and its worst impulses.

The war and its vast appetites for both men and resources forced rapid industrialization. In 1910 BC had 40 registered forest companies; by 1918 there were 140. BC had a single pulp mill before the war; by its end there were six. Copper, used in shell casings, became the province's most valuable mineral commodity. Exports tripled. Zinc production, another strategic military metal, grew seven-fold. In 1914, industrial output for BC was less than $150 million a year. By the war's end it was $400 million, with dramatic increases in both resource extraction and manufacturing. Before the war, only 20 percent of the population was urban. After 1918 the ratio reversed, and more than half lived in cities.

The war uprooted social norms and divided communities. Women, only 36 percent of BC's total population in 1911, flooded into the workforce to replace absent soldiers. They demanded and won the right to vote in 1917, and in the next election the first woman sat in the provincial legislature.

Many young men who had gone to war in a flush of patriotism returned disillusioned and embittered. Some added to the growing strength of trade and industrial unions that battled to secure worker's rights from employers who didn't yet comprehend the changing values. Others saw unions not as salvation but as a threat to the social order. The aftershocks from such tensions still reverberate through the political bedrock of the province.

Fernie at War: 1914–1919 provides meticulous detail and perspective in documenting the profound changes in social, political and economic norms that the distant death struggles of globe-spanning empires and their Great War wrought upon one small, remote mining town.

Stephen Hume

July 2017

INTRODUCTION

This book is an attempt to achieve some sense of what it meant to live in Fernie during the years of the First World War. At the same time, it explores how national themes and controversies affected one small Canadian community. The history of Canada's domestic experience during the war years is largely written from the perspective of people in large urban centres. Fernie, despite its designation as a city, was neither large nor urban. Located in the then remote southeastern corner of British Columbia, it was the centre of a geographically isolated district of perhaps six thousand people. Does that mean it experienced the war years in isolation, or did events taking place beyond the world of the Elk Valley exert significant influence on local attitudes and activities? Was Fernie's history from 1914 to 1919 typical—perhaps a microcosm—of comparable smaller communities in English Canada, or was its experience exceptional, perhaps even unique?

The Fernie of a century ago can be readily imagined. To a very great extent in the downtown area, the buildings and locations of the war years are identifiable and fundamentally unchanged. It is not difficult to have 1914 in mind as one strolls through the community's compact central business district. Of course, social and political realities are much less tangible and more difficult to access. Intervening years have obscured past attitudes and hopes, fears and aspirations. When these in many respects are so profoundly different from our own, their retrieval presents a challenge to any aspiring historian.

That challenge is magnified by the fact that the Elk Valley—a geographically peripheral portion of Canada's Pacific province—is rarely mentioned in the mainstream historical narrative of British Columbia. Its economic and social orientation a century ago was to the east and south. But boundaries being what they are, the region is unlikely to receive attention in histories of Alberta, Montana and Idaho. It is, therefore, neglected on all sides, almost like a historical Bermuda Triangle. Whatever once happened there somehow disappears from radar screens. If this small book can demonstrate to some readers just how undeserved is that neglect, its author will be satisfied.

A few words are necessary by way of introduction to the narrative that follows. Although it was a unique and separate community, Coal Creek is regarded here as essentially a part of Fernie. With barely a trace of "the town up the gulch" remaining today, it is easy to forget that a century ago the two communities shared a common origin and a common destiny. Coal Creek was very much like Michel—a company town built around a colliery—and, despite the genuine affection many residents felt for it, cannot have been generally regarded as a particularly desirable place to live. All community decisions were made by the coal company; there was no mayor or council. Cottages with few amenities accommodated married men with families, rooms in boarding houses everyone else. At the time of the First World War, there were three churches, a general store and a workingmen's club to provide the core of social life for residents, but Fernie was their shopping precinct, their entertainment district and certainly the place to be when monthly paydays rolled round.

That labour issues should command so much attention in these pages may come as a surprise to many. Fernie was an administrative centre with a growing mercantile sector and a significant forestry industry, but its economy was nevertheless fundamentally dependent upon the payroll provided by the Crow's Nest Pass Coal Company and the spending priorities of its workforce. Labour disputes between the company and its employees did not simply inconvenience the city; they threatened its prosperity and perhaps its very existence. For most of the war years, those disputes were frequent, often prolonged and always socially divisive. For four consecutive years, the Crow's

Coal Creek beyond the tipple. The churches and the miners' union provided the bases for social activities in the community. Fernie Museum and Archives 6295.

Nest Pass Coal Company and the miners it employed at Coal Creek were at the very heart of relations between capital and labour on British Columbia's volatile resource frontier. When conflicts emerged in that relationship, repercussions were felt well beyond the Elk Valley.

And between 1914 and 1919 that relationship was intimately connected to the two other great issues of the day. From the declaration of war until well after the signing of the armistice, labour, loyalty and ethnicity were bound in an unnatural dance from which there was no apparent escape. Each in the uncomfortable embrace of the other two, they provided the fundamentally conflicting elements that determined the course of events. The price paid by the entire community for that entanglement—in blood, bitterness and social division—was exceptionally high. Fernie entered the war with optimism in 1914 and emerged from it staggering when the conflict concluded five years later.

The community was uncertain it had an assured future beyond the short time period covered here. The loss of life in the mines at Coal Creek and in the trenches in Europe was high, social divisions were deep and pervasive, relations between capital and labour consistently poor. The prosperous and picturesque Fernie of today may have some trouble recognizing itself in these pages. At the outset, it is perhaps best to remind ourselves that words spoken and actions taken by individuals and groups a century ago are properly judged by the mores and standards of their day—not of ours. If so much described here is found surprising and even shocking, that is simply an indication of how profound and wide-reaching have been the changes wrought by the passage of time.

FERNIE

A CHRONOLOGY OF THE WAR YEARS

1914

August:	war is declared
	British reservists depart
	first Fernie contingent departs
	Proclamation of August 15 issued; War Measures Act passed
	IODE begins Red Cross work
September:	enemy aliens begin reporting to British Columbia Provincial Police
	Belgian and French reservists depart
	branch of Canadian Patriotic Fund formed
October:	arrest of Herman Elmer
	Emil Topay court decision
November:	second Fernie contingent departs

1915

January:	Thomas Uphill elected mayor
	headquarters of the 107th East Kootenay Regiment authorized at Fernie
February:	third Fernie contingent departs
March:	fourth Fernie contingent (11th Canadian Mounted Rifles) departs
May:	Italy joins the war on the side of Britain, France and Russia
June:	strike to dismiss enemy aliens from employment in Coal Creek mines
	internment camp opens at skating rink under provincial authority
	fifth Fernie contingent (54th Kootenay Battalion—first local draft) departs
	Internment Operations take over internment camp
July:	*District Ledger* suspends publication
August:	Patriotic Carnival
	Italian reservists depart
September:	sixth Fernie contingent (54th Kootenay Battalion—second local draft) departs
October:	internment camp moved to Morrissey
	Amalgamated Patriotic Fund organized

1916

January:	Thomas Uphill acclaimed mayor
	seventh Fernie contingent (103rd Battalion) departs
March:	eighth Fernie contingent (143rd Battalion—BC Bantams) departs

May: ninth Fernie Contingent (Army Medical Corps) departs
            tenth Fernie contingent (1st Canadian Pioneer Battalion) departs
June: Elk River in flood
July: eleventh Fernie contingent (225th Kootenay Battalion) departs
            first War Bonus strike
August: Michel mine disaster
September: recruitment prohibited in Elk Valley
            provincial election—Alexander Fisher narrowly defeats Thomas
            Uphill
            plebiscites on Prohibition and votes for women
October: headquarters of the 107th East Kootenay Regiment move to Creston
November: second War Bonus strike
December: inflation commission inquiry

1917

January: Thomas Uphill elected mayor
            third War Bonus strike
March: red-light district closed
April: Coal Creek mine disaster
May: UMWA District 18 contract strike
July: Coal Operations takes charge of mines in District 18
            discharged soldiers begin to return
August: headquarters of District 18 move to Calgary
            Gladstone local union ends payroll deductions for Amalgamated
            Patriotic Fund
September: Wartime Elections Act passed
October: provincial prohibition takes effect
            water supply sabotaged
            Fernie GWVA formed
December: khaki election—Unionist Saul Bonnell elected
            red-light district closed again

1918

January: George Thomson elected mayor
March: GWVA club rooms open
April: federal prohibition takes effect
June: Elk River in flood
August: *District Ledger* resumes publication
September: single-shift strike
October: Spanish influenza pandemic
            internment camp at Morrissey closed
November: armistice in Europe
December: Ukrainian convictions for possession of banned literature

1919

January:	Thomas Uphill acclaimed mayor
February:	agitation to deport enemy aliens
April:	Gladstone local union overwhelmingly favours One Big Union (OBU)
May:	OBU strike begins
	British Columbia Provincial Police sting operation
June:	*District Ledger, Free Press* lawsuits settled
July:	liquor convictions
	Gladstone local union seeks end to strike
	Peace Day

1914

A COMMUNITY GOES TO WAR

Half a world away from southeastern British Columbia, Austria's Archduke Franz Ferdinand was murdered by a Serb terrorist in June 1914. People in Fernie would likely have learned of the assassination from the big-city daily newspapers that arrived by train from Lethbridge, Calgary and Vancouver—often just a day or two late. One Fernie-based newspaper reported on the event; one did not. But the news from Sarajevo would not have caused much of a stir. The geography, the individuals involved and the political forces in play were little understood if indeed they were understood at all. Those who could claim an acquaintance with Balkan politics were probably accustomed to dismissing news from that corner of continental Europe; for nearly a decade, one crisis after another had flared up in the region and then faded away. There was no reason to think the latest would be any different.

A company town: Like their counterparts at Michel/Natal, employees of the CNPCC living at Coal Creek were never far from their place of work. Fernie Museum and Archives 4577do.

Many histories of the First World War point to the splendid early summer preceding the outbreak of hostilities—painting a picture of calm and optimism as people enjoyed tea parties on beaches and picnics under parasols. The mood in the Elk Valley and the Crowsnest Pass was very much darker. People were doing their best to cope with exceptionally bad news—events that had nothing to do with the developing situation in Europe. Ten Fernie residents had lost their lives when the *Empress of Ireland* sank in the St. Lawrence River in late May. On the Alberta side of the Crowsnest Pass, an explosion at Hillcrest on June 19 killed 189 miners. The staggering death toll eclipsed even that of the Coal Creek explosion of 1902, a mining disaster that still ranks as one of the worst in Canadian history. Local residents and their families were reminded once more of connections to miners elsewhere and of the constant dangers faced daily in the region's coal mines.

Hard on the heels of the news from Hillcrest came the announcement by the Canadian Pacific Railway (CPR) that its coal mining and coking operations at Hosmer were to cease on July 3. Businesses and properties in the townsite became practically worthless overnight. The demoralized Hosmer board of trade lamented the town would have to close down. Some of the miners thrown so suddenly out of work were quickly able to find employment in the mines at Coal Creek and Michel and, under grim circumstances, at Hillcrest, but they knew only too well that the coal industry everywhere in

A busy Victoria Avenue, 1915. The building with the pediment at the far left is the Miners' Union Building (Grand Theatre); on the right, the smaller building with a pediment is the office of the *Fernie Free Press*. Fernie Museum and Archives 4888do.

British Columbia and Alberta was struggling. The global financial crisis that began in 1913 had dealt a sudden and severe blow to the booming economy of western Canada. The demand for coal had fallen sharply.

The month of July was dominated by the aftermath and consequences of these harsh realities. Individuals and businesses contributed generously to the growing Hillcrest Relief Fund. Details of the hardships attendant on the abandonment of coal operation at Hosmer were widely discussed in Fernie, but it soon became apparent that the decision would not be reversed and relief for residents would not be forthcoming from the CPR. At the same time, the normal rhythms of local life in the communities of Fernie and Coal Creek continued. Dominion Day activities in Fernie's city park—located on high ground at the south end of town—were much appreciated and well attended; the participation of several members of the Stoney First Nation from Alberta and the Ktunaxa Tobacco Plains First Nation added to the spectacle and the excitement in the horse races.[1] The regular Sunday evening concert on Victoria Avenue by the Italian Band always drew an appreciative audience. Advertisements for the visit at the end of the month of the Sells-Floto Circus—with a promised parade two miles long and a performance by Buffalo Bill himself—caused great anticipation.

Abruptly, local concerns were forced to share the spotlight with international developments. The crisis in the Balkans had not after all faded away like its predecessors. Residents who read the dailies from the big cities would have had good warning—developments in Europe occupied their front pages all week. But those who relied for news solely on the local press would have been profoundly shocked by one of the headlines in the *Fernie Free Press* on Friday, July 31. The brief column titled "Latest War News" advised readers of the rapidly deteriorating situation in Europe and warned, "Hope of localizing the struggle has been practically abandoned." Fernie's other newspaper, the *District Ledger*, gave its readers a less sensational headline but essentially the same message—Europe seemed irrevocably on the verge of a major war.

On the very hot first day of August, dust and smoke from brush fires nearby swirled through the streets of Fernie. Some residents were fearful the situation could lead to a repetition of the devastating fire of 1908, when almost the entire city had burned to the ground. No one could have seen the new threat as somehow suggestive of dangerous crosswinds that would buffet the community throughout the war years to come.

FIRST RESPONSES

Like every community in the country, Fernie understood that the involvement of the United Kingdom of Great Britain and Ireland in war would mean the involvement of the Dominion of Canada. And like every other community in Canada, after an initial moment of disbelief, a wave of patriotism followed the declaration of war by Britain on August 4. Excitement animated all conversation. In England, cheering crowds filled the streets of London; crowds in Toronto and other Canadian cities followed suit; in Vancouver and Victoria, residents waved Union Jacks and sang patriotic anthems. In some quarters, expressions of that patriotism were somewhat more temperate, but doubts and criticism found little expression in the mainstream Canadian newspapers of the day. Almost unanimously, they brandished the flag editorially as vigorously as the crowds in the streets of cities throughout the British Empire.

The weekly *Fernie Free Press* was no exception, presenting its readers with views entirely supportive of the involvement of the Empire in the European war while managing to avoid the jingoistic excesses of much of the reporting at the coast. National and international news was not normally featured in its columns. As a local newspaper, the *Free Press* thrived on local news. It was also a community booster, promoting the district's economic interests and advantages whenever possible. Each issue promoted Fernie as "the Pittsburg of Canada."[2]

The *Free Press* was typical in one other significant respect. Newspapers in Canada at the time openly proclaimed their Liberal or Conservative leanings—in fact, advertising revenues and subscriptions often depended upon those leanings being made perfectly clear. The *Free Press* fit this pattern precisely, touting its Conservative credentials even more aggressively than many of its fellow travellers in larger communities. And it was certainly on the political side of the fence most favoured by British Columbians. Federally, Robert Borden's Conservatives had captured all seven seats in the election of 1911; provincially, Richard McBride's Conservatives won almost every seat in 1912, completely shutting out the Liberals and facing an opposition of just two Socialists elected from Vancouver Island.

In Fernie, however, the comfortable stance of the hometown newspaper did not go unchallenged. The community was also home to a publication that was philosophically positioned well away from the usual political divide between Liberals and Conservatives. The weekly *District Ledger* was certainly partisan, but its allegiance was not pledged to Laurier's Liberals.

Its office and printing plant were located on Pellatt Avenue in the same building that housed the headquarters of District 18 of the United Mine Workers of America (UMWA), which owned and operated the newspaper and had located its administrative office in Fernie since the union's initial organizing success in 1903.

The presence of the office and the printing plant was significant. On the eve of the First World War, with District 18 representing miners in seventeen local unions—four in the southeastern corner of British Columbia and the rest in southwestern Alberta—local union 2314 at Fernie and Coal Creek remained by far the largest and most influential of them all. It was also the only local union in the district identified by more than just a number. Reflecting the strong commitment to Liberal politics that miners brought with them from Britain and named a decade earlier in admiration of British Liberal politician William Ewart Gladstone, local 2314—the Gladstone local union—exerted a dominant influence within District 18 and on its Fernie-based newspaper.

Following the union's formal political affiliation with the Marxist-oriented Socialist Party of Canada—a controversial decision proposed by the Gladstone local union and adopted after much debate at the District 18 convention in the spring of 1914—the *Ledger* redoubled its efforts to educate its readers in the philosophies of democratic and revolutionary socialism. The publication was certainly located in a community potentially receptive to those philosophies. Although the riding was represented by a Conservative MLA, its Socialist vote had been exceptionally strong in provincial elections, and Fernie was home to one of the few active branches of the Socialist Party of Canada. The *Ledger* did include local news, but gave pride of place to articles about political matters in Europe and the United States—primarily from ideological or labour perspectives—frequently translating them into Italian, Polish or Slovenian in a column titled "For Our Foreign Brothers."[3] Considerable space was devoted to analysis of the deteriorating prospects of success in bitter coal strikes on Vancouver Island and in Colorado. Also often included were excerpts from the works of Voltaire, Rousseau and John Stuart Mill. The newspaper claimed to be the most widely read publication in the region, based on its belief that copies were widely circulated amongst readers who could not afford subscriptions.

Fundamental differences in content between the two local newspapers were therefore readily apparent, but so too was a difference in editorial style. The *Free Press* might occasionally include an editorial on a local issue, but more commonly would simply reprint articles from other newspapers or offer a few short sentences of its own on a variety of topics. These reprinted articles in broad outline represented the views of the newspaper's well-established owner and editor, John Rene Wallace. A Fernie resident since 1899, Wallace made no secret of his personal Conservative sympathies and party affiliation. Readers of the *Ledger*, on the other hand, each week found extensive and passionately argued editorials on political and labour issues written by editor Frank Newnham.

The war quickly revealed another difference between the two publications. Within just a few weeks, the *Free Press* would come to regard itself as "the only patriotic newspaper in town" as the *Ledger* challenged the jingoistic sentiments that were animating the community. Both newspapers kept their readers up to date on the course of the war in Europe during the month of August, printing reports from several European capitals, but sharp differences were soon obvious. The *Free Press* initially avoided extensive comment on the war, restricting itself to brief sentences such as the one describing the Japanese as "fine little fellows" for supporting Britain and another concerning the problem of Austrian reservists.[4] In contrast, the *Ledger* did not hesitate to comment directly, extensively and critically on the major issues raised by the war in Europe.

A lengthy editorial in early August made it perfectly clear that the attitude of the *Ledger* to war would not change just because Canada was in one. "So far as the Ledger is concerned," it proclaimed, "we have but one policy, and that is the condemnation of war." Admitting it was "dangerous to write against public sentiment at such times," the editorial nevertheless lamented that the veneer of civilization had been torn away, condemned the churches of belligerent countries—each for blessing its own troops—and cited the loss of life at Hillcrest as reason enough for workers to keep their focus on their real enemy, capitalism. Invoking the internationalist cause that was already dead in Europe, the *Ledger* concluded that workers had no reason at all to be fighting each other. Published just a few days after the declaration of war, the editorial was a clear indication that Newnham would not allow demonstrations of unquestioning patriotism to go uncontested. A week later, he advised readers, "If you feel you are likely to have an attack of patriotism, a mental disease that is affecting many throughout the land, stop a minute and ask yourself a few simple questions." One of his suggested questions was, "Why should I be called upon to sing 'God Save the King' and then be asked to go and smash his uncle?"[5]

The *Ledger* soon observed that patriotic suggestions were "as thick as bees at swarming time." Words and actions intended to demonstrate loyalty and patriotism were indeed everywhere evident in August. Storefronts all featured the Union Jack; the Fernie Conservative Association wrote to the Minister of Militia and Defence in Ottawa pledging its loyalty and offering whatever assistance it could provide. With no branch of the Canadian Red Cross established locally, the recently founded Mount Fernie chapter of the Imperial Order Daughters of the Empire (IODE) pledged to work on its behalf. They quickly sold enough "patriotic bouquets" to raise nearly $600 as a contribution towards the purchase and equipment of the hospital ship its national executive had pledged to supply to the British Admiralty. Not necessarily from the same patriotic motivations, local businesses started mentioning the conflict in advertisements. The Central Hotel invited men to visit the bar to "irrigate" when they got "dry talking war." The Fernie–Fort Steele Brewing Co. pleaded with the same clientele not to overlook the company's beer "in the war excitement."[6]

Residents were proud that Fernie resident Joseph Mackay, the fuel purchasing agent with the Great Northern Railway who had been one of the first to volunteer for overseas service, was instead appointed recruiting officer for both East and West Kootenay. Formerly active with the Royal Canadian Regiment, Mackay retained his rank of lieutenant colonel and was president of the Fernie Veterans' Association. He opened a makeshift recruiting office on Victoria Avenue on the morning of August 12, and by the time it closed that evening, four dozen local men—responding with the same enthusiasm shown by their counterparts elsewhere in Canada, in Britain and in the other dominions—had signed up to join the force Canada pledged to send to the aid of Britain. And on August 18, an enthusiastic civilian crowd gathered at the CPR station to cheer the departure of four British army reservists as they boarded the evening train.

The Fernie–Fort Steele Brewing Company was still closely associated with its German-born founder. Image courtesy of Frank Mrazik.

By the end of August, the number of volunteers had doubled, and the anticipated departure on August 28 of what was proudly named the

Fernie Overseas Contingent caused great excitement. Two days earlier, in honour of the volunteers, a social evening was held at which several local notables gave motivational speeches. The general manager of the Crow's Nest Pass Coal Company (CNPCC), William Ritson Wilson, who was well known for his speech-making abilities, did not disappoint. His remarks were "cheered to the echo" with repeated references to "the glorious traditions of the British soldier." He assured departing company employees that jobs would be waiting for them upon their return. Three Protestant ministers of religion provided the spiritual blessings, while former Fernie mayors Dr. Saul Bonnell and Sherwood Herchmer also gave "stirring addresses." Both the well-established Italian Band and the new Fernie–Coal Creek Excelsior Band—formed by mine employees less than a year earlier and modelled on the colliery-based brass bands of northern England—provided the music, and a parade half a mile long took to the streets following the meeting.

The next day Lieutenant Colonel Mackay privately cautioned the volunteers against the use of intoxicating drink, and urged them to "do nothing

In front of the Trites-Wood store. Sunday concerts by the Italian (City) Band were always well attended. Fernie Mueum and Archives 0591.

to bring a blush to the faces of those who love them." On the evening of departure, the two bands were joined by pipers and the volunteers themselves at the skating rink, located on the river bank at the foot of the Howland Avenue hill. Members of the Fernie Veterans' Association mustered to provide the honour guard. A crowd estimated at thirty-five hundred lined the streets to cheer the ninety-three men on their way to the CPR train depot.[7] The bands played "God Save the King" and "The Marseillaise," and more speeches were delivered. The IODE provided food hampers for the journey, while William Wilson presented each man with a pipe and a pouch of tobacco. Like the speeches, music and blessings of the previous evening, the gifts and the farewells were to become familiar elements in a pattern oft repeated over the course of the next few years. The appreciative crowd cheered as the eastbound train left the station taking the community's volunteers towards the new military training camp at Valcartier. Within a few days, French and Belgian reservists were preparing for the first leg of the journey to report to their military units in Europe.[8] Although unrecorded by the local newspapers, it is possible a number of Russian reservists boarded trains for the same purpose.

Fernie was at war.

Bridges across the Elk River: In the foreground, the Great Northern Railway trestle; in the middle distance, the skating rink, curling rink and the Elk Lumber Company. Fernie Museum and Archvies 2455.

First Shadows

As events would soon demonstrate, Fernie cannot be described as a Sleepy Hollow during the war years, but it certainly was isolated geographically. Despite that isolation and a prolonged economic downturn, the community's hopes for a grand future remained. The board of trade—seeking to draw the attention of potential investors to economic opportunities—provided this description of the city on the eve of war:

> Fernie, near Elk River, on Canadian Pacific, Great Northern, and Morrissey, Fernie and Michel Railways, 700 miles east of Vancouver. Local and long distance telephones. Hotels Napanee, Fernie and nine others, five churches, judicial centre, court house, hospital. Post office and customs house, public and high schools, city hall and fire hall, skating and curling rinks, three banks, two saw mills, brick plant. Large brewery, railway car shops, foundry and machine shops, opera house, baseball and football clubs, commercial and workingmen's clubs, American and Italian consulates. Three livery stables, three automobile garages, four wholesale houses. Crow's Nest Pass Coal Company employs normally 2,000 men ... Customs port of entry, Provincial Police Headquarters for East Kootenay. Outfitting point for hunters ... big game abundant, good

Elk Lumber Company mill and residences in West Fernie: The timber industry was second only to coal mining in importance for the local economy. Fernie Museum and Archvies 1094.

trout fishing. City supplies electric light and power, owns 200-acre natural park with race track. Sewerage treated by septic process. Altitude 3,303 feet. Population 4,000; including tributary population, 7,000.[9]

But outside investment had all but dried up after 1912. Significantly, the only employer mentioned directly by the board of trade was the CNPCC, while the majority of the region's "tributary population" were found in the company's towns of Coal Creek, Michel and Natal.

The initial shock at the outbreak of war and the generally discouraging news of its first few months did not disrupt most aspects of community life. Summer picnics took place as planned; sports teams contested for bragging rights as usual. Neighbours visited neighbours; births and marriages were celebrated. City council dealt with matters pertaining to sewers, lighting, sidewalks and water supply. A complaint regarding speeding automobiles saw the city clerk instructed to advise all three garages that Fernie's eight-mile-an-hour speed limit would be strictly enforced. People could perhaps convince themselves that nothing had really changed. But beneath the surface, potentially dangerous currents of opinion were in play, and even apparently trivial events were suggestive of these dangers.

The biggest ongoing civic issue in the late summer and early fall of 1914 ostensibly had nothing to do with the tensions engendered by the war in Europe. The Italian Band (often referred to as the City Band) had been established in Fernie since 1904 and maintained a high standard of performance that was acknowledged by an annual civic grant. The band's weekly summer concerts were always well received. The newer Fernie–Coal Creek Excelsior Band formed in late fall 1913; by the spring it was advertising its services in the *Ledger* and in summer also applied for a civic grant. Lacking additional funds, city council at first proposed a Labour Day contest to determine which band was more deserving of the existing grant, then debated a motion to divide the grant evenly and finally decided to provide $500 to the Italian Band and a token $100 to the fledgling Excelsior Band.

Taking umbrage, the Excelsior Band immediately donated its $100 to the local hospital. One band member claimed the band had been started in the first place to avoid having English-speaking musicians directed by a foreigner and noted that several Excelsior Band members had recently left Fernie for the battlefields of Europe with the first contingent, whereas no Italian Band members seemed prepared to fight for Canada.[10] Perhaps discouraged by the controversy or perhaps by coincidence, the Italian bandmaster accepted another appointment and left Fernie at the end of September.

It is not clear how representative the attitudes expressed by some members of the Excelsior Band were, but the fact that they formed the basis of a public debate suggests an Italian entry into the war on the side of Germany and Austria-Hungary would have caused serious tensions in the communities of the Elk Valley. Clearly, the European war and local attitudes to immigrant communities was a potentially dangerous mix. Local Italians recognized this fully. When the two lodges of Fernie's Italian Society invited their counterparts from Michel and Coleman to a Garibaldi Celebration in September, discussion of war-related topics was declared strictly off limits.[11]

But it was the immigrants from Germany and Austria-Hungary who were to feel the changed politics born of war most strongly. The federal government took initial steps to reassure them. The Proclamation Respecting Immigrants of German or Austro-Hungarian Nationality of August 15, 1914, while outlining the circumstances that would justify their arrest and detention, assured German and Austro-Hungarian nationals of the protection of the law "so long as they quietly pursue their ordinary avocations." They had only to sign an undertaking agreeing to obey the laws and do no injury to the Dominion of Canada. On September 2, a public notice directed specifically to the attention of "alien enemies" confirmed that a demonstrated respect for the law meant they had "nothing to fear." An alien enemy was defined as an individual born in a country with which the British Empire was at war who had not become a naturalized British subject. All such persons, the public notice reiterated, "so long as they respect the law are entitled to its protection… "[12]

However, the federal government was also responsible for security and for assuring people they were protected from domestic threats in a time of war. At the end of August, enemy aliens were forbidden the use and possession of firearms. Most significantly, the passage of the War Measures Act provided comfort to loyal British subjects, but caused concern in labour circles and in non-British immigrant communities. The legislation received unanimous approval in Parliament and put in place mechanisms to suspend traditional safeguards; these mechanisms permitted the imprisonment of those who failed to show respect for the law and those who otherwise were deemed to threaten national security.[13]

British Columbia's provincial government seemed keen to become involved in the question of domestic security. Premier McBride famously purchased his two submarines for coastal defence early in August and, welcoming a federal request for assistance in dealing with enemy aliens, offered provincial premises at Vernon and Nanaimo for internment purposes. An officer with the militia unit in Victoria, architect Major William Ridgeway Wilson, was quickly appointed as head of the new and grandly named Department of Alien Reservists. With authorization from A.P. Sherwood, Chief Commissioner of Police in Ottawa, the British Columbia Provincial Police then became responsible for administering the undertakings required by the proclamation of August 15 and for ensuring that national subjects of Germany and Austria-Hungary reported to them on a regular basis for the duration of the war. Politicians, military officials and police in British Columbia were poised to play a significant role in protecting citizens from wartime threats to safety and security.

By mid-September, a hardening of tone regarding enemy aliens was apparent. Judge George Thompson at the Fernie fall assizes refused to grant applications for naturalization to local German-born and Austrian-born applicants, regardless of whether they had applied before or after the British declaration of war. In his published judgement, he stated emphatically, "No enemy alien has the right to apply to the civil courts during war. His civil rights are suspended." Encouraged by that ruling, the CNPCC attempted to exploit it. Emil Topay, an illiterate Austro-Hungarian miner severely injured in an accident at Michel, had surprised the company with a lawsuit for negligence. Arguing that Topay had lost the right to litigation by virtue of his status as an enemy alien, lawyers for the CNPCC applied at a hearing in Victoria to have the case thrown out. Citing the proclamation of August 15, the judge surprised lawyers for the company by denying their application. He contradicted the rationale for Thompson's ruling, insisting such rights were not suspended.[14] Nevertheless, it was apparent that the civil rights of enemy aliens would not necessarily be defended by the courts during wartime.

Nor would the police prove too solicitous of those rights. In early October, Chief Constable George Welsby, head of the Southeast Kootenay district of the provincial police, arrested Herman Elmer, the German-born secretary of the UMWA local at Michel. Perhaps inspired to act by Major Ridgeway Wilson, who was then visiting Fernie specifically to advise local police on arrest procedures for those who failed to comply with the new requirements to report, Welsby acted quickly when informed of rumours circulating in Michel that Elmer had been "preaching sedition" at a union meeting. Reporting later to the superintendent of provincial police, he explained that he "thought it best to nip the matter in the bud, before any further trouble arose." The *Free Press* added that Elmer had also been "speaking disrespectfully of the militia."[15]

According to one account of the meeting, Elmer had done nothing more than express his opinion that the international solidarity of working men was more important than military victory by either Britain or Germany.[16] However, it is significant that his arrest occurred in the same week that provincial police officers were required to begin gathering undertakings and information on a form entitled Description of Alien Subjects. In addition to stating age, country of origin, place of residence and occupation, individuals were to specify if they had provided military service or held any rank with the armed forces in their homeland. The *Ledger* urged readers born in Germany and Austria-Hungary to report as required in a respectful fashion to avoid unnecessary trouble, arguing that British justice could be depended upon to protect them from unlawful treatment by authorities. If Elmer was counselling any degree of non-compliance, it was certainly not with the sanction of District 18. The *Ledger* was extremely cautious in reporting the arrest and immediately deleted his name from the list of local union secretaries it published weekly. In its edition of October 10, the newspaper complimented the police for treating him well at the provincial jail in Fernie, noted that District 18 was working on his behalf and expressed the hope he would soon be released on parole; on the same day, Elmer was transferred to the internment camp recently opened at Vernon under provisions of the War Measures Act.[17]

The first Description of Alien Subjects form submitted from the Fernie office of the provincial police was for the week ending September 26, the first from Michel for the week ending October 3 and the first for Natal for the week ending October 10. The overwhelming majority of those reporting were identified as Austro-Hungarian subjects. While some worked in forestry, most were miners or labourers employed by the CNPCC. Throughout the Southeast Kootenay police district, more than three hundred men signed undertakings by mid-October.[18] However necessary federal authorities may have deemed it to gather information from enemy aliens, it would have been seen by those affected as unwelcome and potentially threatening. That some of the foreign-born were required to report to provincial police while some were not underlines the fact that relations amongst the various ethnic communities in the Elk Valley were extremely complex.

A century ago relatively few Canadian-born citizens lived in Fernie, which was fundamentally a city of immigrants. Including almost all those

Canadians, the most numerous group in the Fernie census district was what the 1911 Canadian census records as the "British races." Overwhelmingly Protestant in religion, this bare majority (51.5 percent of the total) identified themselves primarily as Anglican, Methodist or Presbyterian. Whether in business, the professions or employment, they possessed varying degrees of tolerance or discomfort with the non-Protestant religions of their numerous Italian and their few French-speaking Canadian neighbours and of the hundreds of immigrants from little-known regions of Europe. Following the promise of economic opportunity, the "British races" and the foreign-born immigrants found themselves living and working in communities located in an obscure valley on the Canadian resource frontier.[19]

By any measure, Fernie was by far the most significant of those communities. Almost entirely destroyed by fire in 1908, the downtown core had soon been reconstructed in brick and stone. The new shops, theatres and hotels of Victoria Avenue combined to present an impression of a modern and vigorous community. The solid administration building of the CNPCC on Pellatt Avenue represented the coal industry's economic domination of the local economy, while the magnificent provincial courthouse and jail proclaimed that the rule of law prevailed even in remote East Kootenay. With chateau-styled architecture and extensive grounds, the courthouse imparted to Fernie a sense of grandeur and importance that some thought was perhaps greater than the relatively small and decidedly rough community deserved.[20]

Social life was very much focussed upon more modest institutions. For some, the hotel bars were their social centres, while members of church and fraternal organizations were drawn together for meetings, dances and special occasions. To some extent, the congregations of the city's churches were based on ethnic origins (Welsh Methodists, Scottish Presbyterians, etc.), but those tendencies should not be overstated. The several fraternal organizations tended to attract members along similar lines. Women's auxiliaries were active through the churches and the recently formed chapters of the Daughters of Rebekah, the fiercely patriotic IODE and the fiercely protestant Loyal True Blue Association. The large Italian population was brought together socially through the Italian Band and the local Italian Society. Professionals and businessmen enjoyed the exclusive atmosphere of the Fernie Club on Victoria Avenue. Miners could gather socially at the unlicensed Workingmen's Club and Institute in the Miners' Union Building or at the Coal Creek Literary and Athletic Association clubhouse, where a provincial liquor licence permitted the sale of beer. (That licence was under threat;

Welsby complained the barroom had "more the appearance of a saloon than a private club" as he demanded significant and immediate improvements.)[21]

Unlike other mining communities at Michel and throughout the Crowsnest, Fernie shows little surviving evidence of formal social organization amongst the almost exclusively male migrant workers from eastern Europe. Because such organizations were established in the smaller coal-mining centres of the Crowsnest and on Vancouver Island during these years, it is reasonable to assume they existed in Fernie as well. But whatever the social reality may have been within each of the ethnic communities, interactions between them were likely minimal. With the possible exception of the Catholic church, only the local branch of the Socialist Party of Canada—through weekly lectures and dances at its new hall on Pellatt Avenue—seems to have actively fostered an atmosphere in which men and women from the Italian, eastern European and English-speaking communities had opportunities to mingle socially.[22]

Although the British immigrants were fiercely insistent on recognition of their own origins as English, Scots, Welsh or Irish, most of them knew virtually nothing of the ethnic distinctions disguised by the terms "Austro-Hungarian" and "Russian." Poles, Czechs and Slovaks and others were designated as

The Hotel Fernie. While most other hotels were little more than boarding houses, both the Fernie and the King Edward catered to a more affluent clientele. Fernie Museum and Archives 2318.

Austro-Hungarian, but many of those covered by that national identification were ethnic Ukrainians from Austria's eastern provinces of Galicia and Bukovyna. A few were established residents who had taken work in the mines at Coal Creek after the Crow's Nest Pass Railway was completed in 1898; others had come to jobs in mining and forestry after initially farming on the prairies; still others were more recent arrivals from eastern Canada or the United States. The Russian migrants included eastern Ukrainians and Poles, and were predominantly married men from what is now the independent state of Belarus.[23] Their timing was poor, as most arrived in the middle of the economic slump after 1912. Wages earned in the Elk Valley by Russian workers were typically saved or sent home, benefitting families to whom the migrants intended to return after two or three years in Canada.

There was a tendency amongst the English-speaking community to view foreigners collectively, to consider them with some disdain and to be nervous about their reliability in a time of conflict. They were generally seen as a threat to the living standards of the English-speaking working class. Amongst the miners in late 1914, the reputation of Italians in particular was coloured by reports of their recent strike-breaking activities during the bitter Vancouver Island coal strike.[24] With the outbreak of war, the question of loyalty to the British Empire became paramount. The business community was certain that its own loyalty could firmly be relied upon. Although commercial ownership by Italians was increasing, members of Fernie's middle class were typically Canadian-born, with a few British and Americans in their ranks. The perspectives of the war held by the several Chinese business owners (and perhaps those of the city's two Syrian merchants) were regarded with little, if any, concern by businessmen and professionals untroubled by questions about their own patriotism.[25]

Instead it was the question of the miners' loyalty that most troubled them. Vigorous and frequent assertions, especially amongst the union leadership, that miners owed their primary allegiance to the international working class rather than to king and empire were particularly disturbing in the fresh context of war. The loyalty of the English-speaking miner seemed as uncertain as that of the foreigner, and all mining communities in the Elk Valley were dominated by recent immigrants from the coalfields of Scotland, Wales and northern England.

Indications of that dominance are not hard to find. After Elmer's removal from office in Michel, the secretaries of the local unions that comprised District 18 of the UMWA were almost exclusively of British descent.

The social reports from the various mining camps that were published weekly in the *Ledger* rarely included any information about foreign-born residents. When the Crow's Nest Pass Football League organized for the new season in May 1914 with teams from Coal Creek, Fernie, Michel, Coleman, Bellevue, Frank, Hosmer and Corbin—virtually all the region's mining communities—not one team included a player whose name is recognizably of non-British origin.[26] Although they engaged with each other in the world of work, outside that world British and non-British mine employees appear to have had minimal contact.

Coal Creek, like other mining communities in the Crowsnest, had separate residential districts based on ethnicity. Whether the enclaves of Welsh Town, French Town and Slav Town were originally established by the CNPCC, insisted upon by the workforce in general or evolved as preferred locations by their residents is not clear. All situated west of the tipple, they can hardly have been Coal Creek's most desirable neighbourhoods. How strictly observed the separation was by the war years is also uncertain. Welsh Town remains something of a mystery as many Welsh miners lived in the main residential area east of the tipple alongside other British-born miners, while Slav Town was home not only to Slavs, as its name indicates, but also to some Italians and others neither French-speaking nor British. The shacks near the coke ovens at Fernie housed predominantly Russian-born workers, as did the collection of makeshift shacks facetiously named Little New York near the coke ovens at Hosmer. To a very considerable extent, residential separation based on ethnicity was seen as desirable; segregated neighbourhoods may have provided some familiarity for immigrants in an unfamiliar world. But the social distance between ethnically based neighbourhoods suggests the requirement to report monthly to police imposed upon some of the foreign-born may have been barely noticed by many in the English-speaking mining community.

The non-British residents of Fernie and Coal Creek were anything but homogeneous, and like their English-speaking neighbours, they too were burdened by attitudes imported from their homelands. Germans tended to look disdainfully upon the Slav communities, while religious divisions—between Roman and Eastern Catholics and between Catholic and Orthodox followers—further underlined existing animosities amongst Italians, Poles, Czechs and Slovaks, Ukrainians and Russians. Especially in the area near the coke ovens in Fernie, "religious squabbles" between Poles, Ukrainians and Russians were not uncommon.

On fine evenings during the autumn of 1914, a group of men—sometimes numbering up to thirty and described as "patriotic Russians"—practised military drills with sticks for rifles near their homes by the coke ovens in hopes of enlisting with the Canadian Expeditionary Force. The *Free Press* admired them, and Lieutenant Colonel Mackay regretted he could not sign them up, but their public demonstration would certainly have been seen as an unwelcome provocation by many of their Austrian-born neighbours.[27] With the outbreak of war, all foreign-born residents found an additional layer of suspicion laid upon them. Their loyalty to the country they found themselves in when war broke out could not be assumed, and demonstrations of it would be required to allay the suspicions of the predominantly British host community.

Comforted by the "Russian" label, the British residents of Fernie and Coal Creek were equally discomfited by the "Austrian" designation, assuming it provided an indication equally clear as "German" about where wartime loyalties would lie. While the Russians practised with make-believe rifles, Welsby was confiscating real firearms from the few Austro-Hungarian and German residents who possessed them. Other ethnic identities also caused concern as divided loyalties were feared in some quarters and acknowledged in others. Joseph Rudnicki, an employee of the Home Bank in Fernie, was probably not the only local resident who could claim to have some cousins fighting for Russia and others fighting for Austria. In the first few months of the war, confusion about matters of loyalty was as common as certainty.

But respecting neither ethnic distinctions nor supposed loyalties, the ongoing economic slump affected everyone. The CNPCC was extracting considerably less coal in 1914 than it had done in 1913, and company officials were deeply concerned that orders from the Great Northern Railway—chief customer of the CNPCC and its majority shareholder—had fallen further since the outbreak of the war as copper smelters closed in both Canada and the United States.[28] Particularly worrisome was the fact that coke production was also sharply lower because of those closures. The bituminous coal mined in the Elk Valley was ideal for coke production, and the CNPCC—by far the largest coke producer in the province of British Columbia—operated over four hundred beehive coke ovens at Fernie and another four hundred at Michel.

During the last few months of 1914, considerable attention was given to the question of economic distress, unemployment and underemployment. For the third year in a row, company shareholders could expect no dividend, but the local business community was equally worried about the serious slump in the coal markets. In October, Amos Trites—the region's most prominent merchant—declared that "considerable strain would be placed upon the people of the town in relieving distress" if the reduced operations at the Coal Creek mine continued. Prosperity in Fernie depended very heavily on the wages received by employees of the CNPCC.

And just as incomes were being pressured, appeals for funds increased dramatically. The Hillcrest Relief Fund suddenly found itself in competition for donations with the Belgian Relief Fund and patriotic appeals from the Mount Fernie chapter of the IODE, whose two dozen members were working hard to raise funds for the Canadian Red Cross. In response to a request by the province's lieutenant-governor, a local branch of the Canadian Patriotic Fund was launched in mid-October. The fund's declared purpose was to assist financially the needful dependents of soldiers away on active service; the number of local families requiring such assistance was reported to be only half a dozen. Mayor John Gates agreed to act as *ex officio* president, and Trites-Wood Company store manager Edwy Stewart was elected vice-president. The first major fundraiser for the Canadian Patriotic Fund was the successful Grand Patriotic Ball at Thanksgiving.

A meeting held in Coal Creek to consider the lieutenant governor's request decided instead to form a separate benevolent committee to assist needy families, military or otherwise. A benevolent committee was also formed in Fernie to assist non-military families, and miners agreed to donate wages from at least one shift each month for the purpose of alleviating economic distress. The fraternal societies combined to raise charitable funds through a Hard Times Ball in November, and the city of Fernie found work for as many as twenty heads of families in the city park. At the end of December, it was calculated that the mines at Coal Creek had operated for only 172.5 days during the calendar year, providing miners with an average of only three shifts per week. Just before Christmas, Mayor Gates informed the provincial government that as many as two hundred men in the Fernie area were unemployed.[29]

Recognizing the strain being placed locally upon limited and shrinking financial resources, in mid-October the IODE stopped appealing for cash donations to the Red Cross and called instead upon local women to assist in a campaign to knit items that would be needed by soldiers at the front. The women of the IODE were in charge of the organizational effort, and items were to be sent to Europe through the auspices of the Canadian Red Cross.

Both newspapers printed the appeal which included knitting instructions for heelless socks (twenty-five thousand pairs of which were said to be needed), cholera caps, wristlets and balaclava caps. The response was strong. For the rest of the year, weekly newspaper reports included long lists of items knitted, materials donated and the names of donors and knitters. Requirements evolved quickly. In mid-December, the second shipment sent from Fernie included towels, pillowslips, bandages and hospital sheets as well as nearly three hundred pairs of socks. Members of the Rebekahs were also busy, creating small repair kits they called "housewives" that they stocked with items thought to be needed by the fighting man at the front. The items included needle and thread and the *Book of Common Prayer*.[30]

The first group of Fernie volunteers had been divided amongst the new battalions being formed at Valcartier, with a good many of them assigned to the 13th Battalion (Royal Highlanders of Canada).[31] By the time they arrived in England in October as part of the First Division of the Canadian Expeditionary Force, the city was preparing to bid farewell to its second contingent. Canada had promised Britain an additional twenty thousand men, and volunteers from Fernie came forward quickly. This time, they were heading to Victoria for training, but much of the pattern established by the farewell for the first contingent was followed. A social event was held at the Victoria Hall on the evening before departure, and speeches were delivered; William Wilson presented each man with a pipe and pouch of tobacco; the Excelsior Band and the Isis Orchestra provided the music. Instead of food hampers, members of the IODE provided each man with a belt, knitted socks, mitts and a sleeping cap; the Rebekahs presented each with a "housewife."

Thirty-three men from Fernie and Coal Creek assembled at the Drill Hall on Sunday morning, the first of November. Perhaps because the majority of the men were from Coal Creek, the Italian Band left the musical honours to the Excelsior Band, which accompanied the volunteers to the depot in a light rain, adding the newly popular "It's a Long Way to Tipperary" to its repertoire of martial music. This time, the honour guard was provided by men from companies A and B of the 107th East Kootenay Regiment. This was a new militia unit, formed only in May and still in the process of being organized, with headquarters designated at Fernie and intended only for home defence. Like the men they were honouring that morning, the militia escorts were dressed in civilian clothes. Fifteen volunteers for overseas duty from Michel were already aboard the train, accompanied as far as Fernie by well-wishers and the Michel brass band.

The *Ledger* pointedly observed that, as in the first contingent, most of the second were miners. One of the criticisms that found frequent expression in the *Ledger* was that the war was being fought by working men, while would-be patriots who confined themselves to "vaporings" about "king, country and flag" had no intention of enlisting. This was not a topic with which the *Free Press* chose to engage, but the two newspapers did begin to spar over definitions of loyalty in wartime and the expected duration of the war. The *Free Press* most typically reprinted articles from other newspapers, while the *Ledger* usually ran editorials written by Frank Newnham.

Those editorials did not always meet with the approval of the District 18 executive, headed by its new president, Fernie resident William Phillips. In early November, Newnham was summoned to a meeting to explain his rationale for a strongly worded anti-war column. Not at all satisfied with the explanation they received, the executive passed a motion censuring their editor and insisting he adhere more closely to established union policy.[32] It was a curious admonition, given that union policy endorsed the anti-war principle of international working-class solidarity. But it was also a sign that the executive was well aware patriotism was trumping socialism amongst its members.

In a rare editorial of his own, Wallace at the *Free Press* in August hopefully predicted that the war would be of short duration. Arguing that conflicts like the Thirty Years War were no longer possible, he pointed to the Austro-Prussian and the Franco-Prussian wars as the new template for modern warfare, concluding that the current conflict would be over just as quickly. Generally, he preferred to offer assessments from other newspapers insisting that Germany was doomed; from the *Toronto Globe* in December, for example, came a reprint of an article titled "The Allies are Winning."

While the *Free Press* remained optimistic, the *Ledger* predicted death and destruction on an unprecedented scale. Instead of a short conflict, the *Ledger* insisted the conflict would last for years and prove to be the bloodiest war in recorded history. In October, when some still believed the war would be over by Christmas, British statesman Lord Curzon was quoted by the *Ledger* as saying the war would not be over even by Christmas 1915; in December, perhaps testing the limits of his editorial freedom, Newnham fiercely criticized the notion that Germany had a monopoly on militarism.[33]

By the end of the year, Lieutenant Colonel Mackay's efforts as recruiting officer were receiving praise from all quarters. Mackay had been using the property at the skating rink for recruiting purposes in November. City alderman William Robichaud, who privately leased the property from the locally owned Rink Company, was pleased to receive fifty dollars in rent. When it became known that Mackay was personally bearing the expense, Robichaud returned the rental amount to him. Mackay enhanced his reputation further by refusing the refund, donating it instead to the 107th East Kootenay Regiment. In the cold weather of early December, the rink was returned to civilian and skating purposes, and the Rebekahs presented Mackay with a "housewife" rather more splendid than those they typically prepared for the common soldier. His early Christmas present was made of seal leather and grey silk, and its *Book of Common Prayer* was bound in Moroccan leather.[34]

The biggest local event of the year in provincial politics was the visit to Fernie in mid-December of Attorney General William Bowser, heir apparent to Premier Richard McBride and officially acting as premier during McBride's extended visit to England. The visitor was certainly a polarizing figure. Especially in the province's mining communities, Bowser was seen as the clear villain in the strike that had recently concluded in very messy fashion in the coalfields of Vancouver Island. When that strike began in the autumn of 1912, he ordered the hiring of special constables to assist the provincial police in maintaining order, and as the situation deteriorated steadily, in August 1913 he sent the militia into the area. Most of the nearly one thousand troops remained only briefly, but the bitter strike continued. After another year of tensions, the international UMWA announced in July 1914 it could no longer afford financial support for the striking miners, who had no choice but to return to work a month later.[35]

Miners with friends and relatives working in the Vancouver Island coalfields would not have been delighted to learn that Bowser was in town. The highly partisan *Free Press* nevertheless devoted almost its entire front page to a report on Bowser's visit. In his edition of December 18, Wallace printed the entire text of the speech he delivered to local Conservatives at the Victoria Hall. (Curiously, the gathering concluded with a boxing match between a Fernie lad and a fighter from Spokane. The match was declared a draw.) Although it could not have been known at the time of his visit, no individual would have a greater impact on events in Fernie in the year to come than William Bowser.

And then it was Christmas, the holiday season, by which time the cheering crowds of August, the *Fernie Free Press* and just about everybody else had believed the war would be over. Still, not even the pessimistic editor of the *District Ledger* could seriously have imagined that nearly four full years would pass before a victory of sorts could be declared. Residents admired the decorated store windows on Victoria Avenue and prepared to enjoy the holiday with family and friends. The Coal Creek Literary and Athletic Association was relieved that Welsby, satisfied with the "vast improvement" in the barroom, was recommending renewal of its liquor licence.[36]

Everyone must certainly also have looked forward to better times at home and to peace in Europe. After all, it was hard to imagine a worse year than the one just ending. Two men were killed in a cave-in at Coal Creek early in December. The coal markets were showing little sign of improvement. The disaster at Hillcrest, the abandonment of mining activity at Hosmer and the dreadful news of stalemate in the war in Europe affected everyone. To that list of discouraging events, the UMWA would add the debacle of one unsuccessful strike ending on Vancouver Island and another in Colorado.

And yet, for families and friends of several military volunteers and for scores of foreigners newly categorized as enemy aliens, a year very much worse was about to begin.

1915

THE WAR COMES TO FERNIE

The new calendar year began with religious ceremony. A royal decree from the United Kingdom designated January 3 as a day of prayer throughout the British Empire to plead for the success of Allied forces. Not for the last time in 1915, loyal Fernie followed the king's command. Under Mackay's orders, companies A and B of the 107th East Kootenay Regiment—its headquarters officially confirmed at Fernie—assembled at the Catholic church and marched to the Church of England, where an evening service was conducted by the regimental chaplain. Participants hoped the collective prayers of 1915 would have greater effect than had the prayers of the previous year, but just a few days after the service, news arrived from Europe of Fernie's first two casualties of war.

The year also began with twin surprises in civic politics. Mayor John Gates had decided to stand down, and two aldermen stepped forward to contend for the position in what was then an annual January election. Accustomed to dominating civic politics, city merchants and hoteliers were surprised by the convincing victory achieved by the secretary of the Gladstone local union, miner Thomas Uphill. When the outcome was announced, well-wishers gathered in front of the Miners' Union Building (generally also known as the Grand Theatre) on Victoria Avenue to cheer Uphill's victory speech. Members of the Excelsior Band were on hand to play "It's a Long Way to Tipperary."[37]

However, the election result could not be declared official because it was quickly discovered that a clerical error in conducting the poll enabled voters' identities and voting preferences to be easily determined. Awaiting word from the attorney general's office in Victoria about whether a new election would be required, Mayor Gates and the outgoing council would remain in office until the city was advised in late March that the results could be considered valid. Mayor Uphill and his new council held their first meeting on April Fools' Day. Attempted witticisms must have been numerous but sadly went unrecorded.[38]

As always, a mix of the trivial, the mundane and the serious commanded the attention of residents. Concerned at the devastation on the Eastern Front, residents Joseph Rudnicki, John "Jan" Podbielanik and A.J. Paulus organized a local Polish Relief Fund. The CPR announced it would no longer provide toothpicks on tables in its dining cars; the Great Northern announced the express service from Calgary to Spokane would be discontinued at the end of January—another casualty of the economic downturn. Lists of who had knitted what for the military were published regularly in the newspapers; a rumour circulated that German-born Albert Mutz of the Fernie–Fort Steele Brewing Company had been interned in Alberta under the War Measures Act.

Fernie mayor John Gates. With the validity of January's civic election in doubt, Gates stayed in office until the end of March. Fernie Museum and Archives 0196.

In early January, an explosion at the B North mine at Coal Creek occurred just minutes before the morning shift entered the mine. An inspector who entered the gaseous mine prematurely to investigate was the only casualty, but the explosion—said to be the biggest at Coal Creek since the disaster of 1902—seriously alarmed everyone in the valley; a government inquiry was soon announced. William Wilson, in a speech to CNPCC shareholders a few months later, praised the company's safety record, while bluntly asserting the inspector had no one to blame but himself for his death. He also explained that mining in the Elk Valley generated more than twice as much gas per ton of coal mined than did any of the most dangerous mines in Europe.[39]

The band issue continued to simmer, erupting into public controversy once more when District 18 international board member David Rees made a statement implying that the Excelsior group was the only "white band" in Fernie. Italian citizens protested strongly. Thomas Uphill—with the support of Sherwood Herchmer from the board of trade, Joseph Mackay on behalf of the local militia and several other leading citizens—invited the Excelsior Band to a meeting at city hall to find "some means whereby the two local bands may be brought together in peace and harmony to further the advancement of music" in the community. A subsequent vote on a proposed amalgamation of the two bands saw all twenty-five members of the Italian Band in favour, but a clear majority of the nineteen Excelsior players were opposed on the grounds that their aspiration was to play in a traditional northern English colliery band with brass instruments only.[40]

Representations by District 18 on behalf of Herman Elmer met with no success, as officials at Internment Operations saw "no reason to release him." Without a public farewell or explanation, Frank Newnham abruptly ceased to be editor of the *District Ledger* in mid-January, the position being taken two months later by Fernie resident and former *Ledger* editor John Bennett. Nevertheless, the newspaper's columns demonstrated no discernible change in style or content. Just a few weeks after he took over, Bennett felt sufficiently confident to publish an excerpt from Leo Tolstoy's essay "On Patriotism and Government" under the title "The Crime of Patriotism." Without editorial comment, the *Fernie Free Press* abruptly abandoned its weekly boast that the city had an industrial future comparable to that of Pittsburgh. Otherwise, the *Free Press* also maintained a consistent course under John Wallace, who was glad to be able to quash the rumour concerning Albert Mutz: Fernie's best-known brewer was yet a free man.

The women of the Mount Fernie chapter of the IODE doubled their numbers and their efforts. Membership had increased to fifty-three by the beginning of the year, and members were willing to take on any task requested of them. Under the leadership of a new executive headed by regent Eliza Moffatt, they organized a patriotic bonspiel in February and donated the profits to the Canadian Patriotic Fund; their Easter Ball in April brought another significant contribution into the coffers of the fund, and a Sock Day in May—in which they covered the entire city with a house-to-house canvas—resulted in 1,391 pairs of socks for Fernie's soldiers in Europe. Impressive lists of knitted socks, towels, bandages and other items would appear in newspapers every week throughout the year.

The Sock Day and similar fundraising efforts were usually reported as "Red Cross Work" in the *Free Press*, and the items knitted and collected were always sent to the Red Cross offices in Vancouver for distribution to Canadian soldiers in Europe. However, because a Red Cross chapter was not in place in Fernie, the IODE functioned as an agent and acted locally in all respects for the Canadian Red Cross. Interestingly, in Coal Creek, an active Red Cross committee maintained its independence and regularly dispatched more modest shipments to the national headquarters in Toronto.

A third contingent of twenty-seven local men paraded down snow-covered Victoria Avenue to the CPR station at the end of February, each man grateful for the social evening organized in his honour and the pipe and tobacco received from William Wilson.[41] In mid-March a group of nine volunteers departed for Vancouver to train with the 11th Canadian Mounted Rifles. In addition, a dozen local men had enlisted with the 13th Canadian Mounted Rifles at Pincher Creek.[42] Increasingly, concerns were being raised that, because local volunteers were so widely distributed in several military units, the very substantial contribution of troops from the Fernie district was not receiving the credit it deserved. The men of the second Fernie contingent, for example, had been assigned at Victoria to the 30th Battalion, which had just embarked for England, while those of the third contingent were all being absorbed by the 48th Battalion, also mobilizing at Victoria. The news was warmly welcomed, therefore, that a new regiment—the 54th Kootenay Battalion—was to begin recruiting in May throughout southeastern British Columbia and would muster at Nelson. In future, recruits from Fernie would be able to have their Kootenay origins acknowledged.

The Third Contingent, February 1915: These were the last volunteers to leave without first having been assigned to a designated military unit. Fernie Museum and Archives 3766.

The economic depression continued throughout the province, and a stubbornly high level of unemployment persisted. For many British Columbians, the war, unemployment, internment and the foreign-born—typically migrant workers from Italy, western Russia and the eastern stretches of the Austro-Hungarian Empire—were inextricably linked. Under the War Measures Act, internment camps for enemy aliens had been established at Vernon, Nanaimo and Lethbridge in September 1914, and influential voices at the coast were calling for the internment of everyone born in Germany and Austria-Hungary—whether single or married, naturalized or not. The most influential of those voices belonged to acting premier William Bowser. To relieve both unemployment and the pressure on civic relief funds, he urged the federal government to deport unemployed foreigners and to intern enemy aliens. Ignoring promises contained in the proclamation of August 15, 1914, Borden agreed in late April that enemy aliens could be interned simply because they were unemployed. The provincial police immediately began to make arrests in Vancouver, Victoria and the unincorporated districts of the central interior. By the middle of May, more than three hundred prisoners were being transferred to the custody of Internment Operations and to the expanding facilities of the Vernon internment camp.[43]

The level of local unemployment in Fernie also remained high. The number of men seeking work through the city's relief program increased to seventy-five by May, but only half that number had been engaged in road and park improvements. Alderman Robichaud complained that wages of roughly $2.70 for a nine-hour day were too high. To raise money for its relief program, city council in March imposed a reduction of 5 percent on wages for regular employees and 10 percent for department heads. The District 18 executive announced it would not expect members to pay union dues for the months of May, June and July. Meeting at Fernie in May, the same executive then approved the distribution of $2,000 from union funds for the relief of distressed members living in Fernie and Coal Creek and considered sending a delegate to Ottawa to press for federal government action.[44] With advertising, job printing and sales revenues declining, both the *Ledger* and the *Free Press* had reduced their issues from eight to four pages by early May.

The lumber industry remained depressed, but after three years of decreased demand, markets for coal and coke were expected to improve significantly as the year progressed. As a member of the Western Coal Operators' Association—formed in 1906 and representing most but not all coal owners in the Crowsnest Pass and southern Alberta—the Crow's Nest Pass Coal

Company was party to the new two-year collective agreement negotiated with the UMWA at the end of March. An agreement had been achieved without any labour disruptions, and the turmoil of the bitter 1911 strike seemed well in the past. The CNPCC was still operating at a loss, but shifts at the Coal Creek mine were predicted to become more regular. Mine managers and miners alike began to anticipate the prospect of increased production and fuller employment, but each month brought a postponement of the predicted improvements. The high recruitment rate eased the problem of local unemployment only marginally, as little hiring occurred to replace departing volunteers.

Significantly, the smaller Michel colliery was in operation for twice as many days in April and May as were the mines at Coal Creek, where the employment situation remained stubbornly negative. In May, the *Ledger* insisted there had been "no marked change for the better" in work available. Although an official "stay away" notice was not issued by the Gladstone local union, the *Ledger* urged men seeking employment not to come to Fernie. Coal Creek mine manager Bernard Caufield's official report for 1915 supports that assessment. He noted the mines there were in operation on average just nine days each month between January and May, and days worked in May were fewer than those worked in January.[45] Miners at Coal Creek on average were working just two shifts per week, providing them with income perhaps sufficient to cover room and board but little else.

Although much reduced since the prosperous years of 1909 and 1910, the number of men employed remained surprisingly high. Reporting a number that conflicts with other sources, the CNPCC declared 1,280 employees were engaged in its operations at Fernie and Coal Creek in June 1915. Approximately half were English-speaking; a largely British immigrant community dominated the skilled job categories. Also in skilled positions were a few dozen Belgian and French miners, mostly from the coal districts straddling the Belgian-French border. The CNPCC further confirmed that it also employed—typically as unskilled labourers—nearly 300 Italians, 90 Russians, 165 Austro-Hungarians and 25 Germans. Providing numbers that in retrospect seem more accurate, newspapers reported approximately 1,100 men engaged in the mines and at the coke ovens and an Austro-Hungarian figure of only 125.[46] Whatever the actual numbers were, apart from a few unskilled labourers at the coke ovens and nearly four dozen pit bosses, fire bosses, clerks and salaried officials, they were all members of the Gladstone local of the UMWA—the largest and most influential local union in District 18.

The monitoring of enemy aliens seemed to present few initial difficulties for East Kootenay provincial police chief Constable George Welsby and his officers. Austro-Hungarian and German nationals generally reported when required by the local constable, agreed "to do no injury to the Dominion of Canada" and were at liberty to go about their business. In January 1915, the Fernie jail held only two prisoners destined for the internment camp at Vernon. By May, however, provincial lock-ups at Waldo and Fernie recorded increasing numbers of men who had been detained for failing to report or for attempting to cross the border into the United States. Welsby was concerned that the capacity of the Fernie provincial jail—built to hold a maximum of twenty-four prisoners—was being overstretched. He was glad to see all twenty-seven prisoners then held at Fernie sent to Lethbridge on May 21 for internment.[47]

Patriotic fervour rose steadily during May. The new 54th Kootenay Battalion established its office on Wood Street and launched a recruitment drive, and not a day passed without additions to the enlistment roll. Reinforcements were certainly needed in Europe. The war that was supposed to be over by Christmas of 1914 began to produce staggeringly long lists of Canadian dead and wounded in May 1915. The names of men from the Fernie district continued to appear on those lists; by early June, ten men from the first Fernie contingent were reported killed.

Those not entirely sharing in the rising tide of patriotism needed to be careful. For "speaking disrespectfully of the overseas volunteers," William Sherman—son of former UMWA president Frank Sherman—was fined sixty dollars by magistrate William Whimster. The *Free Press* noted that only the appeals of his mother and the memory of his father saved him from a more severe penalty. Regular reports about alleged atrocities against civilians in Belgium underlined widespread suspicions about German and Austro-Hungarian immigrants, who could be blamed for any misadventure. The *Free Press*, without offering any evidence, pinned responsibility for the unexpected death of the canine mascot belonging to the local company of the 54th Kootenay Battalion on an unnamed German sympathizer.[48]

Although it was certainly shared, the outrage occasioned by news of the sinking of the *Lusitania* in early May did not find the same extreme expression in Fernie as it did at the coast. Two days of anti-German rioting in Victoria were ended only by a declared state of emergency and martial law. The *Vancouver Sun* newspaper intensified the agitation for the internment of all enemy aliens, and a number of Lower Mainland organizations—including

Vancouver's Rotary Club and board of trade—echoed that demand. So too did the civic governments of Vancouver, South Vancouver and North Vancouver, the latter also demanding the deportation of naturalized German-born and Austro-Hungarian-born British subjects "who through their acts appear to be unfriendly to the allies."[49] The *Daily Colonist* editorially joined the chorus for interment, while in Nanaimo a brief strike of miners at the Western Fuel Company unsuccessfully demanded the dismissal of all Austro-Hungarians. The *Fernie Free Press* certainly condemned the German action against the *Lusitania* but, in company with the city council, did not link it to the issue of internment.

The neutrality of Italy since the outbreak of war continued to leave the local Italian community on the sidelines. It was widely recognized that the sympathies of most Italian immigrants in Canada were with the Allies; a resolution passed by the Umberto Primo Italian Benevolent Society in Toronto stating bluntly that Italy "should participate in the war on the side of the Allies" was reported prominently by the *Free Press*. The Italian residents of Fernie were jubilant when the long anticipated news arrived on May 23 that Italy would not honour its treaty commitment to Germany and Austria-Hungary. Instead, Italy had declared war on the side of Britain, France and Russia.

Elated and no doubt relieved, local Italians were thereby classed favourably alongside their French, Belgian and Russian counterparts. The Italian Band led a procession around the town, stopping at the 54th Kootenay Battalion's recruiting office, the Italian consular office and other locations where speeches were heard amidst cheers and predictions of victory—Elk Valley echoes of the cheering crowds in the streets of European and Canadian cities of August 1914. Although many proclaimed their intentions to return to Italy to take up arms, the *Free Press* noted rather crankily that only one resident, local merchant Emilio Picariello, intended to enlist in the 54th Kootenay Battalion. Clearly, local Italians were no longer on the sidelines, but just as clearly, contributions to the war effort and demonstrations of loyalty would be expected of them. Not helping in this respect, Picariello failed to enlist after all.[50]

In less than a month, the quota set for Fernie and district for the 54th Kootenay Battalion was met—one hundred local men had enlisted to fight overseas—and the recruiting office was still open and busy. Having achieved the quota, Mackay announced the volunteers would depart Fernie on June 11. At the same time, C. diCastri, the Italian consular agent (and member of the Italian Band), announced he had received instructions to advise all Italian reservists to be ready to respond to a call to the colours. The reservists began to practise their military drills in public spaces while members of the English-speaking community looked on with approval. Fernie had the atmosphere of a war camp about to send its warriors into battle.

On the evening of June 3, an excellent performance of the revue 1915 Follies by a touring British troupe at the Grand Theatre was apparently poorly attended. The main attraction that evening was the "sumptuous dinner" for the men of the 54th hosted by CNPCC general manager William Wilson and his wife in the basement of the Methodist Church. A social event to honour departing volunteers was by then customary. This one took place fully a week ahead of their announced departure date because Wilson's presence at the farewell dinners to honour local soldiers was also by then customary, and he would soon be leaving on a planned trip to the United States. Patriotic speeches were made; Wilson presented the expected pipe and tobacco to each man; emotions ran high. The next day, he boarded the train for his visit to Saint Paul, Minnesota. It was a journey from which he would soon hurriedly return.

REBELLION OF THE MAJORITY

On Saturday, June 5, the superintendent of the Coal Creek mines, Bernard Caufield, was visited by a delegation of eight drivers—five of them Belgian, three of them English-speaking—who, citing safety concerns, told him they were opposed to working underground with enemy aliens. Apparently acting on their own, the drivers did not represent the union, but discussions amongst the miners on the following Monday resulted in a consensus amongst British, Italian, Belgian and Russian employees to back the drivers' position. One observer soon noted that "a bad feeling" had existed for several days amongst English-speaking and Italian miners.[51] Considering what was about to follow, it is not unreasonable to speculate that the bad feeling and the visit to Caufield both resulted from a refusal by Gladstone union leaders to endorse the position given voice by the drivers.

On Tuesday, June 8, miners scheduled for the morning shift at Coal Creek donned their clothes at the wash house as usual and took out their lamps as usual, but only the fire bosses and pit bosses and just a few others reported for work. Most of the men remained at the wash house where they resisted all attempts to persuade them to begin their shift. Their local union secretary, Thomas Uphill, reminded them of the penalty clause in their recently signed collective agreement that would see each man fined a dollar a day for an illegal work stoppage.[52] Caufield told the men the company was operating at a loss and work stoppages could only deepen that loss and threaten their jobs. He quickly realized he had no option but to declare the day idle. The men were adamant—they would not work until enemy aliens were no longer working with them.

An emergency meeting was called for 2:30 that afternoon in Fernie. Convened in the Socialist Hall on Pellatt Avenue, the gathering was quickly moved into an open space outside when the hall proved much too small to accommodate the surprisingly large crowd of approximately six hundred. District 18 president William Phillips and international board member David Rees (both residents of Fernie) were present, as was secretary Thomas Uphill who agreed to chair the meeting. During the next two hours, as many as twenty speakers addressed the assembled miners. Rees and Phillips each stood to argue that the foreign-born had joined in the common struggle against the capitalist class, and having engaged in no misconduct, deserved "British fair play." Constantly interrupted, neither man held the floor very long.

Options proposed at the meeting included a separate mine for enemy-alien miners, immediate termination of their employment or internment. Caufield was granted leave to address the meeting. He stated emphatically that the idea of a separate mine was entirely impractical and insisted the miners were asking the company to perform what was fundamentally the responsibility of the federal government. As secretary for the Gladstone local union, Thomas Uphill knew most of the men who would be affected. He briefly surrendered the chair to repeat the arguments of Rees and Phillips, but the assembled miners were steadfast. They selected six delegates to advise the CNPCC officially of the stand being taken and then adjourned to reconvene at the skating rink in the early evening.[53]

When the delegates called upon company officials at the CNPCC administration building, they were told that in the absence from Fernie of general manager William Wilson no formal response could be given and no action taken. The delegates duly reported back to the reassembled miners at the skating rink but found them unwilling to wait for Wilson's return. After a few references to the *Lusitania* and to atrocities in Belgium, the meeting passed a motion: "We, as Britishers and others, other than aliens, are willing to work and will work, but not under present conditions, that is to say, with alien enemies."[54] The clumsy wording caused the resolution to be reported differently—by the *Free Press* as a refusal to return to work until all enemy aliens had been discharged by the CNPCC, and by the *Ledger* as a call to intern all enemy aliens. Whatever its precise wording, the resolution passed easily. The Gladstone local union was on strike for the first time in four years. Maintaining a business-as-usual stance, Caufield posted notices in Fernie and Coal Creek requiring the Wednesday morning shift to report as usual.

However, the situation was already beyond the control of the CNPCC. As the senior military officer in Fernie, Lieutenant Colonel Mackay wired his superior in Victoria for instructions on the afternoon of the meeting. A response arrived quickly, but not from military authorities, and the instructions were not for Lieutenant Colonel Mackay. While the miners were still meeting, Attorney General and Acting Premier William Bowser instructed Colin Campbell, superintendent of provincial police, "to intern all single aliens working in Mines." Informed of the miners' meeting, Bowser had certainly wasted no time. Nor did Colin Campbell. Chief Constable Welsby at Fernie received his instructions from Campbell in sufficient time to have notices printed the same evening. Conflicting with those posted by the CNPCC, they commanded all unmarried and unnaturalized enemy-alien mine employees of military age to report to him in Fernie the next day. He advised Constable Joseph Boardman in Coal Creek to swear in special constables. Internment was to begin Wednesday, June 9.

With surprising ease, the rebellious miners had achieved their goal, not through a process with the federal authorities legitimately in charge of Internment Operations nationwide, but instead on the almost instantaneous order of the acting premier of British Columbia. Why had he intruded into an area of acknowledged federal jurisdiction so quickly and so profoundly that both military and company officials were apparently deprived of an opportunity to consider alternative courses of action? The answer to that question is found in a particular mix of personality and politics in Victoria and the very recent history of the coal mines on Vancouver Island.

During the extended sojourn of Premier Richard McBride in England, Attorney General William Bowser continued in the role of acting premier. He enjoyed overwhelming control of the Legislature, but was presiding over a government increasingly divided and unpopular as the economic depression took its toll. Anticipating a general election but saddled with seriously high levels of unemployment, Bowser was attempting to regain popularity for provincial Conservatives through legislation and policies intended to attract the support of the working class. His advocacy of internment of unemployed enemy aliens was part of that initiative.

But the most significant impediment to Bowser's hopes for attracting the working-class vote was the deep animosity he had earned by ordering the militia to intervene during the bitter coal strike of 1912–14. Even a year after the strike's conclusion, due to a combination of depressed coal markets and blacklisting of those who had participated in the strike, unemployment was high in the mining communities of Vancouver Island. Nanaimo in particular was struggling with the near exhaustion of its available relief funds and civic financial credit.[55] The strident calls for a broader federal internment policy following the *Lusitania* affair

Hon. William Bowser: As acting premier, he harnessed and exploited anti-foreigner sentiment for political advantage. Royal BC Museum and Archives A-02018.

encouraged Bowser to press Ottawa further; he wanted that policy extended beyond enemy aliens who were unemployed.

With considerable pride, Bowser announced on May 25 in Victoria that, after much effort on his part, he had secured the approval of the federal minister of justice to arrange for the internment of enemy aliens working in the mines at Nanaimo, Ladysmith, South Wellington and Cumberland. In addition to having the appearance of a patriotic action in accordance with demands for internment of enemy aliens, the initiative was calculated to ease Nanaimo's financial burden, create employment opportunities for still unemployed British miners and ease the resentment those miners felt toward him personally and against the foreigners who had taken their places during the strike. To use modern terminology, it had the appearance of a plan that ticked all the right boxes.

Just as Bowser was making his announcement, military officials arrived in Nanaimo to implement the plan. Major Ridgeway Wilson, by then possessing expanded powers to oversee internment matters in British Columbia, was responsible for supervising the operation. The federal authorities had initially been concerned that the small internment camp at Nanaimo and the much larger one at Vernon were already near capacity, but Bowser persuaded them that the new Saanich Prison Farm near Victoria could accommodate the additional prisoners until Internment Operations could accept them. He spoke of removing a menace to the community and claimed his action was very much "to the advantage of white workingmen on Vancouver Island."[56]

Immediately, provincial police in Ladysmith and Nanaimo were ordered to arrest enemy-alien miners.[57] On May 28, sixty-four prisoners from Nanaimo and Extension were sent aboard the *Princess Patricia* to Vancouver en route to the internment camp at Vernon; three dozen more were sent to the Saanich Prison Farm, adding to their number fourteen prisoners from Ladysmith along the way.[58] Bowser then wrote to mine managers urging them to hire unemployed British miners to fill positions vacated by the internees and sent a provincial relief officer to Nanaimo to exert further pressure on them.[59] Apparently pleased with the success of the operation, he then ordered the same process followed at Cumberland. On June 3, thirty-three enemy-alien employees of the Union Colliery Company were handed over to military authorities at Union Bay.[60]

While Fernie was an isolated community in 1915, it is inconceivable that its residents were unaware of these developments on Vancouver Island. William Wilson had certainly been unwise not to cancel his planned trip to Saint Paul. Not one known to shy away from facing a crisis, perhaps he simply gave no credence to the possibility that employees of the CNPCC could be caught up so quickly in the web of Bowser's ambitious plans for internment and re-election. But it must have been obvious that logically the acting premier would have to apply his island policy to the East Kootenay coalfields at some point.

Entries in the June reports of the provincial police constables at Coal Creek and Michel clearly indicate that he was quickly preparing the groundwork to do precisely that. On June 6, two days before the miners' work stoppage, Constable Boardman spent the day gathering all particulars of aliens at Coal Creek, including place of birth and marital status; Constable English at Michel spent that day and the next notifying enemy aliens of the need to report to the police station. The constables were acting on orders conveyed by Welsby from Colin Campbell, who in turn was answerable to Attorney General Bowser. Such entries in the reports of police at Ladysmith, Nanaimo and Cumberland were followed within days by the arrest and internment of enemy-alien miners in those communities. The answer to the question about the speed of Bowser's response to the situation at Fernie is clear. He was able to respond immediately to the miners' demand because his preparations for arrests in the Elk Valley were already made.[61]

If the timing of the miners' revolt can be explained by news of events in the mining communities on Vancouver Island, the dynamics of the mass meeting of June 8 and the nature of the debate are much more open to speculation. The few surviving records of the meeting fail to inform on key questions. They make no mention of the participation of Italian miners or of those from other Allied nations. Nor do they indicate if any of the threatened Austro-Hungarian and German members of the union were present. It is clear that the debate itself was conducted entirely in English, was fundamentally an internal debate amongst the English-speaking members of the local union and was framed in terms of the issue that dominated politics in Fernie during the war. That issue was how to define and how to express patriotism and loyalty.

For many English-speaking miners, the Austro-Hungarian and German employees of the CNPCC had become the face of the enemy. A good number of them were known to be reservists in the armies of their homelands; few of them mixed socially outside the workplace. Demanding punitive action against the readily identifiable and socially marginalized local representatives of enemy states could readily be seen as a patriotic responsibility. A significant minority disagreed. The leadership of the union—comprised of British immigrants both locally and district-wide—was unanimously opposed to the call to dismiss enemy aliens from employment. But with the strong majority at the meeting determined to prevail, the principles of socialism, union solidarity and equality before the law were easily overwhelmed.

Some contemporaries observed it was more accurate to say that the miners were wilfully disguising their true motivation under the cloak of the Union Jack. Both CNPCC general manager William Wilson and District 18 president William Phillips would later insist that patriotism had nothing to do with the resolution passed at the skating rink, each stating that "scarcity of work" was the fundamental motivation of those voting in favour. By that measure, the facade of patriotic motivation became as convenient a disguise for the miners' economic self-interest as it was for the acting premier's political self-interest.[62]

An appreciation of these cross-currents may provide some understanding of what motivated individual miners to vote as they did, but fundamentally their revolt was not necessary. Unaware of Bowser's plans, they were demanding what was about to be freely offered. The internment order Welsby received on June 8 cannot have been entirely unexpected. It was simply delivered sooner than planned. Bowser undoubtedly would have preferred a more orderly process, perhaps dealing first with Coal Creek and later with Michel and Natal and, presumably later still, with Corbin. But the unanticipated job action advanced his timetable. The combination of Bowser's experience of the Vancouver Island strike and his successful action in interning enemy-alien miners at Nanaimo, South Wellington, Ladysmith and Cumberland explain the decision he made about Fernie and the rapidity with which he made it. It had simply become necessary to apply immediately to the East Kootenay coalfields the same policy that had been followed on Vancouver Island.

Fernie's Conservative Association may have been well aware that local enemy aliens were about to be arrested. Meeting at the Hotel Fernie on the afternoon of June 9—just as the first internees were being processed at the courthouse—local Conservatives adopted a well-considered proposal to establish a permanent internment camp at Morrissey. Anticipating up to four hundred prisoners from Fernie alone and citing the high costs that would be incurred in transporting them elsewhere, the meeting resolved "to request the proper authorities to make the necessary arrangements to secure the Morrissey Mines townsite as an internment camp for this district." Owned by the CNPCC, the townsite itself and the privately owned buildings within it were still in good condition, having been abandoned just a few years earlier when mining ceased there in 1909. Acting with such speed and efficiency, the Conservative Association appears to have been a very nimble organization indeed. The resolution was telegraphed immediately to those in charge of Internment Operations and to Fernie's sitting federal and provincial politicians. A response was eagerly awaited.

BOWSER'S INTERNEES

The course of subsequent developments would perhaps have been different had the company been allowed an opportunity to respond to the miners' demand. It is highly unlikely William Wilson would have agreed to fire more than three hundred employees simply because of their national origin, regardless of the strength of what he would later describe as miners' "war sentiment." But Bowser's immediate order to intern meant the company did not have the chance to respond. Had the CNPCC been forewarned? Wilson's absence from Fernie at the critical moment and Caufield's order to report for work as usual at Coal Creek indicate the CNPCC was blindsided by the internment order. Wilson would later assert that neither he nor the company had been consulted.[63]

Nevertheless, in Victoria on June 9, Bowser said he had the full co-operation of mine managers as well as the sanction of military authorities. Echoing his remarks about the internments on Vancouver Island, Bowser stated his purpose at Fernie was to create employment for "deserving men who find themselves out of work." He said, "Full advantage should be taken of the chance to relieve unemployment," adding again that his decision was intended to remove a menace to the peace of the community. The menace he had in mind this time was more likely to have been the prospect of a miners' strike than any subversive activities by disloyal German and Austro-Hungarian nationals. Fundamentally, Bowser knew he could count on the appearance of patriotism and the requirements of wartime home security to justify his decisive action.

But because of the greater number of enemy aliens employed by the CNPCC, the situation at Fernie was immediately more complicated than that on Vancouver Island. The provincial lock-up at Fernie would not suffice on even a temporary basis. Cells in the basement of the courthouse were built to house a maximum of twenty-four prisoners. Welsby scrambled to make arrangements with rink manager William Robichaud and Lieutenant Colonel Mackay, who once again was using the property for military purposes. Both agreed to relinquish the skating rink to serve as a temporary jail.[64]

On the morning of June 9, Fernie residents affected by the posted order of the previous evening began to report to the provincial police office at the courthouse. As a sizeable crowd of onlookers gathered outside the fence surrounding the building, Welsby, assisted by city police chief Albert Brown, took the name and particulars of each man. At three o'clock, the buglers of the 107th regiment were heard leading the volunteers of the 54th Kootenay Battalion to another farewell event, this one organized by the Rebekahs at the Victoria Hall. Sometime after four o'clock, the Fernie prisoners were joined on the grounds of the courthouse by twenty-eight unmarried enemy aliens who arrived on the train from Coal Creek, where Constable Boardman and his two special constables had arrested them during the course of the day. Blankets and personal belongings were searched for alcohol and concealed weapons before the men were escorted the short distance down the hill to the skating rink at the foot of Howland Avenue. One hundred and eight men spent their first night as prisoners of the Province of British Columbia.[65] Following a four-hour meeting on the morning of June 10, miners agreed to return to work.

Provincial police in Michel and Natal attended to the swearing in of special constables, while officers based in Corbin, Elko and Hosmer travelled to Fernie to assist with internment duties. On June 10, Constable Hughes of Natal and four special constables brought sixty-seven enemy aliens to the skating rink. On the same day, four Austrian-born prisoners from Cranbrook, probably temporarily destined for the provincial lock-up in Fernie in transit to Lethbridge, found themselves held instead at the day-old internment camp. One of them made the camp's first escape attempt the following day.[66] Constable English of Michel and his four special constables arrived with eighty-four prisoners on June 11; Hughes returned on June 12 with sixteen more. Constable English may well have noticed Imperial Hotel owners Angelo and Alexander Rizzuto putting a large number of Italian reservists through military drills as he brought in nineteen more prisoners from Michel on Sunday, June 13.[67]

As numbers at the skating rink rose rapidly, providing adequate food and facilities became a challenge that Welsby had to face without delay. The Elk Lumber Company supplied the materials and Trites-Wood the hardware necessary for the quick construction of fencing, latrines behind the building and rudimentary kitchen facilities inside. Welsby made arrangements for groceries, meat and bread with Trites-Wood, P. Burns and Company and John McEwing respectively. Rules, regulations and other arrangements within the compound also had to be quickly established. Internees quickly found they were required to do their own cooking and cleaning.

On just the camp's second morning, June 11, as some prisoners went about assigned tasks and others contemplated or discussed their new circumstances, they heard cheers and music from Victoria Avenue. A civic holiday had been declared and businesses were closed as what was reported as "practically the entire city" turned out to cheer the departing Fernie volunteers of the 54th Kootenay Battalion along their parade route from the recruiting office to the train station. They were to leave on the same train that brought the first internees from Michel. Accompanied by the bugle band and an honour guard of the 107th East Kootenay Regiment, soldiers destined for the battlefields of Europe marched to the train station. There the Italian Band took over musical responsibilities. Whether Mackay anticipated the imminent removal of the Russian government's prohibition on its nationals joining the Canadian army or simply decided to ignore it, for the first time Russian nationals were amongst the volunteers.[68] It seems unlikely that the men listening from their confinement at the skating rink shared in the sense of celebration.

Both local newspapers reacted to the internment with caution. In their editions at the end of the first week of the process, they reported extensively on the developing situation, observing that the prisoners seemed cheerful and philosophical about their situation and were passing the time with card games and music. The *Free Press* commended the provincial police for their handling of the situation and expressed the hope that all parties would "meet the situation with that restraint and consideration which the difficulties demand." The *Ledger* noted the "orderliness and general spirit of give and take" that prevailed and hoped for a quick "return to normality," but it was shocked into a rare silence editorially. The elected leaders of District 18 had been ignored and marginalized by hundreds of members who had insisted on an action that clearly undermined and contradicted the fundamental UMWA principle of union solidarity. Undoubtedly, there were many miners who remained committed to that principle and who were entirely

Departure of volunteers for the 54th Kootenay Battalion: It was reported that almost every resident of the city was on hand to bid farewell. New Westminster Archives IHP-4361.

opposed to the resolution, but the fact remained that a substantial majority at the meeting demanded the ouster of their law-abiding Austrian-born and German-born neighbours from employment in the mines. Proponents of unionism were profoundly discouraged.

Advocates of internment were delighted. In Vancouver, the staunchly Liberal *Sun* newspaper, habitually hostile to Bowser, took the unprecedented step of praising him. The newspaper editorialized that Bowser "had the hearty support of The Sun and all other Canadians who are interested in the welfare of the Dominion." Acknowledging that the acting premier may have exceeded his powers, the editorial insisted he should be "congratulated anyway" and concluded, "Perhaps [the prisoners] have been wrongfully interned without the consent of the government at Ottawa, but the fact remains that they have been put out of harm's way until the end of the war."[69]

The *Vancouver World* agreed, arguing that the miners were forced to act because the federal authorities had long failed to do so and suggesting "many other classes of aliens" should also be interned. The *Daily News-Advertiser* of Vancouver acknowledged the injustice that internment would impose on "non-Teutonic natives of Austria-Hungary" but said blame must be placed on offenders "on the other side of the ocean." Its editorial position was that Britons and Belgian, Russian and French nationals should not be compelled to work alongside "offensive associates." It noted that appeals to union solidarity were "of no avail against the national consciousness and sense of outrage."[70]

Encouraged by these wide-ranging expressions of approval, Bowser in Victoria decided to push further. Welsby was ordered to register all enemy aliens—married as well as single men, naturalized or not. Although the number of individuals affected would be small, the order sent constables scurrying back to their home bases to comply. Registrations took place over the next three days, but no married or naturalized men were subsequently arrested because the CNPCC intervened. As its response to the Topay lawsuit of 1914 had demonstrated, the CNPCC was no champion of the civil rights of enemy aliens, but it was profoundly alarmed at government and union interference with its prerogative to determine the composition of its workforce. General manager William Wilson had hurriedly returned to Fernie. He was able to persuade Welsby—who must have been alarmed at the prospect of supervising even greater numbers at the skating rink—not to proceed with the additional internment. The married and naturalized men were all permitted to remain at work.[71]

However, new prisoners were brought in from Cranbrook and the lumber camps of the south country. Constable Dryden of Waldo brought in four men from the Ross-Saskatoon camp on June 15; Constable Gorman of Elko delivered five men from the Joseph Letcher camp on June 18; and Constable Collins brought two more men from Cranbrook on June 22.[72] Following the patterns established over the previous several months, these men—several of whom had been arrested while planning or attempting to cross into the United States—would normally have been held temporarily at the Fernie provincial jail before being transferred to the internment camp at Lethbridge. Improvising on a daily basis and with limited manpower available, Welsby unsurprisingly decided to confine them, temporarily at least, at the skating rink.

Although provincial police constables at Hosmer and Corbin soon made the same inventories of enemy aliens as had their counterparts at Coal Creek, Michel and Natal, prisoners were not taken. The numbers at the skating rink were severely straining the ability of Welsby and his staff to cope, and therefore the order to intern was not extended beyond the affected employees of the CNPCC. Except for those from Cranbrook and the lumber camps near Elko and Waldo, only CNPCC employees were being held at Fernie.

Reports of the number of affected men varied by source and date. After just three days of the operation, the *Free Press* put the number of internees at 279. The *Lethbridge Daily Herald* placed the number at 321 on June 15, substantially agreeing with a report by an employee of the Department of Labour that 314 Austro-Hungarians and 6 Germans were being held. The *District Ledger* and the *Victoria Daily Times* on June 19 both misleadingly estimated the total number of internees held at the skating rink to be nearly 400. More reliably, the *Ledger* a month later stated the number of men initially detained was 317. If that was a count of only CNPCC employees, as seems likely, there were 187 internees from Michel and Natal—communities where there had been no agitation at all about working with enemy aliens—and 130 from Fernie and Coal Creek. Taking all police reports and other sources into account and including non-CNPCC employees, numbers appear to have peaked at around 330 on June 22.[73]

From Alberta came news that miners at Hillcrest were following the precedent set by the Gladstone local union. Citing safety concerns, they were refusing to work underground with enemy aliens.

THE TROUBLESOME QUESTION OF LEGALITY

By the end of the second week of the operation, the confusion surrounding the whole question of a provincially ordered internment was receiving a great deal of press commentary both at the coast and in Fernie. The confusion arose because Bowser assumed—reasonably but incorrectly—that the co-operation of federal authorities he had secured for Vancouver Island was transferrable to East Kootenay. On that basis, he had instructed Major Ridgeway Wilson to send the internees to "whatever internment camp may be decided upon." But the federal authorities were having second thoughts about the rule of law in a time of war. A representative of Internment Operations met with Lieutenant Colonel Mackay, Mayor Uphill and Chief Constable Welsby in Fernie on June 14 and, as the *Free Press* reported it, advised that there "was no legal authority for interning these men."

Apparently, the proclamation of August 15, 1914, and the broad powers accorded by the War Measures Act were not sufficient to deal with Bowser's internees. The federal measures justified the internment of enemy aliens who had indicated (or were alleged to have indicated) loyalty to Germany or Austria-Hungary, who had attempted to flee to the United States or who by virtue of being unemployed were simply suspected of disloyalty. The men held at the skating rink in Fernie had not professed support for Germany or Austria-Hungary, had not attempted to cross into the United States, had all registered with the police as required and had undertaken to obey the laws of Canada. In addition, they were all employed. And uniquely, they were being detained by a provincial government.

Bowser told Prime Minster Borden he was "greatly perturbed" at the reluctance of Internment Operations to take charge of the prisoners, asking why the situation at Fernie should be seen differently than the detention of enemy-alien miners on Vancouver Island and warning that "riot and strike" could result from releasing the men held at the skating rink. He asked MPs for Victoria and Kootenay to personally lay his concerns before Borden in Ottawa and the MP for Comox-Atlin to wire Borden in support of the province's internment initiative. Placing great emphasis on the seriousness of high unemployment, he hoped to extend his internment policy to the Granby mine at Anyox and the Britannia mine north of Vancouver.[74] In Victoria, during comments to reporters about the situation in Fernie, he rather clumsily attacked federal authorities for their lack of co-operation, criticizing A.P. Sherwood, the chief commissioner of police in Ottawa, for treating internees so well and for being "afraid of hurting their feelings." At the same time, he was pleased with the announcement from the Britannia Mining Company that it had voluntarily discharged its enemy-alien employees.

In Fernie, the *Free Press* asked "Where are we at?" and answered "Who knows?" It noted that individuals representing the federal immigration branch and department of labour and the British Columbia Federation of Labour had all visited and departed without providing solution or resolution. Bowser emphatically denied the report in the Vancouver World that the internees would soon be freed and told reporters he had advised Prime Minister Borden that riots would break out in the mining camps if they were. Agreeing that the potential for disorder was substantial, the Free Press reported that militia units based in Calgary were awaiting orders to leave for Fernie, and noted, "It would be a hardy man who would take the responsibility for turning these [internees] loose in this community now."

Compounding the uncertainty caused by the hesitation of federal authorities was the fact that the internees had been given professional advice that their internment was illegal. Apart from the greater number of prisoners involved, the fundamental difference between the interned miners at Fernie and those arrested on Vancouver Island was that the Fernie internees mounted a legal challenge. No such challenge had resulted from the police operation at Nanaimo, Ladysmith and Cumberland, in part because there had been no delay in transferring the majority of the prisoners to federal custody. But at Fernie, well into the second week of the camp, Internment Operations remained unwilling to accept responsibility for the internees.

It is distinctly possible that the advice about the illegality of the internment originated with the UMWA. Perhaps the supreme irony of the crisis is the fact that the most prominent defenders of the civil rights of enemy aliens were English-speaking executive members of the same union to which the English-speaking rebels owed their allegiance. David Rees and William Phillips had failed to influence the meeting that called for internment; Thomas Uphill in the chair could not play a significant partisan role in that debate but later insisted he saw no reason whatsoever for imprisoning the men at the ice rink. Taking advantage of the union's editorial control of the *Ledger*, the executive mounted what was essentially a counter-attack on Bowser's *fait accompli*.

In a lengthy editorial in its issue of June 19, the newspaper laid out precisely the argument that had so concerned the acting premier. Recalling the proclamation of August 15, editor John Bennett reprinted in full the paragraph guaranteeing that those who "quietly pursued their ordinary avocations" could continue "to enjoy the protection of the law" and would not be "arrested, detained or interfered with." He pointed out that the men held at the skating rink differed from those detained at Vernon and Lethbridge in that they had all signed the undertaking to obey the laws of Canada as required, no charge had been laid against them and they had broken no law. Acknowledging that "dispassionate discussion and calm analysis upon any subject relative to the war" was problematic, Bennett nevertheless drew readers' attention to the principles of habeas corpus as "a precious safeguard of individual liberty against official tyranny."

Unusually, the assessment presented by the UMWA newspaper was entirely consistent with the view held by one of Canada's most prestigious business publications. The *Canadian Mining Journal*, while acknowledging that all known partisans of Germany working in Canadian mines "should be promptly interned," insisted editorially that enemy aliens "striving to live as becomes decent citizens" should not.

> The men employed in the mines have won their positions by their work, and, so long as their work is satisfactory to their employers and their conduct satisfactory to the public, it will be grossly unfair for anyone seeking personal interest to ask that they be refused employment.

The editorial did not specify whether it was condemning the miners of Coal Creek or William Bowser for "seeking personal interest," but its disapproval of the internment is perfectly clear. The *Free Press*, in reprinting the editorial, was stepping back from its initial enthusiasm. By the end of the month, the newspaper would express its own muted criticism of the miners' action but no criticism of Bowser's actions.

Collectively, the internees had attempted to raise $700 for legal fees. Although they fell short of the mark, Cranbrook lawyer Thomas Macredy agreed to apply for writs of habeas corpus in the names of Austrian-born internees Stephan Janastin, employed at Coal Creek since 1908, and Martin Bobrovski, employed at Michel, who had come to Canada as a seven-year-old in 1891.[75] Fernie lawyers, apparently adopting the same patriotic stance as that employed by the miners and the acting premier, had all refused to take the case. Macredy travelled to Fernie on June 16 to serve the affidavit on Welsby but could not locate him. Nevertheless, the affidavit was served the next day, and others were sent to Victoria for Bowser and superintendent Colin Campbell. The applications were scheduled to be heard in the Supreme Court in Vancouver on Monday, June 21.

Internees at the skating rink, June 1915: Under overcast skies, captives and custodians posed for the local photographer. Fernie Museum and Archives 3248do.

Fernie photographer Joseph Spalding managed to secure Welsby's agreement that the internment deserved to be visually recorded. Under overcast skies, the prisoners were gathered on the enclosed grounds behind the skating rink. With a handful of spectators watching from outside the barbed wire fence, with armed guards positioned around the perimeter and with Welsby standing authoritatively in the foreground, the interned men faced the camera. As in a year-end school photograph, the faces of the supervisor and those in his charge were recorded for posterity as Spalding captured a unique image for a new postcard. The photograph was unlike a typical school photograph, however. None of the faces revealed any evident pleasure in the occasion.

As the days passed and uncertainty reigned outside the camp, life inside developed its patterns and routines. Cigarettes and tobacco were delivered to internees by well-wishers. Visitors were allowed into the compound only with Welsby's written permission but could talk to them freely from outside; books and newspapers were permitted if the recipients promised not to litter. Three dozen special constables, on duty twelve at a time in eight-hour shifts, were supervised by one or two regular provincial police officers. The regulars were typically armed with standard issue .38-calibre Smith and Wesson or Iver Johnson revolvers; like the unarmed special constables they dressed in civilian clothes. Spalding's photograph of the camp shows that, while the police also had access to rifles, in appearance they were indistinguishable from store clerks and bank tellers.[76]

Cooking and cleaning were done by small groups of internees, whether as volunteers or reluctant conscripts is not known. The morning meal consisted of bread, porridge and tea; the evening meal of meat, vegetables, bread and soup. Cleaning details kept the facility tidy by dumping accumulated rubbish in the Elk River. Reporters from the Fernie newspapers were allowed full access to the camp. The *Ledger* reporter commented on the sense of fellowship and the "general air of contentment" that prevailed. Indeed, his published column describes almost a holiday atmosphere.

> Games of cards are indulged in, bursts of song enliven the monotony, and as there are quite a number who are musical executants on both wind and brass instruments, the tones of the accordion, cornet, [and] flute furnish excellent media for driving dull care away.

One tune frequently played was "It's a Long Way to Tipperary."[77]

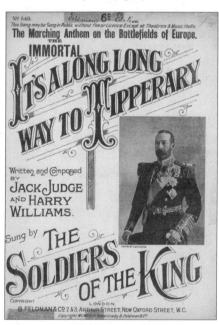

Musicians of the Italian (City) Band, the Coal Creek Colliery Band and the internees at the skating rink all played this song in 1915. Image courtesy of the author.

But of course this was not a holiday camp. The men were still sleeping on the floor, and the lack of bathing facilities was causing concern as "a possible menace" to the health of all. Overshadowing all this was the continuing uncertainty about what was to happen to the more than three hundred men being held. Seven men were released when they produced their naturalization papers. Would they all be released if the legal challenge was successful? If Dominion authorities took over, would the internees be moved to Lethbridge or Vernon or to one of the newer camps, perhaps Revelstoke or Banff? An unseasonable cool and wet June added generally overcast skies to the sense that Fernie was a troubled community. The court date for the internees' legal challenge was postponed for a week at the request of Crown counsel acting on instructions from Bowser. When the week had passed, it was postponed again. The seven men who belatedly had managed to provide their naturalization papers no doubt were relieved to be released. But for those still detained, how much longer could the admired "air of contentment" be sustained?

TRANSFERRED RESPONSIBILITIES

The situation at Fernie presented federal authorities with a serious problem. To continue to refuse responsibility for Bowser's internees meant the legal challenge would proceed with the possible outcome—indeed, the probable outcome—favouring the appellants. That judgement would necessarily also apply to the prisoners arrested from the mining communities of Vancouver Island. The mass release of approximately 450 enemy aliens would cause outrage throughout British Columbia, and that outrage would be directed not only towards Bowser's Conservatives in Victoria. However, by their own assessment, Internment Operations admitted there were no legal grounds for detaining the prisoners at the skating rink.

Bowser was seriously alarmed when advised by the minister of justice in Ottawa that the situation at Fernie was not consistent with that on Vancouver Island. No stranger to the law, he was aware that the application for habeas corpus backed by provisions of the proclamation of August 15, 1914, would certainly succeed. In desperation, he wired Borden on June 25 that he would then have no choice but to issue an order for the release of the internees. Concluding that a release was politically unacceptable, recognizing that its approval of Bowser's proposal for internment on Vancouver Island had been reckless, but with no legal grounds to detain enemy-alien miners, the federal government quietly decided to create those legal grounds.

The internees' day in court—scheduled for 10:00 a.m. on June 28—was yet again postponed. But to the dismay of the internees, Major General Sir William Otter, in command of Internment Operations nationwide, issued orders that day to take charge of the camp at the skating rink from the provincial police. Something had changed. Apparently, Internment Operations was no longer concerned about an absence of legal authority to detain the internees at Fernie; apparently, the applications for writs of habeas corpus were no longer worrisome. Just as he was processing two additional German prisoners brought in from Wardner, Welsby received instructions from Victoria on June 29 to transfer command to federal authorities. He made preparations to comply immediately—probably with a great sense of relief. The transfer of responsibility took effect officially the next day.

The explanation for the Dominion's sudden acceptance of responsibility became apparent to all only when those applications were dismissed out of hand by a judge two weeks later in Vancouver. To the complete surprise of counsel representing the internees, the lawyer for the Crown presented a copy of Order-in-Council 1501 passed June 26 (not yet gazetted, but clearly in response to Bowser's desperate wire of the previous day) giving the minister of justice authority to intern—as he saw fit—enemy aliens working in the mines.[78] Essentially, the order-in-council sanctioned the internment of enemy aliens whose simple presence in a workplace "may lead to disorder." It was devised with the specific situation at Fernie uppermost in mind, but was worded such that there could be no subsequent legal challenge from Vancouver Island internees or anyone else. Swollen with densely worded arguments attempting to justify its conclusion, the proclamation seems just as clumsy as the miners' resolution of three weeks earlier. The *Daily News-Advertiser* in Vancouver summarized its intent.

> It provides in effect, that because of the possibility of danger among enemy aliens and British subjects who may be at work together in mines and at other occupations in Canada, it is considered wise that the enemy aliens shall be taken care of at public expense.

It was knowledge of this new order-in-council that had allowed Internment Operations to suddenly announce its takeover of the camp two weeks earlier. The lobbying campaign orchestrated by Bowser had ultimately succeeded in persuading Borden's government that social disorder was probable in Fernie if the internees at the skating rink were released. Of course, the government in Ottawa also recognized that the legal and constitutional mess created by provincial internment had to be cleaned up. At a single stroke, the protection accorded by habeas corpus was withdrawn from enemy aliens in mining occupations, and the legal authority was created for Internment Operations to take custody of Bowser's internees. Assurances published with such confidence by the *Ledger* during the preceding months that law-abiding enemy aliens would be protected by British justice were apparently naive. The newspaper reported simply and rather weakly that internment at the rink "had been legalized, although this was not originally so."

At Hillcrest, where there had been no provincial intervention to complicate the situation, the new order-in-council was not needed and was not applied.[79] The UMWA local union co-operated with the coal company to have all miners—British and enemy-alien alike—back at work by the end of June, just as federal authorities were taking charge at Fernie. Apart from the handful of prisoners from the south country still in custody, the number of employees of the CNPCC transferred to Internment Operations on June 30 stood at 308.[80] The transfer of the special constables recruited by the provincial police to act as guards did not go as smoothly. Advised they could continue in that capacity, but only at the military rate of pay—namely, $1.10 per day plus a living allowance of eighty-five cents—the guards were unhappy with such a reduction in pay and most refused to continue. Their places were taken by men of the 107th East Kootenay Regiment, initially unarmed and without uniforms.

The officer taking charge of the camp was Lieutenant Colonel Joseph Mackay, much admired in Fernie for his integrity and recruiting work. Like Welsby three weeks earlier, Mackay now had to avoid chaos by taking things quickly in hand. The camp was reorganized to run on military lines, and basic facilities were improved. A medical officer made his rounds each morning; a rotating schedule placed different officers of the 107th East Kootenay Regiment in charge each day; orders were given to treat internees "with uniform courtesy without undue familiarity." Arrangements made with local suppliers had to be approved by Internment Operations, and, while that process was underway, the city of Fernie provided meals to the internees.

Wooden bunks were constructed so sleeping on the floor was no longer necessary; camp boundaries at the rear of the building were extended, stumped and levelled to create a sports field; hot water was finally made available for bathing and washing clothes. Contracts for provisioning the camp were signed with Fernie businesses for terms of "six months or until the end of the war." Mackay was soon applauded by both Internment Operations and the local press for running the camp on an economical basis. Cost of food per man per day was pegged at barely over twenty cents per day; the cost of facilities (showers, kitchen and sanitary arrangements) at thirty cents per day. Ever the community booster, the *Free Press* was proud to report that visiting military personnel were of the opinion the camp was being conducted more economically than any other in western Canada.[81]

Mackay was not an admirer of Bowser's internment order, but military proprieties prevented him from publicly criticizing it. He would later privately advise Otter that he could not understand why such an order was given, describing the local Slavic population as being amongst Fernie's best citizens,

Lieutenant-Colonel Joseph Mackay: A sharp critic of Bowser's internment order, Fernie's leading military man nevertheless took command of the prisoners on behalf of the federal government. City of Vancouver Archives PAM1916.

of no danger to the state or anyone else.[82] Upon taking command, he immediately requested and received permission to examine the justification for internment of each man individually, intending to release those for whom no justification could be found.

However, Mackay did not intend to revive the agitation at Coal Creek; release would be conditional on an undertaking not to return to work in the mines.[83] On June 30, his first full day in command of the camp, he discharged a small number of internees on humanitarian grounds and eight Czechs, described by the *Free Press* as "a tribe of Bohemians friendly to the Allies." With internee Janastin providing translation services for Austrian-born prisoners, Mackay undertook to review the case for internment of approximately thirty individuals per day and expected to complete the process in ten or eleven days. The English-language skills of the few German-born prisoners were apparently such that translation services were not required.[84]

The review resulted in the release by mid-July of 157 men—approximately half the internees. It is likely that Mackay deemed many of those released to be "friendly aliens," a categorization recently adopted by federal authorities to describe ethnic minorities from within Austria-Hungary who were thought to be hostile to that country.[85] Certainly the Bohemians discharged on June 30 had been the beneficiaries of this new policy. The Fernie correspondent to the *Lethbridge Herald* reported that amongst the prisoners released were one American citizen and one Italian mistakenly captured in the initial round-up. The *Free Press* noted only that Mackay had "weeded out" those who were incapable of military duty, and these had "returned to their homes." Many did visit friends and relatives at Coal Creek, but as Mackay had required, none of these men returned to work there.

Soon armed, but still without military uniforms, the new guards of the 107th East Kootenay Regiment were much like the special constables who had preceded them. They were all drawn from the local English-speaking community and had received no special training in supervising a prison camp. The experience of one novice guard may well have served to educate his fellow soldiers. He accompanied two prisoners to a christening, apparently celebrated with them and returned to camp in a clear state of intoxication. Whether this was seen as an example of the forbidden "undue familiarity" or simply as a dereliction of duty, he was relieved of further duties the next day. Two Austro-Hungarian prisoners escaped September 18 when, on an authorized visit home, they slipped out the back door while their escort stood guard at the front. While both incidents have a decidedly comic element, they suggest Mackay was attempting to operate the camp along flexible lines comparable to those established by Welsby. [86]

The acceptance of responsibility for the camp by federal authorities at the end of June thoroughly discouraged those who hoped for the release of the internees. The *District Ledger*—the most severe and consistent critic of the internment at Fernie—ceased publication with a special edition in late July. Stung by criticism from the British Columbia Federation of Labour that the action of their members had been "a travesty of labour unionism," the executive of the UMWA local union responded in a lengthy article published just days before the newspaper's closure. They noted that internment was not union policy, that the Hillcrest agitation had been settled through negotiation with little difficulty and that there had been no agitation at all for internment in Michel and Natal or anywhere else in District 18. But they could not deny the strength of the criticism. [87]

Certainly, the finances of District 18 of the UMWA were seriously strained. Advertising revenues for the *Ledger* had shrunk as the reduction from eight to four pages had shown; for the third month in a row, the collection of union dues remained suspended; and with so many of its members interned, income from local union dues when collection resumed in August was also expected to be reduced at least for the short term. But in its final editorial, the *Ledger* admitted financial difficulty was not the main reason for suspending publication, noting "more potent factors" were "apathy, indifference and illogical opposition." Clearly, the position of District 18 had been seriously weakened; equally clearly, it had not been weakened by conflict with its traditional adversaries, the mine owners of the Western Coal Operators' Association.

The "illogical opposition" represented by the rebellion of the miners of Fernie and Coal Creek indicated that the newspaper was failing to persuade

UMWA members of the benefits not only of "labour unionism" but also of class solidarity and socialism. The apparent success of that rebellion—the first significant work stoppage in District 18 to disrupt the labour peace prevailing since 1911—established the precedent of disregard for union policy that would often be repeated in the war years to come. On Pellatt Avenue, the headquarters of District 18 continued to operate, but without the comforting clatter of the printing press that had been responsible for informing its widely scattered membership of world events and union affairs.

THE ALTAR OF EMPIRE

The summer of 1915 must rank as the oddest in Fernie's history. As the community offered so many of its sons to the war effort, it was also sending its unmarried Austro-Hungarian and German adult males to prison. But while Mackay, Welsby and two levels of government struggled to deal with the situation at the skating rink, community life went on. To a great extent, the focus of that community life remained the requirements of the war in Europe. Towards the end of June, it was announced that dental regulations had been relaxed, and even men with "full dental plates" were being encouraged to enlist. The third Fernie contingent left for England with the 48th Battalion on Dominion Day. Responding to a nationwide initiative to raise funds for the purchase of weapons for Canadian forces, a district-wide campaign was launched in mid-July to raise $1,000 to provide the 54th Kootenay Battalion with a Lewis machine gun. Within a month, over $1,600—in addition to the $1,000 promised from his home in Victoria by city founder William Fernie— was pledged to the Machine Gun Fund.[88] Apparently keen to underline its independence, Coal Creek residents organized a separate effort for the same purpose.

At the same time, the Canadian Patriotic Fund in Fernie was struggling. As early as March, funds raised locally fell $500 short of requirements. Because of the very high level of recruitment, costs of supporting local soldiers' dependents were nearly triple those initially anticipated. Although figures specific to the Fernie district for 1915 are not available, it is likely that dependent families were receiving amounts comparable to the provincial average of $16.52 each month.[89] As it became apparent the war would not soon be concluded, the need for a long-term commitment to supporting soldiers' families was being recognized. Consequently, instead of celebrating Dominion Day, residents planned an ambitious program of events for July 21 to raise money for the Canadian Patriotic Fund. Although the planning was well advanced, the event was abruptly cancelled in favour of what proved to be the biggest social event of the year—the patriotic carnival hosted by Amos and Alice Trites on August 4.

Following the example of the British authorities, the provincial government belatedly urged communities in British Columbia to commemorate the anniversary of the declaration of war by organizing celebrations designed to give "expression to the spontaneous outburst of the will of the People." Fernie participated fully. With a broad community effort, plans for the patriotic carnival were ready just in time for the designated day. Every fraternal organization and union was asked to assemble at the school grounds in the early afternoon. From there, a parade of decorated automobiles interspersed at intervals by the Italian Band, the Excelsior Band, the Michel Band and the 107th regimental bugle band led guests to the Trites residence. With extensive grounds that included a dancing pavilion, that residence was the grandest of all the splendid homes located in Fernie's small up-scale neighbourhood bordering the city park. Its impressive appearance gave substance to Amos Trites's standing as the merchant king of the Elk Valley. Throughout the afternoon, guests were treated to a variety of entertainments, each intended to raise money for the Canadian Patriotic Fund. Attendees were

August 4, 1915: Approaching military precision, the performance of the Girls' Brigade was one of the highlights of the Patriotic Carnival. Fernie Museum and Archives 6043.

particularly impressed by the demonstration of synchronized baton drills presented by the girls' brigade, newly organized and trained by the head of the Mine Rescue Station.

As a Boer War veteran and president of the local branch of the Canadian Patriotic Fund, Mayor Thomas Uphill delivered an after-dinner speech that was followed by unanimous approval of a stirring resolution supporting Canada's participation in the war "against German oppression." The dancing pavilion was opened at six o'clock and remained open past midnight. Just barely down the hill from the Trites property, the internees still in custody at the skating rink may or may not have enjoyed listening to the music, but they could not have avoided hearing it. As an exercise in patriotism, the occasion was declared a grand success, raising more than $1,100 for the Canadian Patriotic Fund. Amos and Alice Trites were applauded for providing the venue and for feeding the large crowd—ten members from each of the IODE, the True Blues and the Rebekahs donating their labour to prepare and serve meals (and probably to do the dishes)—and the gathering was described by the Fernie correspondent of the *Lethbridge Herald* as "the most magnanimous offering yet laid upon the altar of the Empire in this district."[90]

Later in August, the same correspondent informed his readers that the "most frequent occurrence [in Fernie] seems to be the departure of soldiers for the front." Indeed, the pace of departures was accelerating as recruitment became competitive. An officer with the 13th Overseas Mounted Rifles from Alberta rented a room for two days at the Hotel Fernie for recruitment purposes; calls to join the 54th Kootenay Battalion continued unabated. One individual departure that drew much attention was that of former Fernie mayor Dr. Saul Bonnell. Widely considered the likely nominee of the Conservative Party in the next federal election, Bonnell was off to join the Canadian Army Medical Corps. He would soon be assigned to duty in Salonika in northern Greece, where British and French forces had landed in a belated attempt to support the retreating Serb army.

A grand social evening was held to honour the four dozen Italian reservists ready to leave Fernie, first for New York and then for Italy. The list of speakers included the usual notables, and William Wilson's gift of pipe and tobacco to each man was gratefully received, but otherwise the evening was unique. Businessman Alexander Rizzuto delivered a speech in Italian that was translated for his English-speaking listeners, as were the remarks of Italian consular agent C. diCastri, who assured the reservists they were responding to the call of patriotism and certainly not to German-style militarism.

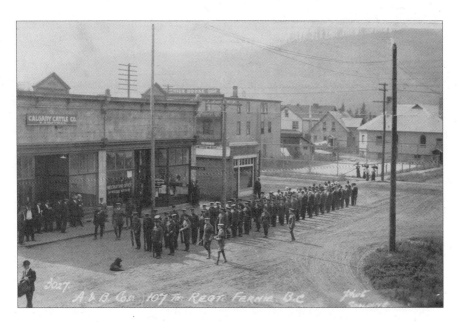

On a late summer's evening, the 107th East Kootenay Regiment prepares to escort Italian reservists to the train station. Fernie Museum and Archives 0969.

The Italian Band provided the music, frequently reprising "The Garibaldi March." The band joined A and B companies of the 107th East Kootenay Regiment in leading the reservists to their eastbound train on the evening of August 19. That departure was followed by a second contingent of Italian reservists thirty strong in early September.[91] A few days earlier, but heading in the opposite direction, sixty more recruits for the 54th Kootenay Battalion left for training at Vernon.

If one frequent occurrence was the departure of volunteers and reservists, another was the almost incessant appeal for funds for war-related purposes. Major events like the patriotic carnival and lesser ones—such as the patriotic dances held every Thursday evening at the Trites's dancing pavilion for the rest of the summer—required considerable effort and energy. The success of the carnival was still being celebrated when the IODE announced a tag day on August 21 (chosen because that was the CNPCC payday) to provide funds for the British Columbia Hospital Corps. More than $500 was raised. Inspired by Fernie's patriotic carnival, Coal Creek residents organized their own for Labour Day, and despite bad weather, raised another $500. Requests for money for the Tobacco Fund and Belgian Relief were steady, and the Machine Gun Fund continued to attract donations, with very substantial amounts coming from the Italian community. Donor fatigue was not yet evident, but its advent could certainly be predicted. The Canadian Patriotic Fund paid out $700 to dependents in August.

Another situation reaching a tipping point was that at the skating rink. With Internment Operations in charge, the long-term organizational aspects of the camp had to be reassessed. For those internees remaining in custody, the question of locating them on a more permanent basis demanded urgent attention. The skating rink would simply not do as a winter camp, but the bid to establish a camp at Morrissey had been quickly rejected. It was understood that internees were likely to be sent to Lethbridge or Banff. In mid-July, another visit by Major Ridgeway Wilson was intended only to inspect conditions at the skating rink, but it resulted in a reassessment of the possibility of establishing a permanent camp locally. With Lieutenant Colonel Mackay and Amos Trites, Major Wilson visited the abandoned Morrissey Mines townsite. He was impressed by what he saw.[92]

At the end of July, citizens of Hosmer saw an opportunity to reverse their community's decline and suggested a winter camp should be located there at the CPR townsite; Mackay promised to consider the possibility. He may have done so, but when Major General Otter arrived at Fernie in mid-August for an inspection of his own, he was greeted with a renewed lobbying effort to locate the winter camp at the Morrissey Mines townsite. Along with the officers of the 107th East Kootenay Regiment, meeting him at the train station were representatives of the Fernie board of trade. No trip to Hosmer took place, but in the company of business partners Amos Trites and Roland Wood, CNPCC general manager William Wilson and assistant manager R.M. Young, three military officers and Fernie mayor Thomas Uphill, Major General Otter travelled by automobile to Morrissey.

That evening, a special meeting of the board of trade was convened to present Otter with the case for a camp at Morrissey. On hand was a telegram from William Bowser urging that internees should be detained locally. Trites pointed out that the region's dangerous mountainous roads would benefit greatly from internees working on improvements and assured Otter that supplies for a camp at Morrissey would be provided by area merchants at very economical rates; William Wilson stated his opposition to the internment, but offered the same assurance for rental of the townsite and noted the company-owned waterworks could easily be made operational again; and Uphill, while also objecting to the internment, nevertheless agreed it would be best to keep local residents close to home. When Otter announced he was willing to consider locating a camp at Morrissey, members of the district Conservative

Association in attendance, recalling their resolution of June 9, must have been very pleased indeed.

As subscriptions to the Machine Gun Fund continued to mount, August 1915 can probably be seen as the peak of grass-roots patriotic fervour in Fernie during the war years. That fervour must have been somewhat deflated by a communiqué received from the Department of Militia and Defence. Fernie and all other communities across the country raising funds to purchase machine guns learned the department was declining their offers and suggesting contributions raised should be donated to the Canadian Patriotic Fund. Discouraged committee members set about consulting donors about refunds and a range of other patriotic options. Coincidentally, William Bowser made a brief stop in Fernie on September 29 on his way to Ottawa. Historical records are silent on whether or not he had the time or inclination to take a look at his internment camp.

That camp was closing. More precisely, it was being relocated. Without publicity, the decision to establish a permanent internment camp at Morrissey townsite had been made and preparations to that end begun in mid-September. The privately owned Alexandria and Windsor hotels were rented, insured and renovated under the supervision of recently promoted Lieutenant Colonel Ridgeway Wilson. A few internees left Fernie on September 28 to assist, and, during the first two weeks of October, the camp at the skating rink was entirely emptied of its prisoners—a half-dozen Germans and nearly 160 Austro-Hungarians. The last few left Fernie on Sunday, October 17. The arrangements surrounding the transfer must have compromised established security procedures—during the last two weeks of September and the first week of October, five prisoners escaped.[93] The skating rink was almost immediately taken over by the 107th East Kootenay Regiment for use as a drill hall. The internment at Fernie was over.

If the rebellious miners of early June calculated that their action would bring more work to men still employed, they were soon proven correct. With coal markets still sluggish, there was remarkably little hiring at Coal Creek throughout the summer months, but men already employed were given additional shifts.[94] As summer drew to a close, however, the short work weeks and concerns about unemployment that had been so pronounced in May gave way suddenly to fears of a labour shortage. As smelters resumed operations, demand for coal and coke began to surge. Mackay suspended a new recruitment drive after just three days when the entire Coal Creek football team enlisted for overseas duty with the 54th Kootenay Battalion. (They were amongst the sixty recruits who left for Vernon in early September.) Remaining miners continued to enjoy additional shifts, even as hiring began to pick up significantly after September. The *Free Press* soon reported regular double shifting by the CNPCC, noting that all men at Coal Creek were able to work full-time again.

When a member of the British Parliament toured the province in October to recruit miners for the understaffed mines of the United Kingdom, editor John Wallace claimed there were no idle men available in Fernie and predicted the MP's visit to the city would meet with little success. The mines were indeed experiencing their most productive month of the year to date.[95] Yet as many as fifty miners called upon the MP when he visited, and, according to the *Cranbrook Herald*, fifteen of them signed on. Perhaps the opportunity of return migration with an assisted passage was simply not to be missed; perhaps steady employment with the CNPCC still seemed uncertain. Even with the sharp late-year increase in coal and coke production, the mines at Coal Creek were worked for a total of only 151.5 days in 1915.[96] For the fourth year in a row, the CNPCC paid no dividend.

The new camp at Morrissey provided a welcome though temporary boost for local employment. The former editor of the *District Ledger*, Frank Newnham, became manager of the military canteen there, and a number of other Fernie residents were hired as civilian employees until personnel from the Canadian Army Service Corps could be assigned. The benefit to local merchants would prove far more lasting. Nearly all accounts submitted to the provincial government—most substantially, those from Trites-Wood, John McEwing, P. Burns and Company and John Quail—for the three-week period of provincial internment in June had been settled quickly in July; Bowser prepared to demand full reimbursement from Internment Operations for the approximately $4,100 expended.[97]

Accounts for goods and services provided after June were also paid in a timely manner by Internment Operations. By the end of the fiscal year in March 1916, the cost of goods and services supplied to the Fernie–Morrissey camp for the nine-month period would amount to just over $18,000. Fernie merchants and suppliers would receive more than three-quarters of that amount. The largest single accounts were from R.G. McEwan (bread—$1,554.16); 41 Market Company (beef and mutton—$3,472.76); and Trites-Wood (groceries, heating supplies, clothing and sundries—$6,338.24). Not all accounts were so large. The Fernie hospital cared for seven ill prisoners for seventy-eight days at a cost of $117, and Joseph Rudnicki received nearly $200 for censoring letters at ten cents apiece.[98]

However, the chaos resulting from Bowser's instant internment order was not quite over. Major General Otter was adamantly refusing to accept responsibility for expenditures incurred by the provincial government. At the time of his refusal, invoices for rental of the rink from William Robichaud and for light and water provided by the city of Fernie during those three weeks in June remained outstanding, and the provincial government refused to settle them. The Government Agent at Fernie and the city clerk wrote separately to police superintendent Colin Campbell in December requesting payment of the long-overdue accounts, but with the provincial and Dominion governments each denying liability, no payment was forthcoming.[99]

A broader issue of finance affected the whole community. The constant pressure of war-related fundraising placed an increasing strain on the ability of most residents to contribute. At the same time, the monthly demands on the Canadian Patriotic Fund were rising steadily. To avoid competing appeals to the public, an approach comparable to the modern United Way—and apparently unique in British Columbia—was adopted in October. Local fundraising efforts of the Canadian Patriotic Fund (providing disbursements to soldiers' dependents), the Red Cross (providing care and comforts to wounded and sick soldiers), the Belgian Relief Fund and the Tobacco Fund (supplying tobacco to soldiers) were all combined in the Fernie district under the umbrella of the appropriately renamed Amalgamated Patriotic Fund (APF).[100]

In exchange for a promise from the APF that they would not be approached for additional contributions, a growing number of individuals agreed to donate a fixed amount each month. Collectively, employees at the Trites-Wood stores in Michel, Coal Creek and Fernie joined the office staff of the CNPCC in agreeing to a systematic payroll deduction. By early December, the Gladstone and the Michel–Natal UMWA local unions had signed on to the new scheme of "systematic giving." Workers earning less than fifty dollars each fortnight would pay 1 percent of earnings; those making more paid 2 percent.[101] Following visits by the APF's new secretary Alfred Cummings, practically every sawmill and logging camp between Hosmer and Waldo had signed on by the end of the year.

The involvement of the miners and lumbermen meant that, for the first time, the finances of the local patriotic fund were on a sound footing. The monthly contribution from CNPCC employees alone would almost match the fund's then current obligations to recipient organizations and to families of local soldiers in the geographic area that stretched from Elko to the Alberta border. With the mines at or near full production, the APF could count on approximately $1,500 per month from CNPCC payrolls alone. For the IODE, the new arrangement meant a significant change in focus. Their final independent fundraiser was a Flag Day in early October. Relieved of the obligation to raise money for both the local patriotic fund and the Red Cross, in future the IODE were to receive payments averaging $250 per month from the APF to allow members to concentrate their efforts on behalf of the Red Cross.

Just as the finances of the APF were becoming firmly established, the rather messy unwinding of the Machine Gun Fund was being concluded. Each donor had been asked to state how his contribution should be handled, and by the end of October, the process was complete. More than $1,000 went to the local patriotic fund as suggested by the Department of Militia and Defence, much smaller amounts to the Red Cross and the Tobacco Fund. However, over $500—nearly a third of the total actually collected—was refunded to donors. The names of all involved—those who required refunds and those who did not—and the amounts each had originally contributed were published in the *Free Press*. More than $300 from Coal Creek's separate fund for the purchase of a machine gun also went to the APF.[102]

Of course, not all local matters pertained to finance as the year drew to its conclusion. In civic politics, Thomas Uphill announced he would seek a second term as mayor. In the world of UMWA politics, William Phillips abruptly resigned during a meeting of the District 18 executive held at the *Ledger* office in mid-November, just before he was expected to be easily re-elected as president for a second term. In military matters, the 54th Kootenay Battalion embarked for England in mid-November, and Lieutenant Colonel Mackay received orders just before Christmas to raise two hundred fresh volunteers for the 102nd Battalion. Full-scale recruiting therefore resumed after a pause of just three months. Ethnic relations amongst workingmen remained tense. Italian employees of the East Kootenay Lumber Company, angry they were being dismissed in favour of better skilled Austro-Hungarians, protested so strenuously the intervention of Chief Constable Welsby was required.[103]

And in provincial politics in December, when Richard McBride accepted the post of agent-general for British Columbia in London, the sitting MLAs of the governing Conservatives in Victoria were obliged to select a new leader—a man who automatically would also become the new premier. Just a few days before Christmas, the selection was made. William Bowser was the premier of British Columbia.

1916

POLITICS AND PROHIBITION

After the trauma of internment and the discouraging progress of the war in 1915, residents of Fernie and Coal Creek understandably hoped for better in 1916. However, it soon proved to be a year of continuing military stalemate and mounting death tolls in Europe and of anxious recruitment drives and labour strife at home. A referendum on votes for women would generate much less local debate than expected; another on the prohibition of alcohol became much more con-tentious. Politics within the UMWA would take some unexpected turns, as would politics at the civic and provincial levels. The war in Europe may have seemed little changed over the course of the year, but the Fern-ie of December 1916 would look remarkably different than it had just twelve months earlier.

January brought week after week of bitterly cold temperatures and high winds, such that outside work was virtually impossible; the hospital in Fernie was kept busy treating the frostbite of workers who attempted to defy the weather. Snow slides at Coal Creek also caused con-siderable damage and further work delays. The region was in the middle of a winter that would ultimately see a snowfall of 210 inches recorded at Fernie, triple that of the previous year.[104] Politically, the year began

A popular politician, Thomas Uphill was re-turned by acclamation to the mayor's chair.
Royal BC Museum and Archives B-06782.

quietly with Tom Uphill being acclaimed as Fernie mayor. The local business establishment that had opposed him in 1915 apparently was reassured by his even-handed stewardship of the city and decided not to run a candidate against him in 1916. Economic conditions continued to improve. The reduction in the wages of civic employees was ended, and voluntary deductions from miners' wages for the relief of the unemployed were deemed no longer necessary. Indeed, in February the committee operating the Coal Creek relief fund was entirely disbanded, with its remaining cash balance being donated to the Amalgamated Patriotic Fund.

THE LOYAL SPIRIT

Consistent with Prime Minister Borden's pledge to raise an additional half-million troops, the year also began with the continuation of full-scale recruitment in Fernie. But serious questions of regional concern were being raised. A good number of the new recruits, like those of the previous year, were members of the 107th East Kootenay Regiment who, once enlisted for overseas service, were being assigned to other British Columbia units. Many people felt that the 107th regiment and the residents of the Elk Valley were simply not receiving the recognition that the extremely high rate of enlistment deserved. Even the 54th Kootenay Battalion, at full strength and completing its training in England, was recognized to be Kootenay in name only.[105] Across the border in Alberta, the recent formation of the 192nd Crow's Nest Pass Battalion based at Blairmore set an example that Fernie sought to emulate.

Following the departure in January of nearly a hundred volunteers for training in Victoria with the new 103rd Battalion (not with the 102nd as originally announced in December), the community organized to support the creation of a locally based overseas unit. A letter to Sam Hughes requested his approval "to immediately mobilize the 107th regiment for overseas service, to be equipped and trained in East Kootenay." With the Department of Militia and Defence publicly encouraging the creation of new military battalions across the country, that approval was quickly granted. The announcement was particularly welcomed in Fernie where the battalion was to mobilize and where recruitment efforts for an overseas unit of the 107th East Kootenay Regiment were already underway.

The announcement was less welcome in Blairmore. Plans for the new military mobilization at Fernie specifically barred the 192nd Crow's Nest

Pass Battalion from actively recruiting in East Kootenay.[106] By late March, it was determined that the new overseas regiment of the 107th would be designated the 225th Kootenay Battalion and that it would recruit as far west as Nelson and Grand Forks. But curiously, and despite the territorial restriction placed on outside recruitment efforts, more than fifty residents of the Elk Valley enlisted in Blairmore with the 192nd in late March and early April. Most of those volunteers were Russian-born lumbermen and miners from Hosmer. The recruitment drive by the new 225th would also attract substantial attention from Russian-born residents, but did not result in a comparable enlistment. Approximately two dozen Russians would sign on with the 225th Kootenay Battalion at Fernie, although few would ultimately accompany the unit overseas.

To concentrate on recruitment and organization of the 225th Kootenay Battalion, the popular Lieutenant Colonel Joseph Mackay was relieved of command at the Morrissey internment camp. It was quickly recognized, however, that Mackay would not have the field to himself. Just as the announcement of the creation of the local overseas battalion was being welcomed in Fernie, a recruiting officer from Victoria visited on behalf of the 143rd Battalion—soon to be known as the British Columbia Bantams—and appealed for men under regulation height who would not normally be eligible for military service.[107] Men working underground in mines were typically short in stature, and he soon had two dozen signed up. He was followed in May, first by an officer of the Army Medical Corps who left town with eighteen new recruits and then by an officer of the 1st Canadian Pioneer Battalion, who left Fernie

The last recruits: Coal Creek members of the 225th Kootenay Battalion at Vernon in the summer or fall of 1916. Fernie Museum and Archives 1202.

with three dozen more. As was always the case, most of them were miners employed by the CNPCC.

John Wallace at the *Free Press*, a strong supporter of the new local battalion, was deeply concerned that the representative of the Pioneer Battalion was but one of three Vancouver recruiting officers who found themselves busy in Fernie at the same time. He complained that "… recruiting agents at the coast seem to have discovered the loyal spirit which exists amongst the miners of the Crow's Nest Pass, and they flock to Fernie in droves." All agents were successful, especially at Coal Creek, which was said to be taking on the appearance of a military centre with so many men dressed in khaki.

Sherwood Herchmer wrote privately to Premier Bowser warning that, unless recruitment in the region ceased, the business community feared "the wheels of industry will be closed down" because the coal mines would have to cease production. He noted that $30,000 per year would then be lost to the local patriotic fund if officers "from all over the Dominion are allowed to come in here and induce men to leave their positions." Bowser replied that military matters were a federal responsibility and, perhaps having learned a lesson from his experience with internment, told Herchmer "it would not do for us to encroach on their territory."[108] The steady erosion of its labour force profoundly worried the CNPCC but was not the only concern William Wilson expressed. He noted that recruiting agents routinely pressed the company and its senior officials for contributions to "defray their expenses."[109]

Mackay was soon hard at work in his new role, competing with the other recruitment officers and finding himself back in command at the skating rink, where the fledgling A Company of the 225th Kootenay Battalion had established its camp. Anticipating continuing needs, Military District 11 (British Columbia and Yukon) rented the rink for a year and authorized renovations of the facility. The Elk Lumber Company and the firm of Kennedy & Mangan supplied the lumber, contractor John Giddings the hardware and labour. As the ranks swelled, so too did the demand for provisions. Trites-Wood, 41 Market Company and R.G. McEwan were pleased with the sharp increase in business. A reading room in the basement of the Anglican church was opened for the men of the new unit, and a series of social evenings was organized.

William Phillips, who had resigned as president of District 18 of the UMWA the previous November, enlisted as a private to the applause of John Wallace. The volunteers paraded throughout the principal streets of Fernie on Victoria Day, led by the Coal Creek Colliery Band, which had dropped both Fernie and Excelsior from its name. The *Free Press* marked the occasion of Victoria Day by publishing the names of 878 local men who had undertaken to serve overseas. The list included twelve Belgian and six dozen Italian reservists. A week later, the list was augmented by seventeen more names, and the *Free Press* admitted that the identities of individuals who had left quietly and an additional six dozen Italian reservists were not known.

The "loyal spirit" of the Crowsnest Pass was evident indeed. Mackay's recruitment efforts continued to bring impressive results. By early June, the 225th Kootenay Battalion as a whole was well over half-strength. Bishop Wilson, the twenty-year-old American-born son of CNPCC manager William Wilson, enlisted with the university battalion at Calgary and was transferred immediately to the 225th with the rank of lieutenant. A dozen members of the Michel branch of a Czech nationalist organization enlisted as a group and formed a unique platoon. They were amongst the fifty-five officers and men from Michel who arrived in Fernie on the first day of the month, raising the strength of A Company to a particularly impressive total of 163 recruits. Lesser figures for the companies recruiting in Nelson, Cranbrook and Grand Forks were nevertheless encouraging, and there was much speculation about when the battalion would be off to Vernon or New Westminster to complete its training. The men were said to be eager to depart.

That eagerness was likely enhanced by the threat of fire and the serious flooding that struck Fernie mid-month. Memories of the fire that almost completely destroyed Fernie in 1908 were foremost in the minds of residents as they watched flames on June 15 spread across both Mount Fernie and Mount Proctor, both closely adjacent to the community. Relief was expressed by all as the fires appeared to be burning themselves out without crossing the river or advancing into the town. But in June 1916 there would be no escape from calamity. Even as the fires still burned, a more immediate threat demanded attention.

Exceptionally warm weather in the first two weeks of June combined with a high snow pack and heavy rain to raise the Elk River to a level twelve feet above its low-water mark. Before the worst was over, the bridge at Fairy Creek, which carried the city's water supply, was entirely swept away. Residential areas bordering the river suffered considerable damage. The companies of the 225th, so recently established at the skating rink, were ordered by Mackay to abandon the site in a hurry on June 16. They commandeered every available vehicle to move approximately seventy tons of equipment to higher ground in the city park. But the makeshift camp established there could only be regarded as temporary. Their anticipated departure from

Disaster narrowly avoided: Fire came perilously close to the city, but did not enter it. Fernie Museum and Archives 1738.

Fernie was probably advanced considerably by the flood that still ranks as the worst in Fernie's history. In short order, the command was received that the 225th Kootenay Battalion was to transfer to the Vernon military training camp on July 8.

Because a large program of first-aid competitions in Coleman was being planned by the St. John Ambulance Association, communities in the region had agreed to suspend their own Dominion Day celebrations. The decision proved a fortunate one for Fernie. Busy coping with the ravages of the flood and with the city park occupied by the 225th Battalion, the community could not have mounted much of a program even with the best of intentions. The Coal Creek mine rescue team returned from Coleman to much acclaim for having taken first-place honours, but otherwise, residents of Fernie marked the day in a fashion more subdued than usual. Many admired the new Savage-Lewis machine gun displayed at the recruiting office of the 225th Kootenay Battalion, but no one could have been aware that a major Franco-British offensive had begun in France while Canada was marking Dominion Day. Eventually people would learn that nearly twenty thousand British soldiers had been killed in the initial engagements of what would soon become known as the Battle of the Somme.

Disaster not avoided: The raging Elk River flooded the yards of the Elk Lumber Company and flowed right though the skating rink. Fernie Museum and Archives 1733.

For the 225th Kootenay Battalion, the very well-established local traditions surrounding military departures were all repeated. The men of A Company—now nearly two hundred in number—were paraded to the CNPCC grounds on July 6, and each was presented with a briar pipe and pouch of tobacco by company manager William Wilson. On the eve of their departure, they were treated to a dinner and social evening at the Victoria Hall, where patriotic and entertaining speeches were delivered by Mayor Uphill, former mayors Herchmer and Bonnell, Wilson and Lieutenant Colonel Mackay. On the morning of July 8, the bugle band of the 107th East Kootenay Regiment led them all up Baker Avenue to the CPR station, where the Italian Band played patriotic melodies and several hundred well-wishers were assembled to bid them farewell. In a *Free Press* column a few days later, John Wallace paid particular tribute to the battalion's departing commanding officer. Noting that before the war Mackay had organized the Fernie Veterans' Association and lobbied for the creation of a local militia unit that became the 107th regiment, Wallace also praised his leadership and involvement with the 54th and the 225th battalions. The city regretted it was losing a much-admired citizen and military figure.

The departure of the 225th Kootenay Battalion marked the beginning of the end of Fernie as a military camp. Apart from saying goodbye to another handful of volunteers for the 225th later in the month and to a dozen for the Army Medical Corps in August, the farewell traditions had been enacted for the last time. The call for volunteers showed no sign of diminishing. Through the office of the *Free Press*, recruiting continued for the 225th. In late July, hopeful representatives of the 228th Foresters Battalion also arrived in town. But the days of extensive and successful recruiting in Fernie were about to come to an abrupt end.

Just as it had the previous September, the ongoing success of recruitment drives brought the emergence of serious concerns about a crippling shortage of labour. The CNPCC found it could not meet the surging demand for coal and coke because it simply did not have the manpower. The overwhelming majority of the 878 recruits listed by the *Free Press* on Victoria Day had been drawn from its workforce. In addition, more than three hundred of its foreign-born employees had been interned in June 1915. Although many had since been released—Mackay had discharged fifty more from the Morrissey camp in January—they were still prohibited from returning to work in the mines of the CNPCC.

The coal company, although experiencing a recent return to profitability, was becoming desperate. In April, it had formally requested the release of the remainder of its interned former employees and permission for them to return to work for the CNPCC. Lobbying in support of its request, the company submitted testimonials to the good character of its interned employees from Lieutenant Colonel Mackay, Joseph Rudnicki and hotel owners Simon Dragon and John "Jan" Podbielanik. To demonstrate how critical the labour situation had become, both Wilson and company president Elias Rogers advised Major General Otter in May that the CNPCC was five hundred men short and "suffering seriously" from an inability to fill orders.[110] The enemy-alien miners—forced from employment with the company less than a year earlier—were sorely missed.

The CNPCC was certainly not the only employer requesting the release of internees. Labour shortages had become acute in many sectors of the national economy. In response, the federal government initiated a policy of release for those internees who were not deemed to pose a threat to security and those who had been interned essentially because they were destitute. However, there were strict conditions to be met. The internee had to be certain of employment upon release; the employer had to guarantee payment at current wage rates and demonstrate the job could not be filled by British subjects. Under these new terms, employment at Coal Creek again became a possibility. In early June, seventeen prisoners were released specifically to work for the CNPCC, six of them in above-ground occupations at Coal Creek.[111]

At the same time, thirty former employees of the CNPCC were released from Morrissey to work for other companies, twenty of them for the North American Collieries at Coalhurst near Lethbridge.[112] William Wilson was furious. When Internment Operations refused to return them to the custody of the CNPCC, Wilson forcefully requested the release of thirty internees from the camps at Banff to compensate and sent a Fernie lawyer to Banff to press the request. By the end of July, fifty internees from Banff were released to work for the CNPCC. Otter noted darkly that complications were "apt to arise" if they were placed at Coal Creek.[113] All of the men released were assigned to jobs at Michel and Natal.

The release policy resulted in other complications, serious complaint and legal confusion. The federal government quickly found it necessary to advise police and courts across the country that released internees could not be reinterned for civil offenses, reminding them that "the only reasons for which aliens of enemy nationality may be interned are outlined in Para. 2 of the Proclamation of 15th August, 1914."[114] Apparently, just a year after the rambling and belated order-in-council justifying the detention of CNPCC employees at the Fernie skating rink, the simple possibility of disorder in the mines was no longer seen as grounds for internment.

In Fernie, the release of internees caused some grumbling. One Coal Creek resident disdainfully noted "a large bunch of strangers" had arrived looking for work in April. But evidence suggests that the six men discharged from Morrissey in June may have the distinction of being the only former internees placed in employment at Coal Creek. The numbers of enemy aliens reporting monthly as required to the provincial police at Fernie show no increase following the release of significant numbers of prisoners in July 1915 and January 1916. William Wilson noted that former Austrian employees at Fernie had "either left entirely or were found other employment by the company."[115] Apart from the company's small rail and lumber subsidiaries, other employment with the company can only have been found at Michel or Natal, where there had been no agitation for internment and where Wilson was more comfortable in adding significantly to the number of foreign-born employees. Provincial police files for Michel show spikes in numbers of enemy

aliens reporting in April and particularly in July 1916, when the fifty internees from Banff and eleven more from Morrissey were released for employment with the CNPCC specifically at Michel.[116]

Apart from the single casual complaint noted from Coal Creek, there
is no suggestion in historical records of discontent amongst the miners there
in connection with released internees. In the Vancouver Island coalfields,
however, the release from the Edgewood internment camp of former island
miners caused uproar. The matter became a major issue at Nanaimo in the
provincial election campaign in September, with all levels of government being sharply criticized for allowing such a "mistake" to happen. In response,
and in contradiction to the recent federal reminder to courts and police,
Bowser sent a telegram to the local Conservative candidate assuring him
that he had personally instructed the provincial police to detain all released
internees and to hold them at the Nanaimo lock-up until they could be returned to federal custody. The Nanaimo city council wrote to Prime Minister
Borden claiming jobs were being taken from British subjects and urging rein-
ternment. When Mayor Uphill and his council received a request for support
of that initiative from their Nanaimo counterparts, the matter received only
a brief discussion before being quietly filed.[117]

Despite the release of practically all company employees originally interned in June 1915, the availability of labour in the Elk Valley showed little
sign of improving. In fact, with recruitment continuing over the summer, the
situation was steadily worsening. The CNPCC claimed that, since August
1914, fully nine hundred men had left company employment to enlist for
military service.[118] Regional recruitment figures are difficult to confirm, but
William Wilson told a meeting of the Western Coal Operators' Association
in September that 1,280 men had joined the colours from the Fernie district
and that almost all had been employees of the CNPCC. Accurate or exag-
gerated, the figures were alarming. So dire had its labour shortage become
that the CNPCC took the unprecedented step of requesting the complete
suspension of local recruiting. In early September, federal minister of labour
Thomas Crothers advised Wilson that step would soon be taken.[119]

Anxious to avoid any suggestion it was being unpatriotic, the company
did not actively publicize its request. However, it soon became an open secret and caused a serious rift between the Fernie business community that
supported it and officers and men of the Morrissey internment camp who
opposed it. The editor of the *Morrissey Mention*, the official organ of the
107th East Kootenay Regiment, slammed the CNPCC as a disloyal, alien

and soulless corporation seeking to curtail recruitment solely to enhance its own bottom line. Alluding to the recent disaster at Michel, he wrote, "This whining, profit-seeking, anti-recruitment crusade will not affect the recruiting situation in the slightest—for it is better to be blown up in Flanders than in British Columbia." He concluded with confidence that military authorities would never agree to such a request.[120]

He was soon disappointed. Following the example of the British government, which in June had forbidden further recruitment of coal miners in the United Kingdom, Canadian authorities acted quickly. Military District 11 issued Order No. 448 in mid-September. It stated that effective immediately, recruiting was "not permitted in Fernie, Cranbrook, Michel or elsewhere in the Crow's Nest Pass Coal Co. mining district, except by the local military unit, the 107th East Kootenay Regiment."

Military Order No. 448 was unique—nowhere else in Canada was recruitment forbidden during the First World War—and it marks a distinct watershed in Fernie's wartime history. A relocation of the headquarters of the 107th East Kootenay Regiment followed almost immediately. In October, the unit was transferred from Fernie to Creston, deemed to be more geographically central for the area served. At the same time, the regiment's responsibility for custody of the internees at Morrissey was renewed. An additional 160 prisoners arrived at Morrissey during the course of the late summer and early autumn as Internment Operations permanently closed camps at Edgewood, Brandon and Lethbridge and reorganized others. The 107th East Kootenay Regiment would retain responsibility for the Morrissey camp until the end of the war, but Fernie's domestic experience as a military centre and as a rich source of volunteers for military duty overseas was essentially at an end.

Of course, the connection of the community to the war in Europe remained undiminished. Neither the request by the CNPCC to end recruitment locally nor the decision to grant it can have been easily made. The news from the front in early 1916 was depressingly like that of 1915. The need for fresh troops was acute. Battles on the Western Front always seemed to inspire hope but result in little advantage, and the names of the dead and wounded appeared with increasing frequency in the columns of the *Free Press*. The 54th Kootenay Battalion, which included many men from Fernie, arrived in France in August after many months of training in England and quickly found itself engaged in the Battle of the Somme. By the end of September, after two full years of war, the Fernie district recorded nearly four dozen dead.

Political Earthquakes

The year brought its share of political surprises. In late February, the annual convention of District 18 of the UMWA was held in Fernie for the first time in many years. Union member and Fernie mayor Thomas Uphill welcomed delegates and granted them the freedom of the city. The internal politics of District 18 fundamentally centred on debates between proponents of often conflicting socialist perspectives and those who argued members would be better served by adopting non-socialist policies. The most controversial resolution before the convention was one that would delete from the constitution the clause committing the union to political action in line with the principles of the Socialist Party of Canada. David Rees and William Phillips had been unsuccessful in their attempt to end that affiliation at the convention of 1915, but continuing objections from international UMWA headquarters in Indianapolis placed the question on the agenda again in 1916.

Speaking at length in favour of retaining the formal tie to the Socialist Party of Canada was CNPCC employee Albert "Ginger" Goodwin. Although only recently hired as a driver in No. 1 East mine at Coal Creek, Goodwin was no stranger to the Elk Valley. He had worked for several months in 1910 at Michel where he was particularly admired for his football skills, helping Michel to the Crow's Nest Pass League championship that year. He then moved to Cumberland but, blacklisted there because of his involvement in the long Vancouver Island coal strike, returned to Fernie seeking employment in March 1914. Perhaps because of his reputation, perhaps because the CNPCC was simply not hiring, he found none. Instead, he devoted his time to political efforts on behalf of the Socialist Party.[121] He quickly realized that the party had no organization whatsoever in the Crowsnest apart from its Branch 17 in Fernie, soon left to look for work elsewhere in the province and returned to Fernie once more—this time finding employment with the CNPCC—just before Christmas 1915.

Anxious to retain the Socialist Party's endorsement by the largest labour organization in the region, he argued strongly at the union convention in Fernie against the proposed change to the constitution. Many years later, David Rees would recall that Goodwin spoke well and made his points forcibly. On the other hand, the *Free Press* reported at the time his speech so annoyed delegates that they declined to offer him the traditional vote of thanks for having addressed them. Whatever the nature of the impression he made, the convention decided to end the affiliation of District 18 with the Socialist Party.[122] Unrelated to the constitutional debate, Goodwin received another rebuff two weeks later. He wrote from Fernie to Premier Bowser objecting to the internment of Cumberland miner Peter Janoni. In reply, Bowser stated, without apparent ironical intent, "I have nothing to do with the internment of any of the aliens … "[123] Perhaps discouraged, Goodwin soon left the Coal Creek mines to take a job at Trail.

The constitutional decision by the District 18 convention was perhaps not a great surprise, but the local Conservative Association was about to make an announcement that would shake up local politics much more dramatically. With the sitting MLA from their party, the district association was strong and had been made even stronger by attracting members of the growing Italian business community to its banner.[124] Emilio Picariello, whose business was expanding to include groceries, bottle recycling and the manufacture of ice cream, recog-

Albert "Ginger" Goodwin: His plea that District 18 UMWA remain affiliated with the Socialist Party of Canada fell on deaf ears. Cumberland Museum C110-002.

nized the commercial advantages of membership and declared his affiliation. In mid-May, however, members both old and new were dismayed by the unexpected announcement that MLA William Roderick Ross would be abandoning Fernie for a Cariboo constituency in the next provincial election, which was expected soon. Putting on a brave face, the Conservative Association immediately scheduled a nominating meeting for the end of the month and promised to select a man of stature and ability equal to that of the retiring Ross.

At that meeting, when the identity of the sole nominee was made public, the association had good reason to be confident their promise had been kept. Amos Trites called the meeting to order, and association vice-president Fred Roo of Elko and Captain Saul Bonnell—recently returned from Salonika, where he had served with the No. 5 Canadian General Hospital of the Canadian Army Medical Corps—shared the nominating duties. Both praised the new man unsparingly. Aware that Fernie was fundamentally a labour constituency, the association had found itself a labour candidate.

As he rose to accept the nomination, Thomas Uphill would have been as aware as his nominators that he was hardly a typical Conservative nominee. After paying tribute to William Ross, he pledged to support the party "on broad principles of conservatism," but reserved "the right to vote against that party on any measure which … is to the detriment of the workers." [125] How comfortable he would be as a representative of the party led by William Bowser—the man organized labour in the province continued to oppose unequivocally—and whether his workmates would back him, time alone would tell. Known for his caution in political matters, Uphill would not have accepted the nomination without being reasonably assured that a significant number of miners from the Gladstone local union would cast their votes in his favour. [126] To focus on the upcoming election, he resigned from his position as union secretary.

If Uphill made his decision thinking that the only route to power in British Columbia was through the Conservative Party, most observers would have agreed. Premier McBride had been in office since 1903, and his electoral victories in 1909 and 1912 had entirely shattered the opposition. Business interests were solidly behind the party, and the broad network of patronage further strengthened its influence. Fernie fit that provincial pattern in all respects, and the community's only newspaper could certainly be relied upon to consistently support the policies of the Conservative Party. Nevertheless, the serious economic downturn and a series of scandals were combining to undermine the government. And locally, it was often noted by the *Free Press* that Liberal meetings in Fernie were attracting significant numbers of Coal Creek residents. The next election, provincially and locally, looked unlikely to be a repetition of the Conservative landslides of 1909 and 1912.

Just two weeks after Uphill's nomination, the Elk River in flood provided an opportunity for the local Liberal candidate to garner some attention. As noted previously, the low ground around the curling and skating rinks was flooded just after the military evacuated. The Annex, the Extension and West Fernie—residential districts made up primarily of modest dwellings that housed miners and labourers and their families—were also particularly hard hit, and the entire city lost its water supply. As mayor, Uphill called an emergency council meeting; a committee was struck, work began on restoring the water supply and a week later a public meeting was held to discuss compensation. The Liberal candidate, Fernie lawyer Alexander Fisher, told the meeting quick and meaningful assistance from the provincial government was essential. The *Free Press* condemned Fisher for politicizing the issue and for allegedly urging "government to compensate every person who had lost a flower bed or a patch of turnips … " On that basis, the newspaper argued, the CNPCC, the Great Northern Railway and every sawmill along the Elk River would have to be compensated. Uphill was praised by the newspaper for providing flood victims with more reasonable and more attainable assurances. The provincial election had yet to be called, but the campaign in Fernie was clearly underway. [127]

Election talk proceeded at a leisurely pace until early August when the lists closed and official candidates were declared. Given the strength of the riding's Socialist vote in previous provincial elections, it was no surprise that this was to be a three-cornered contest. The Socialist Party had identified its candidate well over a year earlier, but when he withdrew unexpectedly, Vancouver bookkeeper John Amos McDonald belatedly entered the local race in his place. McDonald had been nominated by Gladstone local union secretary Thomas France, who surprisingly had defeated the favoured candidate—former Gladstone president and Coal Creek Colliery Band member Harry Martin—in the vote for his position. The *Free Press* immediately blamed the Liberals for engineering McDonald's nomination in an attempt to take miners' votes away from Uphill. With that, local campaigning began in earnest. McDonald held a well-attended meeting at the Socialist Hall; Coal Creek was again noted to be well represented at Liberal meetings; Fisher charged that Conservatives were responsible for trouble with lighting at his meeting at the Grand Theatre; local secretary France wrote to the *Free Press* to point out that Uphill was not the union's endorsed candidate.

To further encourage local Liberal hopes in Fernie, the *Free Press* was once again not the only local newspaper available. Frank Newnham, the former editor of the *District Ledger*, had approached the District 18 executive early in 1916 with a request to lease the idle *Ledger* printing plant.[128] The request was initially tabled, but concern about costs incurred by having the building sit idle convinced the executive later to approve the request. Newnham returned to the newspaper business with the publication of the *Fernie Mail* in mid-August. It immediately became apparent that the fiercely Socialist former editor of the *District Ledger* would be just as fiercely Liberal as editor of the *Fernie Mail*.

Newnham's name had been associated with the Liberal Party just a few months after his tenure ended as editor of the *District Ledger*, so the new publication's political stance perhaps came as no surprise. It certainly did not surprise John Wallace. He alleged that Newnham was available to the highest bidder and that the funds required to lease the printing plant had come from the Liberal Party. Newnham's efforts were apparently not restricted to his columns in the *Fernie Mail*. When the election was long over, a humorous column in the *Free Press* would suggest his participation in the campaign involved the purchase of 25 kegs of alcohol and the promise of "ten acres and a cow" to every Slav who voted Liberal.[129]

Bowser made his only Fernie appearance of the campaign in early August. He was met at the train station by a brass band and members of the Conservative Association. Speaking at the Grand Theatre on August 11, he was apparently given a frosty reception. Uphill's remarks were frequently interrupted, and local MP Robert Green was shouted down when he rose to speak in favour of the Conservative cause. Fisher was given a more respectful hearing than Bowser by a crowd that apparently contained more Liberal supporters than Conservative. The meeting ended abruptly when the audience stood to sing "God Save the King." If it had not been clear till then, it became apparent that Uphill's election was by no means a sure thing.

Interest in the election was so intense that no individual or organization had the time or inclination to make arrangements to celebrate Labour Day in Fernie. A few residents travelled either to Morrissey or to Coal Creek to take part in modest programs. There was considerable surprise when as many as two hundred visitors from Alberta's Crowsnest Pass arrived in Fernie believing that a program of sports events had been arranged. An announcement to that end had somehow been published in a newspaper in Coleman. Merchants welcomed the unexpected boost in trade, and some of the day trippers no doubt enjoyed a legal drink for the first time in two months, Alberta's prohibition law having taken effect on Dominion Day. During the course of their visit, and interested or not, they may have learned all they needed to know about the election contest.

The results of that election were widely anticipated in the rest of the province, but the local result was still a shock in Fernie. Bowser's attempt to woo the working-class voter through legislation and an aggressive internment policy had failed. His thoroughly unpopular government was soundly defeated as Liberal candidates were almost everywhere successful. In both Fernie and Coal Creek, Alexander Fisher outpolled Uphill substantially—the majority of miners had not been willing to follow Uphill into the Conservative camp—while McDonald finished a distant third. The Socialist vote—exceptionally strong in the riding in previous provincial elections—had collapsed. The *Free Press* held out hopes the soldiers' vote might yet elect Uphill, but admitted that was unlikely.

In the labour constituency of Fernie, the Conservative gamble with a labour candidate—and his gamble with the Conservatives—had proved unsuccessful. The workingman's aversion to the provincial Conservatives simply could not be overcome; Uphill's own brother-in-law could not persuade himself to cast a Conservative vote.[130] When the official results were released, Uphill's numbers did increase on the soldiers' ballots as expected, but the boost was not enough. The Fernie electoral district had delivered its first Liberal MLA. In a letter published in the *Free Press*, the *Fernie Mail* and the *Morrissey Mention*, Alexander Fisher thanked electors for putting aside party politics to vote against "Bowserism."

Prohibition and the Woman Question

As men voted in the provincial election, they were also asked to indicate a simple yes or no to questions posed by two accompanying plebiscites. Bowser may have preferred that they be defeated, but both were expected to pass and both did. The substantial affirmative received by one of those questions resulted in legislation that stands to this day. The affirmative given to the other proved to be only a temporary victory for its proponents and provided no solution to a cluster of social problems that British Columbia is debating still. People in the Elk Valley voted substantially in accord with the provincial trend on one question and just as substantially against the trend on the other.

As a mining community, Fernie has a wartime history very much dominated by men, but two political questions of 1916 enabled and encouraged local women to become more involved in the decision-making process. Still without votes in determining how those questions would be answered, they were involved nevertheless in the debates and the campaigns about the two matters being considered—prohibition and female suffrage. Regrettably, their involvement locally went almost completely unreported by Wallace. The only mentions of women in the *Free Press* are almost all to do with social occasions or charity work conducted by organizations such as the IODE. Given the extent of female involvement in the prohibition cause throughout the province, it is ironic that only male names were reported in the crusade in Fernie, most prominently that of William Dicken, a Methodist.

A miner's wife and child in Coal Creek. While women were not able to vote in the provincial election in 1916, they were involved in the debates about prohibition and female suffrage. Image courtesy of the author.

Because the plebiscite question was expected to pass easily with all parties supporting it, the issue of extending the franchise to women was all but ignored during the election campaign provincially. In Fernie, too, it apparently generated little public discussion. The *Free Press* noted there was "very little interest taken in Fernie on the question." When the provincial results were tabulated, more than two-thirds of voters had declared in favour of "woman's suffrage." The local vote was not quite as enthusiastic, but nearly 58 percent of voters in the Fernie district also endorsed the proposal. Only in Hosmer and Natal, where the vote was more than two to one against the innovation, did the referendum proposal meet with significant disapproval.[131] With both the Liberal and the Conservative parties pledged to honour the result, it was clear that the women of British Columbia would have the vote at the next provincial election.

The other question was far more contentious. Pressure on the provincial government from prohibitionists had increased sharply since the formation of the People's Prohibition Association (PPA) a year earlier. Composed almost exclusively of Methodists and Presbyterians from the Lower Mainland and Victoria, the executive of the PPA became impatient with the Conservatives' constant waffling on the question and threatened to endorse the Liberals as a result. That possibility essentially forced Bowser's hand.

He promised to introduce far-reaching legislation, hoping to deprive the Liberals of sole ownership of what had long been one of the main planks in their party's platform. If approved by plebiscite, Bowser pledged prohibition would take effect on New Year's Day. The PPA was delighted, but opponents of prohibition were appalled. The Merchants' Protective Association (also headed almost entirely by individuals from the Lower Mainland and Victoria) organized the business interests that expected to be adversely affected by prohibition and lobbied vigorously against the proposed legislation.

Geographically, Fernie is a long way from the centres of political power concentrated at the coast. Even today, the most modern developments in communication have not entirely erased that sense of distance. A century ago, like a frontier outpost in a far-flung empire, Fernie typically learned of decisions already made or felt the impact of new initiatives only after they had gained traction in Victoria and Vancouver. The community's involvement with the contentious issues surrounding prohibition apparently followed that pattern. The debate at the coast was steady and fierce for months before it attracted serious attention in Fernie.

There had been a relatively good turnout in mid-January when a speaker from Vancouver and another from Manitoba (described by the *Free Press* as "a hustler in the prohibition line") attracted about a hundred people to a meeting at the Grand Theatre. Discussions followed the meeting to establish a local group to work for prohibition, but their subsequent meetings received little attention from the *Free Press*. The distinctly anti-prohibition Wallace was able to claim—probably with some justification—that the "prohibition fever does not seem to be very prevalent in Fernie yet."

To generate some such fever, it was announced by the prohibitionists that G.H. Hardy from Vancouver would arrive in late March to organize local forces on behalf of the PPA. The visit seems instead to have first awakened local opponents. Alarmed at the possibility that the province could be dry by the end of the year, liquor merchant John Pollock and Northern Hotel owner William Eschwig sent telegrams to Premier Bowser urging that his proposed legislation include adequate compensation to holders of liquor licences. They also argued a more reasonable timeline for implementation was essential. King's Hotel owner William Mills followed suit the next day, as did the Imperial Hotel's Rizzuto brothers, who more ominously warned that prohibition in Saskatchewan and Alberta had turned "the trade into other channels."[132]

Before he left Fernie, Hardy spoke to over a hundred miners at a successful meeting at Coal Creek and arranged an interview with the *Free Press*.

LEST WE FORGET—

NANAIMO 1913

JAIL

MINER

FERNIE
1916

That in 1913 Mr. Bowser had nothing better than bullets, chains and prison sentences for the miners; while in 1916 (when he needs their votes) he asks them to consider him their ever loving friend.

An unwelcome legacy: The cartoonist for the *Vancouver Sun* captured the issue undermining Thomas Uphill's bid for provincial office. Image courtesy of Allen Seager.

He predicted a sweeping victory for the prohibitionist movement locally, citing support from businessmen on financial grounds and from church adherents on moral grounds. He also claimed support from the labour movement, which he argued needed its members to be disciplined and keep clear heads if hopes for progressive social change had any prospect of success. Labour organizations at the coast opposed the bill, but trade unionists overall were divided on the question. The UMWA, for example, was notably silent on the matter in 1916, although a few years earlier District 18 had condemned "the evils of the liquor traffic."[133]

Fernie's hotelmen were already unhappy that their hours for liquor sales were to be reduced by provincial regulation from the first of June and, when the details of Bowser's British Columbia Prohibition Act became known in late May, they were further disappointed. The only concession gained was the postponement of the implementation date to Dominion Day, 1917; there would be no compensation for business losses sustained by brewers or hoteliers. With both the Liberals and Conservatives committed to honouring the result of the referendum, the highly divisive issue of prohibition did not become a party issue in the election campaign. As a referendum question, however, it generated much debate. During the last few weeks before the vote, large articles and advertisements appeared in the newspapers throughout the province. Fernie's housewives were warned that the cost of their Christmas puddings would rise significantly if the dry side won; workingmen were told their beer would be unattainable by the glass, while more affluent men could still import liquor by the bottle; everyone was reminded of the evils of the sale and consumption of liquor.

Province-wide, the result of the referendum, while not overwhelming, was a triumph for the prohibitionists. By a margin of roughly four to three, British Columbian voters had approved Bowser's proposed Prohibition Act.[134] Only Lillooet and the rhyming communities of Fernie and Alberni went against the provincial trend. Emilio Picariello, by this time styling himself "The Bottle King," managed to bring a fleeting smile to the faces of Fernie's disappointed wet voters with an advertisement offering for sale "27,000 dozen empty beer bottles." Official results would not be available until the ballots of overseas soldiers were counted, but there was no reason to think their votes could alter the decision to go dry. After all, soldiers stationed in British Columbia had voted more or less consistently with the provincial trend.

Locally, the vote against prohibition in the Elk Valley was not unexpected. The mining communities in Alberta's Crowsnest Pass had voted strongly against that province's plebiscite a year earlier, and it was assumed their counterparts in British Columbia would follow suit. They did, but what is surprising about the local result is not the strength of the vote opposing prohibition, but rather the strength of the vote in favour of it. Approximately 42 percent of local voters approved of the proposed prohibition on the sale and consumption of alcohol. The very substantial number of local Methodists and Presbyterians and their commitment to the cause had delivered that vote. Only Natal provided the overwhelmingly negative vote that might have been expected of mining communities.

All things considered, the first nine months of 1916 brought profound political change to the Elk Valley. Women would have the provincial franchise in the next election; hotel owners were dismayed by the prospect of prohibition; District 18 of the UMWA was no longer officially linked to the Socialist Party of Canada; miners at Fernie and Coal Creek had voted overwhelmingly against the Socialist candidate; Uphill had lost an election for the first time; the local Liberals had won for the first time; and the Conservatives had lost their first election in a long time. Briefly chastened, Wallace at the *Free Press* was quiet on the subject of politics for just a while. But, employing a metaphor from the game of poker, at Thanksgiving he wrote that the people of British Columbia had been "hoaxed by a bunch of coast four-flushers who are not worthy of tying Bowser's shoe-strings." Apparently, the editor of the *Free Press* was not yet reconciled to having Fernie represented by a Liberal MLA. He looked forward to a reversal of fortunes and reported Uphill was in Vancouver in October attending the Conservative convention that was considering the party's future strategy.[135]

Continuing his political wars through the columns of his *Free Press*, Wallace delighted fellow travellers and infuriated opponents. While Frank Newnham, as editor of the *District Ledger*, had elicited no personal condemnation from Wallace, as editor of the Liberal *Fernie Mail*, he was the subject of frequent attack. Wallace described Newnham as a "selfish specimen of humanity" after he persuaded city council to place a tax on publishers in October. When the *Free Press* noted in late November that the *Fernie Mail* had ceased publication, there was no indication of regret and no expression of condolences.[136]

For residents uninterested in (or tired of hearing about) matters of provincial politics, the summer and fall of 1916 provided much else to draw their attention. The number of automobiles in Fernie had risen to twenty-three. One of them—William Wilson's new seven-passenger McLaughlin—was the talk of the town. The Fernie–Fort Steele Brewing Company welcomed Albert Mutz on a visit from Alberta and reported significant improvements in its business operations. Responding to the public's evident preference for "purity" in politics and all else, the brewery began to describe its operation as "immaculate," with vats and machines "kept as clean as the pots and pans in mother's kitchen." In the *Free Press* and the *Blairmore Enterprise*, Fernie's Pollock Wine Company began in September to advertise its products for export to Alberta and Saskatchewan, facing fierce competition from the Michel Liquor Company, which claimed its proximity to the provincial border enabled it to offer better prices to the Alberta consumer.[137]

To counter the widely circulating rumour that he had failed to pay his dog tax, Mayor Uphill—presumably using to advantage the sense of humour for which he was well known—solemnly told a meeting of city council that he did not own a dog.[138] The Italian Band and the Coal Creek Colliery Band were involved in another musical dispute, although this one bore none of the unpleasant undercurrents of the last. Both groups had experienced personnel losses to recruitment. The Coal Creek group held a successful fundraising drive to pay for new uniforms, while the Italian Band was no longer functioning. The city demanded the return of all instruments for redistribution to the more active Colliery Band. It became apparent that some instrumentalists played with both bands, and the issue was resolved such that the two musical units were active again by the end of the year.

The congregations of the local Presbyterian and Methodist churches, perhaps galvanized by their shared hopes for the success of the prohibition referendum, in July voted overwhelmingly to merge. The Presbyterian vote was unanimous and the Methodist vote nearly so.[139] While both congregations were numerically strong, finances were of considerable concern. Their parent churches in Canada had been considering the question of amalgamation for years, and in several prairie communities attempts were also underway to achieve local unions. However, the response of the Methodist governing body in Toronto was swift and clear: the local amalgamation would not be permitted. Both congregations were expected to carry on independently as much as finances would permit until the finer points of theology and governance were settled nationally. Had the amalgamation been allowed to proceed, Fernie would have been home to the first United Church in western Canada, a distinction claimed by Okotoks a few months later. The formation of the United Church of Canada in 1925 did eventually settle those matters of theology and governance, but as their actions would soon indicate, the local congregations were not prepared to wait.

The women of the IODE were very busy indeed. The nominal membership had increased to seventy-four to start the year, with most members apparently active, as the energies of the Mount Fernie branch during 1916 showed no signs of war fatigue. They did not engage in fundraising, continuing to rely instead on the monthly contribution from the Amalgamated Patriotic Fund, unsolicited donations and their own resources. In addition to ongoing knitting and sewing efforts, they sent hampers in April to each local man then a prisoner of war. In October, sixty "comfort bags" containing, combs, cards, games, soap, towels, cigarettes and chocolate went to soldiers in hospitals. A successful "sock shower" in early November enabled them to send dozens of "Xmas socks and trench comforts" to B Company of the 54th Kootenay Battalion in Europe. The stockings were filled with chewing gum, cigarettes and chocolate. As before, all shipments were sent through the international auspices of the Canadian Red Cross.

In an incident that was not made public, Chief Constable Welsby was asked by Superintendent Colin Campbell of the provincial police to warn CNPCC employee Jan Polak that he could be prosecuted for attempting to send funds to Poland. With the local Polish Relief Fund organized in 1915 apparently moribund, Polak acted on behalf of sixteen of his fellow Poles—all of whom would have been classified as Russian nationals and all of whom were likely working at the coke ovens—to send a modest sum of money to an American Polish-language newspaper "for the hungry in Poland." Upon investigation, Welsby was satisfied the money was not intended for Poles in Germany and instructed Polak on the proper channels for any further transmission of funds to Russia. Welsby also noted in his report to Campbell that Polak was contributing a percentage of his wages to the Amalgamated Patriotic Fund.[140]

There were growing indications, however, that even with its successful employee deduction plan working well, the APF was struggling to meet local requirements. Obligations to contribute to the Tobacco Fund, Belgian Relief and Red Cross (through branches of the IODE at Fernie and Waldo and Red Cross committees at Michel and Coal Creek) were being met by the APF, but after the first few months of the year, funds raised locally were unequal to the task of providing disbursements for needy families of soldiers. The situation in Fernie was not unique. The fund was structured to deliver surplus funds from more affluent to poorer districts as required. In fact, throughout the war years, disbursements in British Columbia depended heavily on transfers, especially from amounts collected in Ontario.

The reason for the shortfall locally was not difficult to see. In January, the first full month with the plan of "systematic giving" in place, the Canadian Patriotic Fund distributed $1,241 to fifty dependent families in the Fernie district. Money raised locally by the APF was more than equal to the task, and the provincial headquarters of the Canadian Patriotic Fund in Victoria were no doubt grateful for the surplus funds it received from Fernie. The average amount received by dependent families in the first few months of the year was approximately twenty-six dollars, well above the national average payment of just sixteen dollars per month.[141] By April, however, the number of families requiring assistance had doubled and, following the departure in July of the 225th Kootenay Battalion, the number of new applications increased sharply. By September, 153 families in the Fernie district were receiving payments.

The loyal spirit and high levels of recruitment had created a financial burden that could not be met by the local fundraising efforts of the APF. New national regulations resulted both in reductions to dependents and in letters of abuse to APF secretary Alfred Cummings and members of his committee. The average amount paid monthly to each family after May fell to roughly twenty-one dollars, and even that required a substantial subsidy from the national headquarters of Canadian Patriotic Fund in Ottawa. In his more private moments, Cummings must have hoped the prohibition on recruitment locally would ease the pressure of fundraising, and apparently it did. By the end of the year, only 117 dependent families were receiving payments, while collections in December provided further encouragement, amounting to what would prove to be the wartime peak of over $3,300.[142]

INFLATION AND THE WAR BONUS

Aside from the problems caused by recruitment, labour relations at the mines seemed on an even keel early in 1916. Conditions of full employment prevailed, and, for the first time in several years, the Crow's Nest Pass Coal Company reported it had returned to profitability.[143] However, by late spring—just over a year into the collective agreement between the UMWA and the Western Coal Operators' Association—the rising cost of consumer goods became of sufficient concern that many union members insisted prevailing wage scales were inadequate. At Fernie in early May, a special meeting of the executive of District 18 was convinced by Gladstone local union representatives to demand a 10 percent war bonus to offset inflation.

Complicated negotiations with the Coal Operators, who were reluctant to reopen the collective agreement before it expired in March 1917, brought an offer of a war bonus of 5 percent plus an increase to wages of 2.5 percent. Fully aware of the labour shortage and anticipating further increases in the demand for coal, the operators had no desire to face a full-scale strike. Approval of their offer was not expected to present a problem, and the Gladstone local union voted strongly in favour when the question was put to members in a referendum in July. However, at Michel and throughout the rest of District 18, the vote was even more strongly negative. An impasse had been reached.

The feeling of unease experienced in the Elk Valley at this point was profound. Although service industries and forestry in particular made significant contributions to the local economy, the coal industry, as the cliché would have it, was king. The CNPCC was far and away the region's major employer and the UMWA the largest employee organization. Prosperity depended upon functioning arrangements between the two. But neither company management nor company employees enjoyed the freedom of independent action. The CNPCC was a member of the Western Coal Operators' Association, the organization which included most mine owners in the Elk Valley, the Crowsnest Pass and southern Alberta. However, different priorities between owners of the lignite and sub-bituminous Lethbridge-area mines and owners of the bituminous mines of the Crowsnest Pass and the Elk Valley often caused internal divisions. District 18 of the UMWA often experienced the same divergence of interests, which frequently resulted in disagreement on how best to deal with the Coal Operators. Any threat to labour peace could easily result in widespread economic consequences.

The Gladstone local union returned to its 10 percent demand, and District 18 officials endorsed that position, while the Coal Operators insisted they could go no further than their rejected offer and proposed arbitration. Two weeks of labour chaos followed. The Gladstone local union voted to strike, and the Coal Creek mines were idle; then the men voted to return to work but didn't; when they decided to return to work, union drivers and some coke oven workers refused to co-operate. The UMWA and the Coal Operators agreed to meet, but the meeting was cancelled by the Coal Operators when the Lethbridge local union unexpectedly went on strike.

Mediation efforts conducted at Fernie by Frederick Harrison and J.D. McNiven, fair-wage officials with the department of labour, went nowhere. By the first day of August, camps throughout the district were either on strike or threatening to go out, and the Gladstone local union went out again. All of this was in spite of District 18 officials urging their members to stay on the job. The *Lethbridge Daily Herald* noted that the actions at the different mining camps throughout District 18 showed union officials had "little influence with the mass of the workers if that mass feels like going on strike."[144]

The Coal Operators were feeling the pressures of internal dissension as well. At their meeting on August 2, two Alberta members withdrew from the association.[145] Just as Britain went to war in defence of an existing agreement with Belgium in 1914, the Coal Operators insisted they too were acting to preserve an existing agreement. Willing nevertheless to amend that agreement, they asked why they should talk to a union that could not control its members. Of course, their own organization had no control over mine owners who were no longer members of the association and who preferred to negotiate and settle with their workforces independently.

Almost in desperation, the Coal Operators appealed to John White, international president of the UMWA in Indianapolis. Informing him that District 18 officials "frankly admit their inability to keep the locals working," they insisted they would not negotiate with men out on an illegal strike.[146] White immediately wired District 18 officials to order the men to return to work pending a settlement. His intervention seems to have made the difference. By August 7, all camps were back at work, and the Coal Operators had presented a slightly modified offer with a promise of a further increase when the current collective agreement expired in March. Locals were to vote on the offer on August 10, and there was a general feeling that the crisis was over.

But before the vote, a crisis of still greater significance struck the CNP-CC. During a severe electrical storm, an explosion at Michel's No. 3 East mine just before midnight on August 8 killed all twelve men working on the night shift. General manager William Wilson and the Coal Creek rescue team arrived from Fernie very early the next morning, but it soon was apparent the operation could only be one of recovery. Interestingly, the nominal roll of the dead indicates that the prohibition—still in place at Coal Creek—against Austrian nationals working in underground occupations was not being applied to the mines at Michel.[147]

With loss of more lives serving as another reminder of the realities of their occupation, miners at Michel and Coal Creek showed little enthusiasm for the scheduled vote, but it could not be postponed. After some initial opposition from Coal Creek, the locals in the bituminous mines of the Crowsnest proved to be more enthusiastic about the proposal than the lignite miners of Lethbridge. Overall, the offer was accepted by a clear (if not overwhelming) majority. Labour peace had returned to Fernie and Coal Creek.

It was not to last for long. In November, at another meeting of the UMWA executive at Fernie, the union initiated a process that infuriated the Western Coal Operators' Association. Thomas France, secretary of the Gladstone local union, explained to the *Free Press* that the increases granted by the August agreement had already been entirely used up by rising food costs.[148] In a letter to the Coal Operators dated November 11, the UMWA sought an additional 25 percent war bonus to be applied until the expiry of the collective agreement at the end of March 1917. Should the demand not be granted, the union insisted upon a federal investigation into the cost of living in local mining communities.

The Coal Operators met a few days later and rejected the demand in no uncertain terms. They accused the UMWA of attempting to take advantage of the shortage of labour caused by extremely high enlistment rates. They sent a telegram to Minister of Labour Thomas Crothers in Ottawa claiming the miners' demands were "altogether peremptory in tone ... and absolutely impossible to entertain." The Coal Operators insisted he impress upon District 18 the necessity of living up to agreements and, with their successful tactic of August in mind, suggested that UMWA international president John White would be able to assist in the matter.[149] A week later, confident in the virtue of their stance, the Coal Operators advised Crothers they wanted an investigation into "all conditions surrounding this dispute" and insisted a collective agreement could not be viewed as a "scrap of paper." Their initial inclination to grant concessions had vanished; clearly, the Coal Operators were prepared to fight.[150]

So was the UMWA. Citing the large increases just granted to their counterparts in Nova Scotia, miners right across District 18 prepared to strike at the end of November. At the last moment, district president William Graham and international board member David Rees were called to Ottawa for negotiations with the government and Coal Operators. It is unclear whether, as the *Lethbridge Daily Herald* reported, Graham then issued instructions to cancel the strike. If he did, the miners ignored him. The biggest strike yet experienced in the Alberta and East Kootenay coal mines began on November 27 when five thousand men refused to go to work. After the government agreed to investigate the escalating cost of living as the union had demanded, Graham's fresh instructions to return to work were again ignored for several days. CNPCC mines returned to production on December 4, followed by the Alberta mines a few days later. All of this occurred against news reports that labour unrest over the rising cost of living in the United Kingdom had resulted in a government decision to take over operation of the mines in Wales on the first of December.

Privately, Minister of Labour Crothers advised the Coal Operators that granting the demand for an enquiry into the cost of living was the lesser of two evils.[151] The Coal Operators did not get their full-scale enquiry. The miners did get their investigation. The discussions in Ottawa resulted in an order-in-council issued December 10 authorizing an investigation into the cost of living specifically in the mining communities served by District 18. Frederick Harrison, who had been active in attempting to mediate during the troubles of July and August, was appointed as the sole commissioner. Initially, he was given a deadline of December 15 to conclude his work, but that date was soon extended to the end of the month. For the second time in just eighteen months a federal order-in-council had been required to address a labour issue that had been initiated by disgruntled miners at Fernie and Coal Creek. It would not be the last.

Commissioner Harrison started his work with sittings in Alberta and arrived in Fernie just before Christmas. At Calgary, there had been mention of subpoenas to compel reluctant businessmen to testify; at Lethbridge, the weak testimony of a prominent UMWA official must have disappointed and embarrassed the union. At Fernie, there were no such difficulties. Prominent city merchants complied fully with Harrison's requests; Canadian Pacific's Lewis Stockett represented the Coal Operators; Thomas France and Thomas Biggs of the Gladstone local union gave well-considered evidence.

Concluding with a final sitting on Thursday evening, December 21, Harrison immediately made public the statistics he had gathered at Fernie. Prices from early July for food, dry goods, clothing and shoes were compared with prices for the same items in late November. As increased food costs had been specified by the union as the chief cause of its cost-of-living concerns, he focussed on the foodstuffs available at Trites-Wood, the Crow's Nest Pass Trading Company, the Fernie Co-operative Society and P. Burns and Company. These were published in full in the Christmas edition of the *Free Press*, which noted that the comparisons provided very little support for the union's demand for a significant cost-of-living increase. Apart from sharp increases for eggs and dairy products, prices had remained exceptionally stable over the five-month period.[152]

Commissioner Harrison returned to Ottawa to prepare his report. He left Fernie with question marks hanging over future labour relations. Was the Canadian government at all inclined to follow the example of Britain in taking control of the coal mines? Despite the labour shortage and disruptions over the cost of living, the CNPCC had enjoyed a very good year, paying a dividend of 6 percent due to increased demand and production. The Coal Creek mines worked 248.5 days during the calendar year. Would these conditions continue? Colliery band member Thomas Biggs—generally thought to be more radical in politics than Graham by virtue of his membership in the Socialist Party—had been elected president of District 18 by a narrow margin in early December. What would that mean for internal UMWA politics? Of course, the seemingly interminable war in Europe presented another question. When would it end? The Battle of the Somme had claimed the lives of more local men as trench warfare marked its third Christmas. And the Coal Creek mines had claimed five more lives in separate incidents during the year.

Miners, mine managers, merchants and everyone else seeking some fleeting distraction from such serious concerns could enjoy the silent film *The Shooting of Dan McGrew* at the Orpheum. The Trites-Wood store gave out a thousand treats to delight children at Christmas. Curlers were active again in their repaired facility. Children and hockey players too were pleased the ice rink had been repaired following the floods of June, and, with winter weather co-operating, was once again available for skating.

The internees, the 107th and the 225th had all moved on.

1917

LABOUR, LOYALTY
AND MORAL REFORM

The new calendar year began as usual with civic issues to the forefront. A referendum was scheduled on the question of when to implement a half-holiday in Fernie—Wednesday or Saturday—as required by a new provincial law. The *Free Press* urged a vote in favour of Wednesday, noting that Saturday was always CNPCC payday and therefore an important day for local merchants. Wednesday was the clear choice of voters. Sporting a new handlebar moustache, so was Thomas Uphill in his bid for re-election as mayor. His opponent, William Dicken, had led the local prohibitionist forces in the provincial campaign and called for strict police enforcement of existing liquor and gambling laws. Although he received a considerable vote, the "purity planks" he advocated were not particularly popular with Fernie voters, and Uphill, unlike most of his fellow Methodists, was known to advocate a more tolerant approach in such matters.

Nevertheless, the strength of the moral reform movement was being felt in Fernie. The new Liberal provincial government announced it would vigorously enforce existing laws on gambling and prostitution. After receiving direct instructions from the superintendent of provincial police early in February, Chief Constable Welsby immediately undertook a campaign to improve the moral tone of East Kootenay. Gambling establishments in Cranbrook had already been raided in January, and—armed with his fresh mandate—Welsby issued orders to shut down that community's red-light district. He travelled to Cranbrook to assist the local constable in carrying out the order.[153] Commenting on the crackdown, Wallace at the *Free Press* wrote that the displaced women were "scattered all over the city wherever they could find lodgings and prostitution is known to be more common than ever."

Wallace's statement resulted in another episode in the long-standing civic rivalry between Fernie and Cranbrook. (When some residents of Cranbrook referred to Fernie as "the Coal City," their intent was not to be purely descriptive; the clean air they enjoyed in Cranbrook was often favourably compared to the smoky atmosphere created by Fernie's coke ovens.) The Anglican rector in Cranbrook mistakenly attributed Wallace's comment to Uphill. He wrote to the *Free Press* advising that "decent British public opinion [was] sufficiently strong in Cranbrook to see that these houses of beastliness are wiped out" and insisting that the prostitutes had indeed "been sent from the town." He urged the "clean-minded public of Fernie" to follow suit. Recognizing the offending statement was properly attributable to Wallace, the *Cranbrook Herald* also insisted that every single prostitute had left town and noted it was "a poor lame business of the editor of the Fernie paper to endeavour to bolster up [Fernie's] own bad case by trying to blacken another's character." Wallace replied that he had no intention of slighting the reputation of Cranbrook but was simply pointing out that the preachers who advocated driving prostitutes away were not "providing them with work."[154]

The debate was not restricted to newspaper editors. In Fernie, following a presentation by four local ministers of religion in March, the police commission (comprised of three members—the mayor as chair and two appointees of the provincial government) made the decision to follow Cranbrook's example immediately. City police were to co-operate with provincial police to accomplish the task. Knowing full well there would be a financial consequence for civic finances, they may have taken that decision reluctantly. For years, the practice of fining known prostitutes for vagrancy every month meant that what was often obliquely referred to as "the social evil" was effectively licensed in Fernie. The penalty was always a fine or one month's hard labour. According to city police records, no one so penalized ever did the hard labour. The eleven-dollar monthly fines for prostitutes and the twenty-two-dollar fines for madams were always paid promptly; city coffers were duly enhanced, and those charged were free to go about their business.[155]

That arrangement was about to end. Chief Constable Welsby served notice that, after one final legitimate weekend, the city's red-light district—located at the foot of Cokato Road in the area known as the Old Town—was to be closed on Monday, March 19. A result parallel to that he claimed had occurred in Cranbrook was soon noted by Wallace. He wrote that some of "the inmates left town, some are at hotels, and some have taken rooms around town." He also predicted city police would have difficulty "supressing the vice entirely." Of course, he was correct. Two weeks later, a lengthy discussion at a city council meeting was sharply critical of local police efforts in the matter and voted funds to send one prostitute, apparently arrested in the crackdown, to a church-sponsored home in Vancouver.[156] When police in April announced that Fernie was finally free of prostitutes, the always feisty editor of the *Free Press* couldn't resist posing the question about where they might have gone. He suggested the answer could be ... Cranbrook.

Rivalry with Cranbrook also extended into the world of sports. Fernie's curlers were proud of their brand-new building, located right beside the skating rink on the east bank of the Elk River. Led by former mayor Sherwood Herchmer, the club defeated its Kootenay rival there in late February to capture the Fleishman Cup, the symbol of local curling supremacy at the time. While ice hockey received little attention, curling was always front-page news in the *Free Press*, no doubt because editor John Wallace was an active club member. Amos Trites seemed to agree the roaring game deserved attention—the Fleishman Cup was proudly displayed in one of the large windows at the Trites-Wood store. But the curling club was not alone in making Fernie familiar to other British Columbia communities. Businessman Emilio Picariello, while still maintaining his bottle and grocery businesses in Fernie, supplied ice cream to Crowsnest Pass communities and opened ice cream parlours in both Trail and Blairmore in early 1917.[157]

Of course, the domestic war effort continued to command much attention. The fundraising structures established by the Amalgamated Patriotic Fund in late 1915 continued to work well, and another tour of the logging country to the south by APF secretary Alfred Cummings had persuaded hitherto reluctant managers of some camps at Bull River to sign on. Civic boosters were proud that the monthly amounts collected in the Fernie district continued to compare so favourably with subscriptions in communities of comparable size. Although there was to be no published annual report from the APF for 1917, the average $3,000 monthly collections were again able to provide adequately for local dependent families without subsidy from the provincial headquarters of the Canadian Patriotic Fund. With the number of families in need significantly lower than the peaks of 1916, Fernie and district collections were creating substantial surpluses.

As secretary of the APF, land surveyor Cummings was an influential and persuasive figure. He apparently attempted to exert that influence when he met with the local IODE executive in January to complain that they were simply not being sufficiently productive on behalf of the Red Cross. He explained that he thought "a special effort should be put forth toward getting every woman in town to devote their spare time to this work." Reporting on the meeting, Wallace (whose wife Laura was an executive member of the

IODE) may have been inviting public reaction to the criticism as much as he was endorsing the call for new members to join the IODE. He certainly knew Cummings's complaint was curious in light of the weekly reports in the *Free Press* indicating that remarkable numbers of items for the men in the trenches were consistently being produced by the Mount Fernie chapter.

In response a few weeks later, the executive of the IODE let their annual report for 1916 speak for itself. Although membership had declined to fifty-one by the end of the year, both their efforts and their results seem little short of astonishing. Acknowledging particularly contributions from Michel, Natal, Corbin and Waldo—and of course from the Amalgamated Patriotic Fund—the report completely itemized the number of hampers sent to prisoners of war in Germany, comfort bags sent to men in English hospitals, monthly shipments of trench comforts, Christmas socks and their contents.[158] No further public criticism of the Mount Fernie chapter of the IODE would be heard from Cummings, the Amalgamated Patriotic Fund or anyone else for the duration of the war.

News of the progress of the war itself was largely left to the big-city dailies, but local details continued to be featured in the *Free Press*. Letters from men serving in Europe were printed regularly, especially those thanking the women of the IODE for the welcome supplies received through the Red Cross. Wallace noted (incorrectly, as time would reveal) that his former antagonist, Frank Newnham, had enlisted at Calgary. From New Westminster came the news that the 225th Kootenay Battalion left for Nova Scotia en route to England in January, but without its commanding officer. Lieutenant Colonel Joseph Mackay had been declared medically unfit for overseas duty.[159] Every week brought fresh reports that caused pride for some Fernie residents, concern or dismay for others—word of local soldiers decorated, wounded or killed. Former District 18 president William Phillips wrote to David Rees from England noting whimsically that he would "soon become one of those who are but a hazy remembrance to you and all the folks in Fernie." Phillips was killed in France soon afterwards.[160]

Fernie merchants continued to benefit significantly by supplying the needs of the internment camp at Morrissey. Providing primarily hardware and building supplies, Trites-Wood, Kennedy & Mangan and John Quail did substantial business with Internment Operations during the fiscal year ending March 1917. Providing groceries, so too did the Crow's Nest Trading Company. However, Major General Otter was struggling to control costs as inflation began to take its toll. To supply internment camps throughout the western provinces, he turned for groceries to A. Macdonald and Company of Winnipeg and to P. Burns Company of Calgary for meats. Invoiced through their Fernie outlets, the $23,000 in products these companies jointly provided was of only token benefit to the local economy. The city's bakers were also out of trade as the Morrissey camp began to bake its own bread. Interestingly, the CNPCC—supplying no coal and charging no rent according to the financial records of Internment Operations—did not share in the commercial advantage the camp at Morrissey brought to the Fernie business community.[161]

As a footnote to Bowser's internment order of 1915, the recently elected Liberal administration in Victoria finally conceded that costs incurred prior to the transfer of the prisoners to Internment Operations were indeed a provincial responsibility. A memorandum for the new attorney general noted the adamant refusal of federal authorities to reimburse the province for its expenditure on Bowser's internment camp and explained that the "late Attorney-General decided it would be better to arrest and detain these aliens than to run the risk of a strike at Fernie." Avoiding a more accurate explanation of the internment and any overt criticism of Bowser, the province finally settled accounts with the city of Fernie for light and water and with William Robichaud for rental of the skating rink.[162]

ANOTHER GOVERNMENT INTERVENTION

All matters of local interest, however, were overshadowed by the ongoing and escalating labour dispute between the Western Coal Operators' Association and the UMWA. Commissioner Harrison reported in early January to Minister of Labour Thomas Crothers in Ottawa that his investigation of prices at Calgary, Lethbridge and Fernie indicated a war bonus of 29 cents per day, retroactive to mid-November, was justified. This represented an increase of approximately 5 percent for the highest-paid workers and 13 percent for the lowest.[163] A far cry from the 25 percent initially demanded, Harrison's recommendation was accepted by the District 18 executive, but fears were quickly expressed that the Coal Operators would reject it. Representatives of the Coal Operators (including CNPCC president Elias Rogers, William Wilson and Lewis Stockett) and District 18 (Thomas Biggs as president-elect and UMWA international board member David Rees) were all summoned to Ottawa for a wage conference to discuss the Harrison award.

The conference did not go well. The two sides were entrenched in opposing if predictable stances. The union expected to receive the full amount determined by Harrison; the Coal Operators—insisting they would not reopen the collective agreement a second time—regarded the award as "unjustifiable and exorbitant." They submitted an angry statement to Crothers outlining their position. The Coal Operators accused the American-based UMWA of being controlled by foreigners who did not have Canadian interests at heart and who were taking advantage of the labour shortage by treating signed agreements like "mere scraps of paper." The UMWA, they said, was an "alien organization" that should not be allowed to dictate to mine owners or Canadian governments. Pointing to the future, they concluded that granting a cost-of-living increase under threat of a strike would only encourage "further aggression on the part of this foreign union."[164]

A long-serving union official in District 18, Thomas Biggs's credibility as president-elect was undermined at a critical time by news his election was being contested. Fernie Museum and Archives DL-PF-1909-0292.

As the Coal Operators sought to undermine the credibility of the UMWA, the union itself seemed to do its best to help them. David Rees infuriated many with a widely reported speech to the Ottawa Trades and Labour Council in which he revived the complaint that the workers of the world had not had the "opportunity of saying whether they wanted war or not." He compared his own position to that of Lloyd George in opposing the Boer War. The *Calgary Herald* made his comments front-page news under the headline "Rees Hurts Miners Cause at Ottawa."[165] The speech was portrayed as an indication of disloyalty, and Rees was quickly and widely condemned for his remarks. More significantly, Thomas Biggs received word that the votes cast in December for union executive positions at Lethbridge and Drumheller had been thrown out "due to irregularities." Both locals had strongly favoured Biggs, a Socialist Party member. The old executive was to remain in place until fresh elections could be held. Biggs was not president-elect after all, and his authority to act for the union during the negotiations in Ottawa was seriously compromised.

Lacking firm assurances that the Harrison award would be paid, miners at Coal Creek went on strike. At an emergency meeting at the Miners' Union Building on the morning of January 16, they heard moderate president William Graham, moderate local secretary Carter and radical vice-president Thomas Biggs—just off the train from Ottawa and probably still coming to terms with his ouster. All three men delivered the same message: return to work. The miners were reminded of the financial penalty for illegal work stoppages; they were urged to await the final outcome of the Ottawa conference; they were told only miners at Frank had joined their work stoppage, with all others abiding by the union directive to remain on the job pending a decision about the Harrison award.

But the members of the Gladstone local union refused to listen. By a margin of two to one, they voted to remain on strike. The situation was highly reminiscent of the internment vote of June 1915, with union officials pointing to the collective agreement and unanimously urging a return to work, miners rejecting that advice and only one other UMWA local inclined to follow their example. However, this time the situation throughout the district changed over the next ten days as other locals decided to follow Fernie's lead. At the *Free Press*, John Wallace—seldom sympathetic to the UMWA in labour disputes—was not inclined to change his views. "Miners on Strike Again" proclaimed his impatient headline.

Wallace was not alone in his impatience. Many observers, government officials and miners alike began to consider and to welcome the prospect of a government takeover of the coal mines. Citing the example of the UK, where in similar circumstances the government had taken control of the Welsh coal mines in December, the *Lethbridge Herald* ran the headline "Government May Take Over Coal Mines." The *Free Press* raised the same possibility soon afterwards. The provincial police in British Columbia were particularly nervous about the strike situation. Welsby received a shipment of forty pairs of handcuffs, twenty leather batons and forty badges that would be needed if the situation required the swearing in of special constables.[166]

After nearly two weeks idle, the Coal Creek miners on January 28 voted overwhelmingly in a secret ballot to return to work. Most other striking locals in the Crowsnest soon made the same decision. Bitterly cold temperatures had resulted in a serious shortage of the domestic coal supply, but a severe winter blizzard made an immediate resumption of production almost impossible. It was not until the first day of February that full production could be resumed at Coal Creek. The wage conference—reconvened in Calgary, but still making no progress—was awaiting the arrival of Minister of Labour Crothers. The entrenched union and the equally entrenched Coal Operators were talking only through government mediators Frederick Harrison and Kootenay MP Robert Green. Like everyone else, Crothers proved unable to secure a compromise. But on Saturday, February 3, he advised the Coal Operators that the full Harrison award would be paid retroactively to November 16—not by them, but by the federal government. He added that after February 3 and until the expiry of the collective agreement at the end of March, the Coal Operators were to be responsible for the payment and should raise their price of coal accordingly.[167]

District 18 union officials could claim a victory, but the Coal Operators initially refused to endorse the government plan. Like the union, the owners' organization was experiencing internal stresses. Within the previous several months, three companies had gone out of business and three others had withdrawn to make policy decisions independently. The fourteen companies remaining often struggled to reach agreement, but they shared an increasing consensus that a major battle with the union was necessary. At their annual general meeting a few days later, after electing William Wilson as their new president—in itself an indication of that consensus—the Coal Operators accepted the imposed arrangement under protest. They agreed to comply only because Crothers insisted a "national crisis" existed and because the government was prepared to pay the retroactive portion of the bonus.

In a bitter press statement released following their meeting, the Coal Operators insisted the crisis had been caused by government interference and made it clear that they would have preferred a full-blown confrontation with the UMWA.[168] Ottawa had not after all taken control of the mines, but it had intervened to impose its will. Coal companies, union, government and everyone else knew that, in modern parlance, the can had simply been kicked down the road. And that road was known to be a short one. The collective agreement (and the government's peripheral involvement in it) would expire in just eight weeks' time.

District 18 held its annual convention in Fernie for the second year in a row beginning on February 19. Mayor Uphill again welcomed the delegates and granted them the customary freedom of the city. Over the course of the next ten days, the forty delegates were again entertained in Fernie and at Coal Creek and treated to recitations, speeches and performances by the Coal Creek Colliery Band. They attended the monthly patriotic dance put on by the Amalgamated Patriotic Fund. But the convention was faced with a full agenda. While considering the Harrison award, delegates heard substantially different reports on the recent negotiations from Graham and Biggs. Delegates confirmed the union's opposition to employment of Asians, postponed a decision on resuming publication of the *District Ledger* and, at the request of the British Columbia Federation of Labour, recorded their opposition to "conscription in any form." To address the voting "irregularities" of December, they also managed to agree upon a process to hold fresh elections for executive positions.

However, the main task was to prepare for negotiations for a new collective agreement. The war bonuses would both expire with the current agreement on March 31, and delegates were well aware the Coal Operators were not in a generous frame of mind. Coincidentally, just as the conference was wrapping up, Harrison and an assistant visited Fernie to make arrangements with local banks for the payment of the government war bonus to all members of the Gladstone local union. Perhaps out of consideration for the community acting as their host, one controversial decision appears not to have been made public by the delegates while in Fernie: District 18 headquarters were to move to Calgary. Just as the military considered Fernie too far east to be East Kootenay's military centre, District 18 decided Fernie was too far west for its growing Alberta membership. But the decision was taken for reasons not entirely geographic. The Gladstone local union—the first, the largest and still the most influential in the district—was witnessing a shift in political power away from the Elk Valley to the coalfields of Alberta. By August, the move would be completed. And with no tenant, the union building on Pellatt Avenue became a liability.

The negotiations for a new contract opened in Calgary in early March and dragged on for the rest of the month. Again Minister of Labour Crothers found himself involved in the negotiations, and again there was talk of the government taking control of the mines. Union leaders promised no work stoppages as long as talks were ongoing, but when the collective agreement expired at the end of the month, miners walked out at Michel, Bellevue and Hillcrest. Again the Coal Operators asked why they should negotiate with an organization that could not control its members. For a change, the Gladstone local union had voted to return to work on the advice of its leaders, but the mines at Coal Creek also fell silent on April 5. That stoppage had nothing to do with contract negotiations.

At 10:30 in the morning, what was later thought to be the greatest explosion ever to occur at Coal Creek ripped through the No. 3 mine. All thirty-four of the men at work in the mine at the time of the explosion were killed. It was soon recognized that there could be no rescue operation and that recovery work would be extremely dangerous and slow. The horror had a profound impact on the whole community. Sydney Hutcheson, a nine-year-old Fernie schoolboy at the time, would later recall viewing the severely burned bodies of victims with his classmates at George Thomson's funeral parlour.[169] The first four funerals on April 9 drew a huge attendance; the dirges were supplied by the Coal Creek Colliery Band. The Gladstone local union's plans to host a "monster Mayday" in Fernie for the entire region were cancelled. It was not a time for celebration. Chief Constable Welsby noted the disaster had "cast a gloom over the district."

Like all misfortunes—large and small and nationwide between 1914 and 1918—the disaster at Coal Creek aroused suspicions of wartime sabotage. Just a few days later, CNPCC President Elias Rogers revealed to shareholders that the company had received anonymous letters concerning terrorist actions.[170] One note received in August 1916 at Michel claimed responsibility for the recent explosion there; at the same time, another threatening a future act of sabotage had been stuck into the door jamb of the Mine Rescue Station at Fernie. The existence of the notes was not made public.

Without any apparent knowledge of the threats, the coroner at Fernie contacted the attorney general in Victoria to urge that guards be placed at all mine entrances to search everyone before allowing access.[171] Welsby quickly assured his superiors in Victoria that the coroner was an alarmist and that both William Wilson and Thomas Uphill scoffed at his allegations of sabotage. The nominal roll of the dead indicates that the prohibition against Austrian-born and German-born nationals in underground occupations was still in effect at Coal Creek. To demonstrate the loyalty of local enemy aliens, Welsby noted that three Germans were assisting with the rescue efforts.[172]

The fire at the Parliament buildings in February 1916 and the Halifax harbour explosion that would soon shock the country in December were quickly found to be the results of accidents. So too was the disaster at Coal Creek. It was certainly no coincidence that the CNPCC just a few weeks later replaced its oil-burning Wolfe safety lamps with Thomas Edison's new battery-powered electric lamps. Nor was it a coincidence that the British Columbia minister of mines asked the director of the Dominion Meteorological Service to place "a delicate seismograph" in the mines at Coal Creek in hopes of identifying dangerous conditions. Fernie's coroner was not assigned to conduct the inquest, that responsibility being given instead to the coroner from Natal. However, beyond pointing to gas and dust, the extensive hearings held in Fernie throughout April led to no definitive conclusion about the cause of the explosion. The lack of certainty allowed doubts to linger and speculation to continue. Fernie's coroner was not alone in harbouring fears that saboteurs were operating in the region.

A good many of those killed left wives and families, and the Coal Creek Colliery Explosion Fund was quickly launched. Trustees were Mayor Uphill, MLA Alexander Fisher and Gladstone local union secretary Thomas France, who all assured potential subscribers their donations would be as well administered as those raised following the 1902 Coal Creek disaster, which had only very recently ceased to provide payment to eligible dependents. The appeal was successful, with donations ranging from a modest fifty cents from many individuals to the very substantial amounts contributed by William Wilson and the UMWA. By the end of the year, bolstered by a contribution of $10,000 from the federal government, the fund stood at over $20,000 and was making payments to bereaved dependents.[173]

With strikes still ongoing in the Alberta Crowsnest and rumours circulating of a government takeover of the mines, contract negotiations in Calgary between District 18 and the Coal Operators were difficult. Progress was finally made in mid-April, and an agreement was reached late in the month. In summary, the miners were to retain the war bonuses and receive an increase of 3 percent on wages and a reduction in hours for some job categories. From a contemporary perspective, the proposed collective agreement seems astonishingly complicated. Pay rates for the same job category varied from one company to another and even varied from mine shaft to mine shaft at the same mine. Rates at Michel were not the same as those at Coal Creek. Of course, this had been true of the expired agreement as well, but clearly members of the Coal Operators did not always share the same priorities. Just as clearly, the same was true of the UMWA locals. The fact that an agreement had been reached nevertheless was cause for optimism throughout the coal mining districts. The *Free Press* offered its congratulations to both miners and owners when it published the proposed agreement in full. Miners were to vote on the proposal on Saturday, May 5.[174]

The optimism was misplaced. While miners at Michel substantially approved, Gladstone and most of the sixteen local unions in Alberta just as substantially rejected the agreement. Overall, it was turned down by a margin of approximately two to one. A report received at the last minute that a better agreement had been achieved in Pennsylvania gave support to those who argued the wage increase offered was inadequate. The Coal Operators advised Crothers it was "useless to negotiate further" and appealed to the government to put the agreement into effect "to get the mines in operation and save the country further embarrassment during the period of the war." The *Free Press* claimed the negative result was due to "bitter contention among the leaders" over the disputed District 18 elections. Until that was settled, it predicted, "the miner will continue to be the goat."[175]

Whatever the cause, a complete shutdown of all mines in the district followed. The union demanded fresh negotiations, additional concessions and a significantly better wage offer; the Coal Operators adamantly refused on all counts; the federal government's proposal of a royal commission was favoured by the Coal Operators and scorned by the union. Both the Coal Operators and the government were encouraged by the intervention of UMWA international president John White in late May. He wrote directly to District 18 locals ordering a return to work on the basis of the rejected contract pending the conclusions of a royal commission. He placed the blame for the strike directly on District 18 president William Graham and said no strike pay would be forthcoming. Ironically echoing an argument of the Coal Operators, Graham replied that District 18 should not be dictated to by the foreign international UMWA organization and ordered locals to ignore the order. Citing "district autonomy," he denied that White had the authority to command a return to work.[176]

The Coal Operators were hopeful the internal union dispute would weaken the strike and allow the mines to reopen without a government takeover. Nevertheless, during what the *Calgary Herald* described as a "secret meeting" at Fernie on May 26, they replied to the minister of labour's fresh request that they resume negotiations with an emphatic refusal. Interestingly, they also invited him to intervene.

> If the men will not accept what their own representatives and the representatives of the President of their [international] Union consider fair and reasonable, we urge that the Government immediately take effective action to put the mines in operation.[177]

The strategy meeting at Fernie demonstrated that, under the leadership of William Wilson, the resolve of the Coal Operators was strengthening. The *Free Press* reported the CNPCC seemed "prepared to fight to a finish." The company may have been further encouraged by news from Natal where "Bohemian miners" were breaking ranks with the union leadership and demanding to be allowed to return to work. Concerned about ethnic tensions there, Welsby travelled to Natal to talk to the dissident faction in hopes of forestalling trouble.[178]

Reluctantly acknowledging that intervention was required, Crothers appointed Kootenay MP Robert Green as a one-man commission to investigate and report. Green arrived in Calgary on June 5, and ten days later had proposals to present to District 18 and the Coal Operators. His talks with union officials coincided with another communication from the UMWA international president, who repeated his order to return to work and his refusal to consider strike pay until that order was obeyed. White was aware that relief was desperately needed in the mining communities. The long strike was demoralizing; perhaps as much as half the membership had left to seek employment elsewhere. Like the Coal Operators, White saw the prospect of a complete collapse of the UMWA in District 18. At Fernie, the Gladstone local union was attempting to organize its own system of relief for needy members and their families. No one could disagree that a resolution of some sort was essential.

Green's proposals did not provide that resolution, but they changed the situation entirely. He proposed a one-year deal including a commission to investigate the cost of living every four months, the elimination of the penalty clause and a 7.5 percent increase over and above what had already been offered. As the proposal included practically everything they wanted, District 18 officials immediately said they would recommend acceptance to their members. The Coal Operators rejected the package just as quickly, advising Green that "the importation of a few thousand foreign labourers would solve the whole difficulty."[179] But the Coal Operators were having trouble of their own. The Drumheller mine withdrew from the organization and settled separately with its workforce.

Having failed to achieve a settlement, Green returned to Ottawa. In a long discussion with Crothers on June 20, he recommended the legislated imposition of his proposals and the appointment of a commissioner to set wage rates, coal prices and hours of work throughout District 18. Within days an order-in-council was passed to do just that. William H. Armstrong, head of a Vancouver construction firm and owner of the Nicola Valley Coal Company, was appointed as the sole commissioner.[180] Events had moved forward so quickly, Armstrong would later claim he first learned of his appointment through a newspaper report. As the head of what would become known as Western Coal Mining Operations, he issued orders on June 27 to reopen the mines on Tuesday, July 3 under the terms of Green's proposals which were to apply until April 1919.

The government had indeed taken over the mines, albeit indirectly. The Coal Operators' demand for intervention had been granted, but hardly on the terms they had hoped for. They would continue to operate their mines, but under a commissioner's direction and an imposed collective agreement they thought punitive. Furious with Green, the Coal Operators complained the government had seen fit to "give the men all they ask (and more than they expected)."[181] Nevertheless, they immediately wired Crothers that they would "loyally comply" with the order. The miners voted overwhelmingly to comply as well, but were profoundly disappointed by the role their international union had played in the dispute. District 18 officials had been rescued from continuing a dispute with their parent body, the probability of a lost strike and the possibility of a complete collapse of the UMWA in British Columbia and Alberta.

The mines to which the rank and file returned needed maintenance work before they could safely be made operational, and the workforce immediately available was much reduced. Miners had taken employment wherever they could find it, and it was estimated that it would take considerable time to reassemble a workforce sufficient to resume full production. Many families

A thriving economy: Like coal, timber was much in demand in 1917. Fernie Museum and Archives 1099.

had had their credit cut off at local stores; others had substantial debts to honour. During the shutdown, Trites-Wood advertisements offered "Strike Prices" as the store owners claimed to be "doing our bit to relieve the existing pressure of the times." The popular Isis Theatre on Victoria Avenue closed temporarily due to a lack of patronage.

But over the course of the summer, life returned to normal in Fernie. Lumber camps were affected by labour shortages as miners gradually went back to better-paid employment in the mines at Coal Creek and full production resumed. As was so often the case in Fernie, normal life meant the death of workingmen. In late July, seven men were killed when a fire devastated the Elk Lumber Company's logging district at Spruce Creek. Joseph Mackay was welcomed back as he resumed his duties as fuel purchasing agent for Great Northern. Coal Creek, the "town up the gulch" as it was sometimes referred to, welcomed home ten returning soldiers in July and treated them to a banquet at the Northern Hotel in Fernie. A brief early summer strike by employees of the Fernie–Fort Steele Brewing Company was settled with a 15 percent wage increase before any supply shortages occurred.[182] The Gladstone local union announced it would host a splendid program of events on Labour Day. When Wallace noted the city's customary smoke-filled air had returned, it seems his sense of humour had as well. In mid-July, he wrote that the "coke ovens have resumed operations and consequently the mosquitoes, which have been doing a flourishing business in Fernie for the past two weeks, will have to move on."

There was also an element of excitement. For the first time, the travelling American entertainment and educational organization known as Chautauqua had arranged appearances in western Canada. The leading citizens of Fernie needed little persuasion that Fernie could benefit from the program of cultural and moral improvement promised by tour organizers and booked the show for the standard six days in mid-August.[183] Mayor Uphill headed the new Fernie Chautauqua Association, and the *Free Press* urged everyone to attend at least some of the program. Under the touring company's famous brown tent, the performances and lectures proved such a substantial success that plans were launched immediately for a return engagement the following year.

MONEY AND LOYALTY

With the strike finally over in July, District 18 conducted the elections needed after the disputed results of the previous year were declared invalid. In the election for president, the outcome was precisely the same: Thomas Biggs of

Fernie by a very narrow margin was chosen over William Graham of Coleman. At the local union level, Thomas France did not seek re-election. Harry Martin, long involved in union affairs at Coal Creek, took over as secretary. Whether the new man sought to make his mark or whether he was responding to pressure from his members, Martin soon involved the Gladstone local union in an ugly and very public dispute with Alfred Cummings, the secretary of the Amalgamated Patriotic Fund in Fernie.

Nationally, criticism of the system providing relief to the dependents of soldiers was growing. Impressive though they were, funds raised in British Columbia were insufficient for the purpose of providing relief for the dependent families of absent soldiers. Amounts collected surplus to requirements in Ontario provided a subsidy for British Columbia and Alberta. The demand was growing that individual donation should be replaced by a system of national taxation. In British Columbia, the Vancouver Trades and Labour Council called upon members to end voluntary contributions in December; in Alberta, the government was preparing to introduce a tax to provide that province's allotted quota.

Payments to dependents varied considerably from district to district, and the monitoring of families receiving disbursements also created tensions. In Fernie, where class distinctions were keenly felt, that task fell unofficially to the same relatively small number of middle-class women who made up the ranks of the IODE. The families most commonly requesting assistance were those who had lost their primary wage-earner, typically miners and loggers. Presumably, both the APF and the IODE were sufficiently aware of potential problems to avoid arranging visits to coal miners' homes by wives of coal mine officials.

In step with the demands for reform, the local union's support for a national system of taxation was expressed in a surprisingly awkward fashion. In late August, Martin advised the CNPCC that, ostensibly as a protest against a proposed new provincial poll tax, the Gladstone local union had decided to immediately withdraw consent for payroll deductions for the Amalgamated Patriotic Fund. After a one-day strike on the issue shut down the Coal Creek mines in mid-September, the executive of the APF agreed to refund contributions for August if requested by individual miners and to stop the automatic deductions after September. However, Cummings was incensed. In an article given front-page coverage in the *Free Press*, he asked, "Has the Union Gone Mad?" He argued that the action would have no effect on the provincial government's implementation of its proposed poll tax and threatened to publish the names of those who wanted a refund, stating such a list "would make interesting reading for the boys at the front." He insisted the choice should be an individual one, not something imposed by a union resorting to "Germanism."[184]

In an open letter replying to Cummings, Martin agreed the choice should be left to the individual and should not be something imposed by the CNPCC, the APF or the Gladstone local union. He alleged the "Germanism" was all on the side of Cummings if he felt the deduction should be mandatory and attacked him personally for taking a salary as secretary of the APF and for hiding behind the cloak of patriotism. The bitter exchange did not alter the outcome. More than half the miners did request refunds for their August deductions, and only a few agreed to the levy in September and afterwards.

The secretary of the national Canadian Patriotic Fund would later complain that the province's splendid record of contributions had been "marred by the action of a few agitators, influenced more by prejudice and selfishness than judgement." He shared Cummings's understandable dismay as well as his curious definition of "voluntary" but also went much further in his postwar report.

> The miners were largely of foreign nationality, while their unions were generally officered by men of alien birth or of pronounced socialistic tendencies. There is reason to believe that the agitation against the voluntary method might be laid at the door of the foreigner, who naturally wished to escape as much of the burden of the war as possible, or of the socialistic official who regarded taxation as the best method of placing the burden on the hated rich.[185]

If such an analysis in any way derived from opinions held by Cummings, those opinions were expressed privately. Reference to foreigners and socialism did not form part of the public debate between Cummings and Martin in their letters to the *Free Press*.

The monthly pre-strike contributions to the APF from Fernie and Coal Creek had averaged nearly $1,300. September's figure was $1,308, but October's was just $337.[186] Clearly, the regular deductions from miners employed by the Crow's Nest Pass Coal Company had provided by far the largest source of income for the fund. As with the campaigns to raise funds for war bonds, amounts collected for the Canadian Patriotic Fund in Fernie were often compared to amounts raised by rival communities. Wallace at the *Free Press* liked to compare Fernie with Cranbrook in this respect, but would soon lament that Fernie's standing in the monthly list published province-wide for patriotic fund donations had plunged to village status, with Waldo's contributions exceeding those of Fernie in December.

Recipient individuals and organizations were also concerned. The IODE, for example, did not receive its usual monthly contribution of $300 from the APF in November and soon announced it might have to resume its own fundraising efforts. Unrelated to local controversies, an international appeal was issued by the British Red Cross, and the IODE was asked to organize the effort in the Fernie district. With some apology for deviating from its usual practice of not appealing to the community for funds directly, the IODE conducted the tag day for the British Red Cross very successfully. Offering a particularly hearty thanks to the miners for their generous donations, the published report of the event from the IODE included the observation that those who refused to contribute "were Austrians, a few Italians and three or four English-speaking subjects." Clearly, donation was regarded as a measure of patriotism, and refusal to donate—viewed through the ever-present lens of ethnicity—a measure of disloyalty.

Local controversies were often intimately connected to the war. The principal of the school drew the ire of some parents who thought he was too generous in his assessment of German cultural achievements. The internment camp at Morrissey, with virtually none of the original CNPCC detainees remaining, also drew criticism. Under international law, the prisoners could not be compelled to perform work unrelated to their own "comfort, cleanliness and health." With visits from international observers occurring frequently, military officials at Morrissey were careful to adhere to that requirement. Nevertheless Fred Roo, the regular Elko correspondent of the *Free Press*, frequently used his column to complain that the internees were not working on the much-needed improvements to area roads. Wallace echoed that complaint, noting that it made his blood boil to "see this lazy bunch of pampered prisoners living like lords" while Canadian POWs in Germany were compelled to work.[187]

Then, suddenly, there were renewed fears of sabotage by enemy aliens. One early morning in October, the community was shocked by an explosion at Fairy Creek. The pipe supplying Fernie's water supply had been intentionally blown up. Police chiefs Brown and Welsby and a special provincial detective co-operated in investigating the incident as a wave of anxiety and anger swept the city. Officials with the CNPCC were interviewed about security measures in the storage and disbursement of explosives materials. With no apparent progress being made in their investigation, city council offered $500 for information resulting in the arrest and conviction of those responsible.[188] To this day, the reward remains unclaimed and the crime unsolved.

PROHIBITION OR NOT?

To the great annoyance of many on both sides of the issue, prohibition became the question that simply would not go away. The reason was Richard McBride. As premier in 1909, McBride had sabotaged the province-wide plebiscite about local option by manipulating the wording, withholding the results and not printing sufficient numbers of ballots. As agent-general in London in 1916, he was responsible for supervising the voting in Europe, where agents of the liquor interests were still campaigning and soldiers were able to vote on the referendum question until the end of December. As early as Christmas 1916, Vancouver newspapers were reporting that the anti-prohibitionists were claiming the soldier vote in Europe had overturned the provincial result. When the official figures were made public in March, it was clear that the dry victory of the previous September had been reversed. Voting roughly nine to one against prohibition, the soldier vote was so overwhelmingly negative that the referendum question had failed.[189]

However, the barely credible numbers were not accepted at face value by the new government in Victoria. McBride was widely suspected of having manipulated the process and the results. A commission was appointed to investigate, and it returned from England with a report that disqualified most of the soldier ballots. The commission found that many soldiers had voted often, dead soldiers had voted, soldiers not resident in British Columbia had voted and soldiers imprisoned in Germany had voted. Many votes were recorded from individuals of whom there was no trace in military records. When these and other questionable ballots were disqualified, the final tally gave the prohibitionists a victory, although it was a very narrow victory indeed. British Columbia would go dry after all. The final outcome alarmed the Michel local union, which immediately began a campaign calling for beer to remain available, pointing out that the majority of its members, while certainly affected by prohibition, had not been qualified to vote in the referendum of 1916.[190] But it was too late. The new date for implementation set by the provincial government was the first of October 1917.

It is not surprising that the planned Labour Day festivities in Fernie took on an aura of being an opportunity for one final big party. Events were to be held in the city park, and plans were in place for a chartered train from Lethbridge to bring in people from all along the line. As many as fifteen hundred guests were expected to arrive on that train. From already dry Lethbridge came word that attendees were looking forward to what they regarded as their "last big wet trip" in British Columbia. The police commissioners and the mayor expected a request to "take off the lid" for the weekend of the Labour Day events. Ironically, at the same time, city police announced (again) that they had finally "put a lid" on the red-light district. A delegation of local ministers was assured by the police commissioners that no formal request to relax enforcement had been received. Welsby also refused a request to allow gambling games to take place.[191]

The Labour Day program was regarded as successful, although fewer people attended than had been predicted. It was a relief that no one was arrested for disorderly conduct and no brawls were reported. Wallace noted that "most of the visitors were from the desert of Alberta while Fernie is still in the wet belt." But Fernie was not to be in the wet belt for much longer, and prohibition was a big topic of discussion again. A fire in Michel in early September destroyed an entire business block that included the Michel Liquor Company, which was quick to assure customers it would reopen immediately with new stock already on the way. Mid-month, the government announced that the province would have only two liquor stores—one in Vancouver, the other in Victoria. Pollock Wine Company advertisements suggested every family "should have a small supply of Wines and Brandies on hand," but warned there was no guarantee of delivery after September 24. The company's sales representative, Emilio Picariello, resigned and began to contemplate a move to Blairmore. The curling club took steps to ensure it would have a good supply of spirits available for its winter bonspiel.

With the rest of the province, Fernie went officially dry on the first of October. A delegation of local hotel owners soon appeared before city council to request the refund of their liquor licensing fees for the months of October, November and December. Council readily complied.[192] Similarly, the district's two provincially licensed clubs—the Coal Creek Literary and Athletic Association and the Fernie Club—applied for and received proportional refunds from Victoria. The loss of revenue from liquor sales was a serious blow to local hotels. The only beverage they could legally make available to their customers was a weak concoction soon referred to with little affection as near-beer, a brew that contained less than 2.5 percent alcohol.[193] The Napanee Hotel on Victoria Avenue would soon be forced to shut down completely.

After the introduction of prohibition, bar tokens became virtually worthless—none were issued after 1917. Images courtesy of Ronald Greene.

Indications were soon evident, however, that not everyone was accepting of the new regulations concerning the availability of alcohol. In mid-October, city police were investigating a break-in at the Pollock Wine Company and the theft of three or four cases of liquor. Wallace at the *Free Press* reported that there seemed to be no shortage of alcohol in Fernie, noting that there were "as many drunks on the street as ever." Charges were laid against the Cranbrook Brewing Company for selling beer well over 5 percent proof, and the Elk Valley Brewing Company in Michel was suspected of doing the same. The owner of the Queen's Hotel was sentenced to six months in jail for selling liquor to a man identified by the *Free Press* only as "a Slav," who was subsequently arrested for drunkenness in Waldo.

The sale of alcohol continued to thrive as an export business. Cross-border sales could not be prohibited by provincial legislation. The Pollock Wine Company had been enjoying a substantial trade with residents of Alberta and Saskatchewan after prohibition took effect in those provinces. With British Columbia's legislation in effect, purveyors of alcohol in eastern locations saw an opportunity to sell in a new market. In time for Christmas, a full-page advertisement in the *Free Press* offered local residents a wide range of products from a Saskatchewan liquor company.[194] Despite prohibition, liquor was readily available in Fernie to anyone able to pay for it.

THE KHAKI ELECTION

As Christmas drew closer, the availability of alcohol was not the only issue drawing the attention of local residents. The oft delayed federal election date had been set for mid-December. But much had changed since Borden's victory of 1911. Significant electoral redistribution meant the number of ridings in British Columbia had increased from seven to thirteen.

The old constituency of Kootenay was divided in two. The sitting Conservative Kootenay MP Robert Green—perhaps keen to avoid the wrathful gaze of William Wilson—decided to contest the new riding of Kootenay West, leaving the equally new riding of Kootenay East open for hopeful candidates. But the campaign was not to be simply the usual contest between Liberals and Conservatives; instead it proved to be unlike any other election before or since. The war in Europe and Prime Minister Robert Borden in Ottawa combined to make it the most divisive—and its result the most conclusive—in the young country's first half-century.

With recruitment falling sharply nationwide and the demand for fresh troops in Europe rising, the controversial issue of conscription received ever-increasing attention. Britain had introduced conscription the previous year in January 1916. Having promised that Canada would provide up to an additional hundred thousand soldiers, Borden introduced his War Service Act in June 1917. The ensuing debate shattered the unity of the Liberal Party, as many of its leaders and supporters joined the Conservatives to form a coalition that quickly became known as Unionist. Those opposed to conscription were forced to defend themselves against charges of being disloyal and unwilling to commit Canada to a full war effort. The allegation of disloyalty was directed against even former prime minister Sir Wilfrid Laurier.

To bolster the Unionist cause, Borden introduced legislation to disqualify potential opponents from voting and to expand the numbers of those who were likely supporters of conscription. The Wartime Elections Act was aimed primarily at the solidly Liberal immigrant communities of the prairie provinces and Ontario, and Liberal leader Laurier spoke eloquently against it during the parliamentary debate. But the legislation passed easily. All foreign-born residents from enemy nations, including those who had become naturalized British subjects after 1902, thereby lost the franchise. Many longtime residents of the Elk Valley—eligible voters in the provincial election of 1916—became ineligible to vote in the federal election of 1917. The Wartime Elections Act also gave the vote to mothers, wives, sisters and daughters of soldiers. A companion piece of legislation, the Military Voters Act, ensured that all soldiers in Europe would be able to vote. When the election date was finally announced, the Unionists were confident that patriotic feeling would give them almost exclusively the votes of military families.

The *Free Press* seemed to reflect accurately both the prevailing local mood and the national mood. John Wallace, relatively quiet on the political front since the defeat of Bowser a year earlier, returned to form when the federal

Saul Bonnell: Back from Salonika, Fernie's longest-serving doctor won an easy victory as a Unionist in the khaki election. Royal BC Museum and Archives G-08327.

election was still being anticipated. The Gladstone local union in June went on record opposing conscription, but Wallace supported it fully, arguing that the coalition forming around the issue brought together "the forces in both parties that are sincerely and whole-heartedly in favour of vigorous prosecution of Canada's part in the war." The $200,000 quota assigned to the Fernie district for the new Victory Loan was quickly exceeded, and Thomas Uphill, chairman of the committee responsible for raising the local funds, optimistically announced a new target of $300,000. That too was exceeded.[195]

Saul Bonnell had been touted as a likely Conservative candidate in Kootenay well before he left for Salonika in 1915. After a year abroad with the Canadian Army Medical Corps, his return revived that speculation, but he was not destined to carry the Conservative banner. With the support of many local Liberals, he was handily selected as the Unionist candidate for Kootenay East at the nomination meeting held in Cranbrook in mid-November. Pictured in military uniform, he was the epitome of the front-running candidate in an election that was all about loyalty and indicating support for the soldiers in the trenches.[196]

The Laurier Liberals offered the local electorate Robert Beattie, a pharmacy owner, but Liberals and Unionists would not have the field to themselves. Although Branch 17 of the Socialist Party of Canada had effectively collapsed, many remained committed to the philosophical principles it represented. The fledgling Independent Labour Party of Canada made an unsuccessful bid in mid-October to organize in Fernie and then attempted with an equal lack of success to persuade Thomas Uphill to stand as its candidate. With a further effort in November, the party organized and nominated District 18's newly elected union president Thomas Biggs as one of its six candidates in British Columbia.

Biggs had been an active union member in Fernie since 1903 when he emigrated from his native Monmouthshire in Wales. A miner since the age of fourteen, he was said to be "a life-long abstainer."[197] The party platform did not emphasize issues pertaining to prohibition, but did include various labour-oriented planks, proportional representation, equal pay for women doing equal work and equal military pensions regardless of rank. However, it was the party's strong opposition to conscription—an issue that would bedevil labour for the rest of the war and beyond—that would gain the most attention for Biggs and cause him the most grief. His earlier vocal and instrumental performances in support of local volunteers for overseas service were effectively forgotten, and with an apparently less than nuanced espousal of his party's anti-conscription plank, he would soon find himself open to the accusation of "insulting the boys who are fighting overseas."[198] Such wording strongly suggests he was expressing opinions very similar to those which had resulted in a fine for William Sherman and the imprisonment of Herman Elmer three years earlier.

With the election underway, a steady stream of endorsements for Unionist candidates was unleashed. At Victoria, Liberal Premier Harlan Brewster expressed his support; in Fernie, the new local branch of the Great War Veterans' Association (GWVA)—established in October by fourteen returned soldiers and one of the first branches formed in Canada—eagerly endorsed the candidacy of its best-known member, Captain Saul Bonnell. In the adjacent riding of Kootenay West, former District 18 president William Graham, having moved to Nakusp, was in a riding with a strong Labour Party candidate. Nevertheless, he declared his support for the man who had so recently recommended government control of the mines—Unionist Robert Green.[199] At the *Free Press*, Wallace urged "everybody who has Canada's welfare at heart" to vote for Bonnell. The Mount Fernie Chapter of the IODE did not formally endorse Bonnell, but did publicize a resolution of the national executive in Toronto proclaiming it was the duty of every member who could vote to mark her ballot to "secure a government that will press the war aggressively to a victorious conclusion." The message could not have been clearer.

The participation of women voters was, of course, unprecedented. The *Free Press* noted that 250 local women were registered to vote and that probably 225 of them would support Bonnell. In an editorial just before the mid-December election date, Wallace wrote of the "grave responsibility" that had been placed on their shoulders, but assured them he was confident they were sufficiently mature to handle it well. He repeated that, of course, they seemed almost all for Bonnell. That they would overwhelmingly be "patriotic voters" had been Borden's belief in including close female relatives of soldiers in his Wartime Elections Act, and as the campaign unfolded, it was apparent that belief was well founded.

With Wallace at the helm of the *Free Press*, whatever organized events or expressions of support there may have been for Beattie and Biggs were simply not reported. But the results—nationally, provincially and locally—can never have been in doubt. Borden's Unionists achieved a stunning majority, with few seats outside Quebec going to the Laurier Liberals. All thirteen of the ridings in British Columbia were easily won by Unionist candidates. In Kootenay East, Saul Bonnell overwhelmed his opponents with 63 percent of the vote; Beattie had 29 percent, and Biggs, who lost his deposit, just 8 percent. The *Free Press* would subsequently report that, when the soldier votes from Europe were counted, Bonnell had outpolled Beattie by a margin of eleven to one and Biggs had received no votes at all.[200] A comparison of election night tallies and official results indicate that is probably not true, but the statement does underline what is undeniable: the appeal of loyalty to king and country and the desire to indicate support of the soldiers in Europe were unstoppable in Kootenay East.

Fernie residents must have been relieved to see the end of what had been a very difficult year indeed. Memories were still fresh of the bitter coal strike, the tragedy at Coal Creek and the sabotage of the water supply. Just as 1916 had proved to be the best year of the war for the CNPCC, 1917 was its worst. The continuing shortage of labour and days lost from work stoppages combined to sharply reduce production and profits. The CPR cancelled all orders with the CNPCC when prices increased to cover the war bonus, stating it could get cheaper coal elsewhere.[201] The coal company could pay no dividend in 1917.

Yet a sense of optimism was strong. The khaki election had revived flagging support for the war. Coal Commissioner Armstrong announced in late October that his first cost-of-living review justified another 20 cents per day for District 18 members. The prospects for labour peace were good, and prosperity had clearly returned. Merchants reported the best Christmas trade in years. A local Rotary Club had been formed, and the city could also boast of being home to three dozen motor cars and a new automobile association. With very cold weather prevailing, William Robichaud was able to open the skating rink in mid-December. Despite the war in Europe, some simple pleasures were still available at home.

Pleasures of the flesh were also apparently still available for a price in the Old Town brothels. The issue that had so engaged the community at the start of the year still drew attention at its conclusion. City police records indicate no arrests of prostitutes after March, but policing the red-light district (or, as it was then cautiously referred to, the former red-light district) proved sufficiently problematic that city council agreed to transfer responsibility for law enforcement there to the provincial police in December. Just a week before Christmas, Welsby proudly reported, "Received instructions from Superintendent re taking over old restricted area. Went there ... and ordered inmates to leave the district. Closed it down tight."[202] It was the fourth reported closure in just over eight months.

1918

OLD PROBLEMS, NEW POLITICS

Indications that Fernie was entering a modern age were widespread early in 1918. Two women's ice hockey teams—one comprised of teachers, the other of "lady clerks"—took to the ice in January, their second game resulting in a twenty-four-dollar donation to the IODE for the Canadian Red Cross. Local curlers—apparently convinced that one frustrating game was not enough—formed a committee and were making plans to establish a golf course at the north end of the city. By late spring, an executive had been elected, fees were set at ten dollars annually and all members were urged to donate time and effort to preparing the course. A new executive at the board of trade tackled the question of driving in East Kootenay. Drivers in the adjacent jurisdictions of Montana and Alberta were required to keep to the right-hand side of the road; in British Columbia, traffic kept to the left. The board regarded cross-border driving as dangerous and resolved to ask other East Kootenay boards of trade for support in lobbying the provincial government to allow East Kootenay to drive on the right.[203] Soon to become a director of the Good Roads Association of British Columbia, Sherwood Herchmer would be well placed to participate in that lobbying effort. And with four dozen registered automobiles in Fernie, the local automobile association endorsed the campaign fully. Local drivers were pleased to see the speed limit within city limits increased from eight to fifteen miles per hour.

A significant shakeup in civic politics was further evidence that modern trends were having an impact on the city. Questions raised by the moral reform movement with little effect in 1917 were certainly not ignored by voters in 1918. Supporters of "purity plank" issues were pleased to see William Dicken elected to council, but their greatest triumph was in connection with the police commissioners. New provincial legislation called for the election of the two commissioners for the first time, and both men elected in Fernie were vocal supporters of moral reform. Joining them as *ex officio* chair of the commission was a new mayor. It is difficult to say if undertaker George Thomson likewise owed his victory to the same forces of moral improvement. He had not campaigned on them, preferring to emphasize that, although he was secretary of the Fernie Liberal Association, he was "independent of any influence." That was clearly directed at the former mayor's connection to the miners' union; after the labour turmoil of 1917, perhaps some voters had become wary of Uphill's membership in the UMWA. Significantly, although the electorate was still overwhelmingly male, women were able to vote for the first time, and Thomson did subsequently thank voting women—generally thought to favour the moral reform of society—for giving him their "practically solid" support. Whatever the explanation, Uphill's vote dropped sharply from the previous year, and, in a three-cornered race, Thomson was elected by a comfortable margin in what was described by the *Cranbrook Herald* as the community's quietest election in years.

It didn't take long for the new men at city hall to make their presence felt. Just one week after their election, the police commissioners instructed city police chief Brown and his two deputies to strictly enforce "the laws regarding the illicit sale of liquor, the social evil, gambling, pool rooms and the curfew." They were given thirty days to show "satisfactory results." To the dismay of some parents, several boys were nabbed at the skating rink on a school night and taken to the police station, where they were warned for being out after the nine o'clock curfew. A new curfew bylaw then raised the age to sixteen and stated that, after three warnings, parents would be fined if their children were out and about fifteen minutes after the nine o'clock curfew bell sounded. The names of individuals convicted at police court for liquor infractions began to be published in the *Free Press*.[204] City police, provincial police chief Welsby and Constable Boardman of Coal Creek raided every hotel in Fernie on the evening of February 2, but found no illicit liquor. John Wallace, always sceptical of attempts to improve behaviour through legislation, frequently mocked morality convictions in a *Free Press* column on police court proceedings that he often titled "Mills of the Gods Grinding."

But the new police commissioners were not inclined to change course. As Wallace was soon to lament, the impressive results in bylaw enforcement achieved by Chief Brown were "not sufficient for these narrow-minded gentlemen." The commissioners demanded Brown's resignation when the thirty days had passed and offered the position of city police chief to Welsby, who must certainly have been aware his new masters were not easy men to please. In town—and watching these developments with perhaps both bemusement and concern—were thirty delegates of District 18 of the UMWA, which was holding its annual convention in Fernie for the third year in a row. With the freedom of the city extended to them by Mayor Thomson, it was not their place to comment on local civic matters; indeed, they had their own problematic issues to deal with.

Chief Welsby and the City police force: Local law enforcement was far more political by war's end than it had been in 1914. Fernie Museum and Archives 0517-a-01.

The chaotic labour situation of 1917 had neither served nor pleased anyone. The UMWA international executive orders had been ignored by District 18 officials; in turn, the district orders had been frequently rejected by several locals, and, just as the delegates were gathering in Fernie in February, an unauthorized strike at Drumheller provided yet another example of how dismissive of union policy members and locals could be. As usual, deep political divisions existed amongst the delegates. The records of the convention have not survived, but one participant later noted that the convention spent considerable time struggling to deal with the politically radical directions advocated by some delegates.[205]

Publicly, the convention at Fernie in 1918 was all about mending fences. A long-serving international board member from the United States reminded District 18 delegates that they were not an independent body and that local actions had repercussions far beyond southern Alberta and southeastern British Columbia. Federal fair wage officer Frederick Harrison, also in Fernie at the time, was invited to address the convention. He pointed out that 262 disputes had been settled under Coal Operations. The convention sent a cable to Prime Minister Borden expressing its full confidence in William Armstrong, the coal commissioner. When a letter from Armstrong arrived urging the union to discipline the strikers at Drumheller, Thomas Biggs replied that the convention had already gone on record condemning that strike as "unconstitutional and against the policy of our organization." He wrote that District 18 favoured "drastic action against any of our membership in any future contingencies of a like nature. Our policy is to keep our contracts and be the last to violate them."[206]

William Armstrong: The coal commissioner brought a welcome measure of stability to relations between District 18 UMWA and the Western Coal Operators' Association. Royal BC Museum and Archives G-07977.

Towards the end of the convention, two decisions were made that would have a direct impact on the future of Fernie. With the majority of

NON-INTOXICATING LIQUOR

TEMPERANCE

BOTTLED ONLY
AT THE BREWERY.
EVERY BOTTLE
STERILIZED

WINNING
THE WORLD
WITH
ELK QUALITY

BREW

WE GUARANTEE
THIS BEER TO BE BREWED FROM CHOICEST MATERIALS.
ELK VALLEY BREWING CO. LTD.
NATAL, B.C.

Thomas Fisher Rare Book Library, University of Toronto.

the membership in Alberta and with headquarters located in Calgary since the previous summer, delegates decided their convention of 1919 would take place in Calgary. City businessmen would be losing a gathering they had become accustomed to hosting. More favourable economically was a decision concerning the *District Ledger*. Delegates agreed with the recommendation of vice-president Phillip Christophers that publication should be resumed "on a business basis." Then, after much debate, they agreed the newspaper would be produced in Fernie. The location of the existing idle printing plant in Fernie was the deciding factor, but the convention did acknowledge that the entire plant could be moved to Calgary if deemed advisable.[207] Delegates left Fernie anticipating labour peace at least until new contract negotiations were to begin a year later.

The city turned its attention to yet another development in the ongoing saga of prohibition. On the first of April, federal regulations took effect outlawing cross-border sales of alcohol. All through March, full-page advertisements from liquor vendors located in the prairie provinces appeared in the *Free Press*. Apparently, the citizens of Fernie responded enthusiastically. Large consignments of alcohol arrived by train daily throughout the month. The Fernie–Fort Steele Brewing Company reported a surge in sales amounting to $7,000 for the month of March. It is unlikely the company's products

Thomas Fisher Rare Book Library, University of Toronto.

all crossed the border into Alberta. Wallace noted that the new chief of police would have his hands full trying to keep drunks off the street. Emilio Picariello took a further step in changing careers as he purchased a hotel in Blairmore in January, moved his bottle operation there and became a sales agent for the Lethbridge Brewing Company.[208] His new advertisements for the company's products in the *Free Press* promoted only temperance drinks.

Welsby was not the only police chief with his hands full. His replacement was assigned dual responsibilities. A twenty-year veteran of the provincial police, Assistant Inspector W. Owen was transferred to Fernie from Vancouver; he would continue to perform the duties of an inspector while also being the acting chief constable for Southeast Kootenay. In that latter capacity he was faced immediately with a serious situation at Michel. Several Italian miners there had assaulted the local constables, and the potential for continuing unrest in the community was such that Owen reassigned Constable Joseph Boardman from Coal Creek to Michel for nearly three weeks. By the time Boardman returned home, convictions for assault and obstruction had been secured and substantial fines paid.[209] Another incident at the end of May proved awkward for Owen and indicated just how difficult enforcement of prohibition had become. Acting on information received, Owen ordered constables at Michel to intercept former Fernie city police chief Albert Brown, who was en route by automobile to Alberta. A search of his car found thirty-five gallons of whiskey. The result was confiscation, another conviction, another substantial fine and considerable civic embarrassment.[210] City police were further embarrassed when a prisoner from Morrissey in their temporary custody escaped in early June.[211]

The new federal rules about prohibition fit well with the ongoing wave of purity sweeping the city. Accepting the changed circumstances, liquor merchant John Pollock (who had long served as American vice-consul in Fernie) prepared to conclude his business operation and made plans to return to the United States. Mayor Thomson announced he would not accept his $500 salary, preferring to donate portions of it to the Amalgamated Patriotic Fund, the IODE and other good causes. Rumours circulated that the police commissioners were planning to close ice cream parlours and cigar stores on Sunday. Wallace facetiously suggested the use of automobiles and going for a walk on Sunday should also be prohibited, predicting Fernie could soon resemble "a Quakers' prayer meeting." When the police commissioners, over the objections of Mayor Thomson, voted to require Chief Constable Welsby to enforce with equal vigour "each and every by-law," it seemed that Wallace's prediction could have substantial merit. But the equal enforcement policy seems to have resulted in little more than prosecutions of residents who failed to control their chickens and dogs.

Of course, the city at large was still very much occupied with its own domestic war efforts. The Amalgamated Patriotic Fund was struggling to find its feet after the cancellation of automatic contributions by the Gladstone local union and the public quarrel that resulted. The new mayor did not follow the example of his predecessors in assuming the role of APF president, that position being filled instead by Trites-Wood store manager Edwy Stewart. Alfred Cummings resigned as secretary in March to devote more time to his business, his place being taken in quick succession first by Sherwood Herchmer, then by two returned servicemen and finally by Thomas Uphill. Significantly, a salary was no longer attached to the position. Monthly contributions remained steady at about half previous totals, with the largest amounts now coming from the camps of loggers and lumbermen at Jaffray and Waldo. Disbursements to needy dependents of local soldiers continued to rely heavily upon the subsidy from the Canadian Patriotic Fund office in Ottawa.

Concerned at the sharp drop in contributions, the provincial secretary of the Canadian Patriotic Fund visited Fernie to admonish local miners for the precedent they had established. At the conclusion of a patriotic concert

in March he delivered a lengthy speech, noting that while miners at San-
don had followed that precedent, coal miners on Vancouver Island had not.
Echoing the analysis Cummings had originally expressed, he said:

> In its essence any opposition to war work was really pro-Germanism,
> at least to the extent that it assisted the enemy. When the boys come
> home, when history is written, will Fernie have the notorious distinction
> of being a slacker? [212]

It was not the first time the loyalty of miners in the Elk Valley had been ques-
tioned, nor would it be the last.

Hard on the heels of the international appeal from the British Red
Cross the previous November, a call for funds from the Italian Red Cross
proved very successful in January, raising over $2,000 primarily (but by no
means exclusively) from the Italian residents of East Kootenay. Although
there was no reduction in APF funding for the IODE, the Mount Fernie
chapter did resume its own fundraising in 1918, sponsoring teas, raffles and
a dance, holding one tag day in March and another on behalf of the Canadian Red Cross in July. Established in new workrooms at the closed Napanee
Hotel—and assisted by free coal supplied by the CNPCC and free electricity
from the city of Fernie—the five dozen members of the IODE in 1918 continued their undiminished efforts.[213]

The IODE also began to devote attention to the comforts of returned
soldiers. As the veterans' numbers rose steadily, their concerns attracted
increasing attention. Citing similar moves in larger cities, the local branch
of the Great War Veterans' Association immediately began to press for a
designated burial area to be set aside at Fernie's St. Margaret's Cemetery
and for a monument to be erected there to commemorate what people were
commonly referring to as the district's "noble dead." Assisted by the IODE
and a grant from city council, the returned soldiers took possession of club
rooms in the 41 Market Company block in March. With IODE regent Eliza
Moffatt at its head, a GWVA women's auxiliary was formed in April, and
a series of fundraising summer dances were begun after Amos Trites again
offered the use of his pavilion.

The sense of disillusionment with the war that affected the whole country by 1918 is nowhere indicated in the pages of the *Fernie Free Press*. That is
neither surprising nor unique. Censorship rules forbade the publication of
criticism of military affairs in Canadian newspapers, and editors, having no
desire to draw the critical attention of federal authorities, rarely challenged

those rules. If indeed he had criticisms of the Canadian military, John Wallace at the *Free Press* preferred self-censorship to government oversight. Nevertheless, the extent to which the initial eager enthusiasm for the war had eroded since 1914 was being revealed by the implementation of conscription, the policy that had brought Borden's Unionist party its overwhelming patriotic victory in the recent khaki election.

Young men eligible in the first draft were called up in January. The tribunals responsible for applying the legislation were kept busy all across the country as more than 90 percent of those eligible for conscription were applying for exemptions. Applications from Fernie fit that pattern, and Judge George Thompson faced a full schedule of requests for exemptions when he presided at the first local tribunal in January. On the surface, the purpose of the tribunals seemed clear and straightforward, but the political undercurrents were strong. Local Conservative stalwart Fred Roo alleged decisions were made based on personal spite and politics, and Harry Martin said that they gave too much consideration to the interests of the CNPCC. Judge Thompson knew his decisions would be closely scrutinized.

To avoid unnecessary duplication, the appeals of thirty-six miners from the CNPCC were heard as one. Frederick Harrison and Harry Martin appeared to present the case that these men were essential to the war effort in their capacity as coal miners. Judge Thompson granted the appeal, but made it clear an exemption would be cancelled if a miner missed more than one shift in any given month or failed to report for work due to a work stoppage. He stated it was the duty of the UMWA to see that no such stoppages occurred, advising Harrison and Martin, "These applicants must understand they are now soldiers … And the only way they can continue to be of greater value as coal miners than as soldiers is by producing coal."[214] On the same basis, a tribunal in Calgary a week earlier had approved the appeals of Alberta miners. It was clear that a strike or any other absence from work would cancel the exemptions granted. An editorial in the *Free Press* reprinted from the *Toronto Globe* endorsed the judgements, noting there must be "no malingering" by exempted miners. John Wallace agreed. He wrote, "To malinger is to be unpatriotic."

Several men from Fernie drafted in March were trained and ready to leave Canada in May; at the same time, a few who had avoided that draft were reported about to leave the Fernie jail under escort to join military units at the coast. A second contingent followed the same route in June, as did a number of Italian-born "slackers" in August. The Italians were quickly returned to

Fernie when it was realized the regulations of the Military Service Act could not compel them to join the Canadian army. Wallace noted it was expected those regulations would soon be changed. Following its delayed entry into the war, the United States was struggling with its own regulations concerning the foreign-born. When rumours once again circulated in Fernie of the detention of brewer Albert Mutz, this time their accuracy was confirmed. Mutz was held at the Kingsgate border crossing in Idaho for ten days by American authorities who were suspicious about his travel plans in the United States.[215]

A new embargo placed on the importation of American coal was welcome news, but the summer of 1918 also brought some grim reminders. Another death at the Elk Lumber Company in May underlined the fact that coal mining was not the only local industry that brought danger to its workforce. In June, fourteen months after its deadly explosion, the No. 3 mine at Coal Creek resumed production after finally having yielded the last four bodies of its victims. Casualty rates in Europe were declining, but notices of local men's deaths and injuries continued to arrive. After four years of newspaper reports of dramatic Allied advances and imminent German collapse, the headlines in the big-city dailies announcing more of the same in July and August may not initially have seemed too significantly different. The war in Europe had simply become an accepted fact of life.

Other more benign themes were also revisited. For the second time, the determined congregations of the Presbyterian and Methodist churches voted overwhelmingly in favour of union. The vote was almost identical to the result of 1916, but this time no veto was received from parent organizations in Toronto. Styling itself the United Church, the combined congregation located itself at the Presbyterian church on Victoria Avenue, renting the former Methodist building to the school board for high school classrooms. And for the second year in a row, the Chautauqua returned to Fernie. Although the lectures received less enthusiastic reviews than those of the previous year, the performance of the Kaffir Boy Choir proved sufficiently popular that the travelling show was booked again for the summer of 1919.

One spectacle residents particularly did not want to see repeated was the Elk River in flood. Nevertheless, in June the city's modest efforts at riverbank protection failed, and flooding again damaged homes and forced the temporary closure of the Elk Lumber Company. While the flood of June 1916 resulted in much greater damage, the less severe flood of 1918 produced greater anger. MLA Alexander Fisher had promised much and delivered nothing, leaving the city government solely responsible for flood protection.

Property owners of the Annex and West Fernie organized and demanded Fisher's resignation; city council did not endorse that course of action, but also went on record vigorously demanding assistance from the provincial government. The campaign worked. Provincial minister of lands Thomas "Duff" Pattullo and a government engineer met with Annex and West Fernie residents in August, and the government in Victoria soon agreed to finance 50 percent of future work intended to prevent flooding by the Elk River at Fernie.[216]

Locally, perhaps the most significant renewal in the summer of 1918 was the revival of the *District Ledger*. The decision to resume publication resulted in the hiring of Nova Scotian Peter Lawson as editor. Formerly an organizer with the Socialist Party of Canada, Lawson arrived in Fernie in July, and, as an outsider, may not have recognized that much had changed in Fernie in the three years since the *Ledger* had suspended publication. John Wallace at the *Free Press* had certainly changed. He had not altered his attitudes to the miners' union, but he had abandoned his reticence in expressing those attitudes in print. In the debates over loyalty and commitment to the war in 1914 and 1915, Wallace had studiously avoided direct criticism of the UMWA, the *District Ledger* and its editor Frank Newnham. By the summer of 1918, the *Free Press* had become more of a pulpit for his personal political opinions. In welcoming Lawson to town, Wallace rather disingenuously wrote that he hoped the union would give him a free hand—and then made it clear he expected otherwise.

> Hitherto the policy of the Ledger has nearly always been controlled by the selfish intrigues of those in office … or by the red-eyed bolsheviki element who are of the opinion that anarchy is the only remedy for the existing order of things.[217]

It was a shot across the bow that Lawson must have heard clearly. And the news of the one-day general strike in Vancouver protesting the apparent murder near Cumberland of former Coal Creek miner Albert "Ginger" Goodwin provided a timely indication that labour unions were moving away from their wartime practice of general co-operation with employers and governments. Wallace commented only that Goodwin was well known in Fernie but had taken to the hills rather than serve king and country. It was later noted that, at the time of his death, one of Goodwin's few possessions was the medal he had received in 1910 as a member of that year's champion Michel team of the Crow's Nest Pass Football League.[218]

The issues surrounding local union politics were also much changed. When the newspaper suspended publication in July 1915, District 18 of the UMWA was affiliated with the Socialist Party of Canada, and, for the first time, the advice of its officials had been entirely ignored during the internment agitation by its members at Fernie and Coal Creek. When it resumed publication in August 1918, District 18 had no formal political affiliation, was bitterly disappointed with its international parent, saw the orders of its elected officials ignored almost routinely and had seen the centre of its organization—along with union headquarters—move from Fernie to the coalfields of Alberta. Significantly, employees of one Lethbridge-area coal company had recently downed tools *because* an Austro-Hungarian worker had been fired—not because they were demanding his dismissal.

The decision to revive the *Ledger* was certainly an attempt by District 18 officials to exert greater control of its membership through improved communications. The printing plant on Pellatt Avenue was in operation once again, but almost immediately the Gladstone local union provided the hopes of the district executive with a setback.

THE SINGLE SHIFT

In early July, miners began to press the argument that accumulating gas significantly increased risk of explosions during the second shift at Coal Creek. The No. 1 East mine was of particular concern. The previous November, all miners on shift had managed to escape when another severe bump hit that mine, and everyone was aware that work had just been completed to recover the bodies of victims from No. 3 mine following the disaster of April 1917. The Gladstone local union—with a membership then at 735—adopted a position in favour of a single shift to allow gases to dissipate safely. In mid-August, the District 18 executive advised Minister of Labour Crothers and Coal Commissioner Armstrong that they supported that position.[219]

Union local president Thomas Biggs promised William Wilson there would be no industrial action over the issue before the first of October, but in early September miners at Coal Creek and Michel walked out, choosing their moment when General Manager William Wilson was away in northern British Columbia on personal business.[220] The politically radical Biggs apparently exercised as little control over the rank and file as had his more moderate predecessor. As if on cue a severe bump in No. 1 East mine caused no damage or injury, but seemed to add credence to the miners' claim, while

Wallace was able to reprise his "Miners on Strike Again" headline. CNPCC president Elias Rogers was in Fernie at the time and expressed the company's outrage that the collective agreement had been violated, along with Biggs's promise and the union's commitment to maintain wartime production. He would later claim the strike was "probably the most inexcusable" of any that had ever occurred in the district.[221]

Talks in Calgary achieved no resolution and, for the first time since June 1915, the British Columbia government intervened. Encouraged by Commissioner Armstrong, provincial minister of mines William Sloan called the parties to Vancouver for negotiations in mid-September. Delegates from Coal Creek and Michel were selected to accompany Biggs and district secretary Ed Browne for talks with the company and the government. At a ninety-minute meeting with the provincial cabinet in Victoria, Biggs insisted the single-shift system would not harm production; Premier John Oliver and William Sloan each indicated that was their chief concern.[222] Wilson was in Vancouver, but refused to participate in the talks until the miners ended their strike. The company was not wavering from its belief that a major showdown was needed to resolve labour matters once and for all and sensed that the issue of the single shift would provide favourable grounds on which to force that showdown.

During the talks, Biggs threatened a general strike throughout District 18 if the Gladstone local union's demand was not met. Mines minister Sloan offered to introduce legislation to bring in an eight-hour single shift if a commission of enquiry recommended it. That offer was turned down by a large meeting of the Gladstone local union at Fernie on September 21, forcing Biggs to leave Vancouver with nothing to show for his efforts. Talks reconvened a few days later in Calgary, where Sloan suggested that No. 1 East alone should either be operated on a single shift or closed down entirely. The miners' negotiators were not enthused about the proposal, and Wilson still refused to talk about anything until work resumed. An impasse had been reached.

Recognizing that a district-wide strike on an issue affecting only Coal Creek would be ill-advised, Biggs turned to Coal Operations. At the request of District 18, Coal Commissioner Armstrong issued an order that the CNPCC must reopen its mines on the basis of a sixty-day trial of the single-shift system, while Sloan was to appoint a commission to examine the issue. When Biggs presented the terms to yet another meeting of the Gladstone local union, he initially received yet another refusal. Apparently, workers in several outside occupations were unhappy at the complications a single-shift system would require. Finally, following a confused series of votes at both Coal Creek and Michel, the miners of the CNPCC returned to work on October 8.[223]

Because of the involvement of the provincial government, the strike had attracted more attention at the coast than was usually the case for events in East Kootenay. One organization in Victoria—struggling with the question of whether to call itself the Anti-Hun League or the League of Patriots—was particularly incensed about the situation at Fernie. At a meeting in Victoria towards the end of September, members alleged enemy aliens were responsible for the strike and demanded action from the federal government. One member said the pay should be $1.10 per day—the same as a soldier received. A representative of the GWVA said the rate should be 25 cents per day—the same as internees at Vernon received if they chose to work. Another suggestion was to convert the mines into internment camps where enemy aliens would be forced to work. A minister of religion, building on his reputation in Victoria as a champion of the returned soldier, said if the striking miners won't work, "let us get some returned men with bayonets behind them." Former provincial premier Edward Prior, as president of the league, was tasked with drawing these views to the attention of federal authorities.[224]

The diverse reactions of Fernie's newspapers to that meeting in Victoria are instructive. As the strike dragged on, John Wallace had become increasingly distressed at the inaction of the federal government. Almost echoing the call for a settlement by bayonet, he asked why Dominion police had not been involved if the federal government was responsible for coal production and even went so far as to say the Borden government's policy of laissez-faire in the matter was starting to make it "look like a bunch of pikers." However, he parted company with the Anti-Hun League when it argued the strike was due to the influence of foreigners. "The alien enemies who are employed here are almost as tame as any old cow. The real trouble-makers are about six old country Englishmen... " A week later he was more specific; the troublemakers were identified as Harry Martin "and his half-dozen noisy boys."

Lawson at the *Ledger* avoided engaging Wallace on the matter of government intervention, but joined him in dismissing the Anti-Hun League's allegation that enemy aliens were responsible for the strike. Describing the Victoria clergyman as more dangerous than a German spy for advocating an action that would result in bloodshed, Lawson argued he was therefore "more deserving of being stood up against a wall." He offered to provide the Anti-Hun League with the names of all those who had been prominent in advocating the single shift to prove they were all English, Irish, Welsh, Scottish or Canadian-born, without a single German or Austrian amongst them. He ended by extolling the patriotism and bravery of local miners and alleging that, if workingmen were turning away from religion, "lickspittle clergymen" with no regard for facts were responsible.[225]

The month-long strike had clear consequences. Two dozen miners granted exemptions from military service in January were told their exemptions were being reviewed because they had violated Judge Thompson's order requiring them to remain on the job. That order permitted them only one day idle in any given month and they had been on strike for twenty-nine working days. Fernie and Coal Creek were not the only communities experiencing labour unrest. On October 11, the Borden government issued an order-in-council banning strikes right across the country for the duration of the war. The executive of District 18 emphatically refused to surrender the right to strike, and when Harry Martin endorsed that refusal, Wallace noted that perhaps the "Gladstone local has had more to do with the promulgation of this drastic order than any other union in Canada." The timing is certainly interesting. While the allegation rather grandly places Fernie at the centre of national labour relations, it makes a point that cannot entirely be dismissed.[226]

Also difficult to assess is the impact of the strike on the reputation of Thomas Biggs. The annual election for officers of District 18 soon followed, and Biggs faced three challengers for the president's job—one was his vice-president Phillip Christophers, and another was fellow Fernie resident and long-time international board member David Rees. After all the turmoil surrounding the single-shift issue, the results must have been a considerable disappointment for Biggs. In the coalfields of Alberta's Crowsnest Pass and at Lethbridge, where the issue had little relevance, and in Fernie, where the issue was paramount, Biggs polled poorly.[227] Because no candidate secured the required majority, a second vote would later be required, but the name of Thomas Biggs would not be on that ballot.

THE NEW POLITICS

While the drama of the single-shift strike was being played out, the community saw continuous evidence of patriotism and a few more indications of progress. Another patriotic organization, established earlier in the year, announced that its membership rolls had exceeded expectations. With 71 adult and 230 junior members, the Navy League conducted a very successful tag day in September and was making plans for a Trafalgar Day dance in October to "keep Lord Nelson's memory fresh." Thomas Uphill and Harry Martin received approval from city council to organize Labour Day events in the city park as a fundraiser for the Amalgamated Patriotic Fund. With an extensive parade and Union Jacks everywhere, a program of races and a first-aid competition judged by Lieutenant Colonel Mackay, the day had the atmosphere of another patriotic carnival. Exceeding financial expectations, the day resulted in a much-needed contribution of $1,200 for the APF.

Other familiar themes were revisited. With the labour crisis of 1916 but a distant memory, it seems overseas recruitment was again permitted; the local medical officer of the 107th East Kootenay Regiment was authorized to enlist men for the Canadian Siberian Expeditionary Force. Under the title "Our Noble Dead," the *Free Press* began to publish each week a list of men from Fernie and Coal Creek who had been killed in the war. The IODE appealed for money and cigarettes to sustain what had become their annual preparation of Christmas socks for the troops in Europe and were once more pleased with the response. The number of automobiles continued to increase steadily. Introducing a note of freshness and novelty very late in the season, the city's first game of golf took place on the newly laid-out course.

But political issues continued to dominate the news. Perhaps it is fairer to say that they dominated at least the local newspapers. The revival of the *District Ledger* brought a new dynamic to journalism in Fernie. In one of the newspaper's first new issues, Lawson examined the revised attitude to Czechs and Slovaks—hundreds of whom, Lawson noted, were members of the union in District 18—commenting on the irony of how they had apparently ceased to be regarded as enemy aliens by virtue of military efforts by their countrymen against Bolshevik forces in Russia. He provided geographic and ethnic detail of the region in Europe, picking up themes current when the *Ledger* ceased publication in July 1915 and making it clear that the break in publication had not meant a break in advocating equality before the law.

The *Ledger* was barely a month old before a newspaper war broke out. Introduced as an eight-page publication in August, the newspaper was quickly reduced to just four pages in September as initial revenues fell short of expectations. But then the provincial government awarded the contract to print the annual notice of provincial land sales for East Kootenay to the *Ledger*, which blossomed to twelve-pages for the next month as it included the extensive lists of properties in four columns out of seven on each page. Wallace was incensed. He raged that the *Free Press* could have handled the

Pervasive patriotism: A Union Jack is held by a First Nations woman attending the races on Labour Day. Fernie Museum and Archives 6678.

contract easily, whereas the *Ledger* needed to bring in Frank Newnham from Calgary and a machinist from Seattle and had to borrow an additional pressman from the *Free Press*. He took the opportunity to remind readers that the *District Ledger* was "a propaganda organ of bolshevism," emerging once more "from under the dung heap of Socialism, where it has been buried in silence for three years…"[228]

The *Cranbrook Herald*, which had also hoped to print the notice of the land sales, printed an open letter to its MLA urging a reversal of the decision. Editorially, the *Herald* alleged one week that the union newspaper was Bolshevik and insinuated it was pro-German the next. The newspaper called Fernie MLA Alexander Fisher "a damned traitor" for giving the contract to the *Ledger*, adding that the money paid for the notice "might as well be thrown into the Fernie coke ovens and burnt up" because the union newspaper was not distributed west of Fernie.

Lawson's editorial response was initially concentrated on only the criticism from the *Cranbrook Herald*. He reprinted the *Herald* articles in full, referred to its small circulation figures and pointed out that MLA Fisher would never consider awarding such a contract to a disloyal newspaper. However, as the remarks of the *Free Press* echoed those of the *Herald*, they too demanded a response, and with Lawson's editorial of October 3, the Fernie newspaper war became fully engaged. Lawson chided Wallace for his overheated remarks and, dismissing the charges of Bolshevism alleged by both the *Free Press* and the *Herald*, insisted that what their editors didn't know about that philosophy would fill far more space than the notice of land sales they had failed to secure. Political sniping aside, there can be no doubt that the government contract provided a significant boost to the finances of the *Ledger*, enabling the newspaper to return to its original eight-page format in November.

The gloves were also soon off on a topic of a less parochial nature. The Russian Revolution and its subsequent struggle for survival were shaking the world in respects other than the purely political. One of those respects was ethnic awareness, and in Fernie an evolving understanding of ethnic distinctions also brought new problems. The term "foreigner" covered a great deal of ground in the Elk Valley in 1914. It still did in 1918, but there was a growing recognition of ethnic differences amongst the non-English-speaking communities. The most significant understanding pertained to the Ukrainians. It was not widely recognized in 1915 that many of those interned at the skating rink and categorized as Austro-Hungarian nationals were from western regions of Ukraine. Indeed, it is only in 1918—in large part due to reports of events in Russia—that the term Ukrainian finds its way into the local public discourse. Ironically, it was also recognized that some of those designated as Russian nationals were actually ethnic Ukrainians from territory within the Russian empire. Unfortunately for the entire resident Ukrainian community, a new political divide was emerging—also largely a consequence of events in Russia—as many Ukrainians in Fernie again found themselves regarded with suspicion and accused of disloyalty.

Political developments and philosophies were having the same effect in Canada as they were in Russia—dividing Russian and Ukrainian communities into factions either favouring or opposing the revolution. Also part of a rapidly changing political landscape, war veterans were emerging as a conservative and often reactionary force. In September, the president of the local GWVA sent a telegram to the military intelligence officer in Victoria complaining that concerts were being held in Fernie to benefit a Ukrainian Labour Temple in Winnipeg. He complained that Mayor Thomson was permitting "these enemies to assemble in numbers." Asked to investigate, Inspector Owen interviewed Thomson, the local GWVA president, the Ukrainians organizing the benefit concerts and Peter Lawson of the *District Ledger*. He advised the new superintendent of provincial police that he could find no evidence at all of disloyalty or sedition.[229]

Just a few days later, through Orders-in-Council 2381 and 2384, the federal government banned a number of organizations judged to be of a revolutionary character and made illegal the possession of literature promoting revolution and printed in "enemy languages."[230] The Winnipeg group responsible for the recent concerts in Fernie was found to be associated with one of the suppressed organizations. At the same time, police raids began against Russian and Ukrainian socialist groups across the country, and in

154 — FERNIE AT WAR

October several Ukrainians living in the Annex were arrested in a raid by city police. They were known members of the Ukrainian Social Democratic Party, one of the newly banned political organizations. Police chief Welsby confiscated Ukrainian-language literature by Karl Marx and Friedrich Engels, bilingual banners, newspapers, the contents of a desk and, oddly, two suits of underwear belonging to one of those arrested. He placed four men in city cells and ordered the arrest of four others.[231]

The arrests quickly became another source of contention between the local newspapers. In language reminiscent of its advocacy of the internees of 1915, the *Ledger* championed the right of the prisoners to receive "British justice." Surprisingly, Wallace at the *Free Press* had recently seemed to express an appreciation of the factors that were leading enemy aliens towards revolutionary politics in the coal mining districts of Alberta. He quoted paragraphs from an article in *The Albertan*, one of which read:

> Almost every public policy in the past twelve months has tended to alienate, exasperate and rouse the foreign population. They have been disenfranchised, suspected, and in some instances exploited; almost everything that could be done to alienate them has been done.[232]

However, he showed no comparable understanding that those same public policies could be responsible for the emergence of Bolshevism in Fernie, preferring instead to applaud "anti-revolutionary Ukrainians" for criticizing those arrested.

The very use of the term Ukrainian by the two newspapers is another indication of change. Just as Lawson had provided readers with details about the aspirations of Czechs and Slovaks in August, so too did he take the opportunity provided by the arrests to educate readers about Ukraine. Stating that hundreds of members of District 18 were Ukrainians, he asked, "What is the Ukraine?" He then proceeded to explain its geography and history to his readers. Lauding the prisoners in the city jail as revolutionary and anti-clerical, Lawson identified their critics as Ukrainians still under the influence of their priests and Germany. All the cross-currents of a disintegrating Austrian empire and the Russian Revolution were clearly being felt in Fernie.[233]

The accused were members of the Gladstone local union, which hurriedly held an emergency meeting directing the executive to seek legal advice and to raise bail. At the preliminary hearing, police magistrate William Whimster set surprisingly harsh bail conditions, and even when the confusion was dispelled (as only four men were charged), those arrested remained in custody for several days before bail was accepted. Over the next several weeks, Whimster received strong criticism from the *Ledger* for his attitude and treatment of the men, Lawson even calling for a replacement by a "man better qualified by intelligence and suited by temperament" for the duties of a magistrate. Apparently bowing to this pressure, Whimster withdrew from the case. After several postponements, the trial was held on December 9. One charge was dismissed, but W. Moysiuk, W. Symanchuk and Nick Tkachuk—all finally described by Wallace as "pets" of the *Ledger*—were found guilty of possessing seditious literature and fined seventy-five dollars each.[234]

Spanish Influenza

The drama of the single-shift strike was barely ended and the debate on banned organizations barely begun when Fernie was threatened by another crisis. The pandemic Spanish flu was sweeping across the country, devastating communities wherever it went. By October 11, it was reported to be in the south country at Waldo and Elko and in Alberta at Lethbridge. Fernie knew the contagion was closing in, but unlike a medieval city, it could raise no drawbridge to offer even an illusory sense of protection. Inspector Owen noted considerable alarm in anticipation of an outbreak, especially amongst what he described as the "foreign population." Two weeks later, with several stricken lumbermen from Jaffray in the Fernie hospital, the city reported about twenty cases. The *Free Press* initially reported the illness was being found "mostly among the foreign element." As in politics, so in health: threats to social stability were still readily associated with the non-British community.[235]

But this threat would prove oblivious to ethnic distinctions. Mayor Thomson issued a proclamation on October 23 closing schools and banning all public gatherings. Churches, the meeting rooms of fraternal organizations, theatres, poolrooms—no public social place was exempt. The hospital was quickly overwhelmed. Just a week after the first cases were reported, the number of those afflicted had reached seven hundred, and the first death was recorded. Urgent appeals were issued for volunteer nurses. An emergency hospital and a soup kitchen were opened in the closed Napanee Hotel. Two more almost contiguous hospital sites quickly followed—one at the Victoria Hall, the other right across the street at the King's Hotel adjacent to the Napanee. By November 8, the *Free Press* reported that over half the population was sick and printed public health notices in English, Italian and Polish. The *Ledger* did not publish at all the last week of October, and "under flu handicap," reduced its size to just four pages for much of November. A number of deaths were occurring daily.[236]

The pandemic added further twists to the still unfolding consequences of prohibition. Supplies of medicinal brandy were low. Mayor Thomson asked the attorney general in Victoria if the city's store of confiscated alcohol could be used. Expressing concern about the unknown contents of bootlegged liquor, the attorney general said it could not, so the hospitals were forced to rely on donations. When one of Fernie's wealthier citizens was laid low in hospital, his private supply of wines and spirits was stolen from his home. These bottles were no doubt intended for the thief's private consumption, but it is probable that a glass or two of this contraband liquor might have been raised with his friends in toasting an event that had finally occurred four years later than at first predicted.

Germany had surrendered. When news of the signing of the armistice reached Fernie on Monday, November 11, the mayor (from his sickbed) declared a civic holiday and "everybody that could possibly crawl sallied out to join the procession" of pipers, automobiles and pedestrians that made its way to the Victory Loan office at the Napanee Hotel. (The building was still in use as a hospital; presumably no one entered.) There they heard speeches from MP Saul Bonnell, MLA Alexander Fisher and CNPCC general manager William Wilson, new Italian consular agent Louis Carosella, new American consul Norton Brand and Polish agent Joseph Rudnicki. In the evening, a torchlight procession led to a huge bonfire opposite the King Edward Hotel. Celebrations got a little out of hand, with the windows of the John Quail store being broken and a young boy injured by an exploding firecracker. But the war—the seemingly interminable war—was over.[237]

Occurring as they did in the middle of the pandemic, the public gatherings of November 11 may well have extended its life somewhat, but the Spanish flu in Fernie was on the wane. The hospitals at the King's Hotel and the Victoria Hall closed a week later, leaving the Napanee and the Fernie hospital to handle the rapidly declining number of new cases. By the time the hospital at the Napanee closed on November 28 and the ban on social gatherings lifted two days later, the pandemic had claimed fifty-one local victims. And at the end of the month, it was reported that Jim Corrigan—one of the four army reservists who were the first men to leave Fernie for the front in August 1914—had been killed in the war's last battle. Including his name, the list published weekly in the *Free Press* under the heading "Our Noble Dead" increased to seventy-six. November 1918 in Fernie was a time for counting the dead. The war was over and the flu well past its peak, but in neither case was the death toll completed. By the time the final tallies were taken, the number of local lives lost to influenza in just a few weeks would almost equal the number killed during four years of fighting in Europe.[238]

Attracting little comment as the Spanish flu consumed all the energies of its residents, a significant pillar of Fernie's wartime economy was lost when the internment camp at Morrissey closed in mid-October. Although the camp employed virtually no civilians after its first few months, the $4,000 monthly payroll for the guards of the 107th East Kootenay Regiment disappeared as they demobilized and returned to their homes throughout East Kootenay. For three years, members of the regiment and of the Canadian Army Service Corps stationed at Morrissey had looked to Fernie for personal necessities and entertainment.

City merchants accustomed to supplying the camp felt the loss of trade. However, if the contracts with Burns of Calgary and the Macdonald firm in Winnipeg are excluded, that loss may be regarded as significant but not crippling. The Fernie business community provided only approximately 10 percent of the goods and services required by the camp in the eighteen months prior to the closure in October 1918, with Trites-Wood, Kennedy & Mangan and John Quail continuing to be the main local beneficiaries. In the same period, Burns and Macdonald together were paid over $42,000 for provisions received at Morrissey, a sum accounting for 40 percent of the camp's total operating costs.[239]

Matters of commerce aside, the closure of the Morrissey camp represented the official end of perhaps the strangest chapter in local history. The camp had long ceased to exist for the sole purpose of containing Austro-Hungarian and German employees of the CNPCC. Virtually none of the approximately 250 prisoners being transferred to camps in Alberta and Ontario in 1918 were amongst those initially held at the skating rink. But the facility would never have been located at Morrissey in the first place without the demands of the miners and the orders of William Bowser in June 1915. With the camp closed and the armistice ending the fighting on the Western Front just a month later, residents of the Elk Valley no doubt hoped they could put both the internment and the European war behind them. For several of the guards assigned to shut down the Morrissey camp, that hope was temporarily frustrated when they had to be hospitalized in Fernie with the flu.

The issues surrounding ethnicity and enemy aliens did not leave with the internees. Alderman Robichaud, just a few days after the armistice was signed, found himself having to make a public apology for mistakenly alleging that Fernie pharmacist Norman Suddaby was German by birth.[240] But the formerly clear understanding of what constituted an enemy alien was blurring quickly with the end of hostilities on the Western Front and the chaos in Russia. Nevertheless, the official wartime definitions remained, and many of those long designated as enemy aliens were increasingly reluctant to report to police regularly as required. Inspector Owen's reports and Fernie city police records indicate substantial fines were collected for "failing to report."[241] The other major source of income to police coffers came from fines for liquor infractions. Owen noted that the nearly $1,400 collected in police court fines in July was probably a record; if so, the record was broken by the $1,500 collected in October.

The provincial police were pleased to move from the basement of the courthouse to new rooms on the ground floor in October. Unfortunately, the enjoyment was limited as all the clerks and constables in the force except for Inspector Owen were down with the flu. The pandemic also put a halt to a major initiative by Owen to intercept smugglers. Constable Boardman spent much of October helping Constable Gorman in guarding the bridges near Elko "to prevent Whiskey peddlers from getting through from Montana." There are no reports of seizures of alcohol as a result of the operation, but Owen was pleased to note over $2,000 worth had been confiscated in November.[242]

Despite some clouds on the horizon, the local economy remained strong. Even as the flu inhibited nearly all activities, the target for the latest Victory Loan was met and exceeded in the Fernie district. For having met its quota, the community received a flag from the federal government; attached was a crown to indicate the quota had been significantly exceeded. The more than $400,000 raised was seen as another indication of loyalty, but it was also a measure of prosperity. The cost-of-living increases awarded to the miners of District 18 in January, April, August and December contributed significantly to that prosperity. The awards amounted to seventy-two cents per day per man. Although there were wide variations between job categories, the average wage for an underground coal miner at Coal Creek had increased to over seven dollars per shift.[243]

Prosperity was sharply tempered by inflation. Each decision by Coal Commissioner Armstrong to increase wages was followed by an increase in the price of coal. Even customers like the city of Fernie, which received a preferential rate, expressed concern as their fuel costs rose substantially in 1918. But fundamentally, increases to miners' wages and the price of coal were following inflation locally more than they were driving it. The financial records of the recently closed Morrissey internment camp indicate how dramatic the price increases of certain items could be. P. Burns and Company had provided bacon to the camp in mid-1916 at a cost of twenty or twenty-one cents per pound; its final delivery two years later was billed at thirty-four cents a pound. A pound of butter from Burns cost the camp thirty-one cents in 1916, the last shipments forty cents or more.[244]

Serious concerns were expressed at the end of the year that the lifting of the embargo on importation of American coal would suppress both production and prices for the CNPCC. The return of men from the fighting in Europe was also expected to create a labour surplus and perhaps a return to worrisome levels of unemployment comparable to those of 1914. But these were the concerns for the new year. For the moment, discussions about an appropriate location for a war memorial were reaching no clear consensus. City council resolved to work with the local GWVA to erect a suitable memorial, and Mayor Thomson donated the last uncommitted $100 of his salary to that purpose. At the same time, he made it clear that he would not be standing for re-election. William Wilson indicated that his support for Fernie's military men would not be ending with the war. He hosted a dinner for returned soldiers at the Hotel Fernie just before Christmas and announced he intended to repeat the gesture from time to time. In recognition of his past gifts to departing soldiers and his future intentions for returned men, Wallace gave him the well-deserved title of "the soldiers' friend." The soldiers also had friends in the GWVA and the IODE, which combined to provide Christmas turkeys to the wives and mothers of the ninety local men not yet returned from Europe.

While victory continued to buoy the spirits of the English-speaking community, optimism was also high at the end of the year amongst the emigrants from continental Europe. Czechs, Poles and Hungarians were excited as the creation of independent states seemed a likely outcome at the Paris Peace Conference. Italians expected significant territorial expansion in the Adriatic. Russians followed the ever-changing developments in the civil war with concern, but also with a sense that their homeland was experiencing a new beginning. And the Ukrainian-language newspapers from Winnipeg told their readers of the bright prospects of an independent state that would encompass the Ukrainian provinces of both Russia and Austria-Hungary. It seemed to many immigrants that the brighter future for them lay not in the Elk Valley but in their European homelands.

1919

A COMMUNITY AT PEACE?

Very early in the year, two normally unremarkable occurrences—yet another fundraiser and a regular meeting of city council—demonstrated the paradoxical truth that things can change but also remain unchanged. As president of the Amalgamated Patriotic Fund, Edwy Stewart received a letter as part of a nationwide appeal from the Canadian Red Cross for funds to assist the forty-three thousand sick and wounded Canadian troops still in Europe. With the end of hostilities in Europe, fundraising fatigue was everywhere evident. The week-long national campaign drew little response from neighbouring Cranbrook and Lethbridge, but Fernie responded energetically after a bit of a push from some local women. Perhaps hopeful of resuming at least some of their peacetime activities, the IODE expressed the opinion that, for the purpose of this new appeal, it was "now the duty of the men to jump in."[245]

And jump in they did. A special committee of leading citizens (Mayor Thomson, Thomas Uphill, MLA Alexander Fisher and members of the GWVA) was formed to conduct a campaign to raise the $3,300 goal set for the Fernie district. The committee quickly announced it intended to exceed that amount and just as quickly urged "the female organizations within the city to co-operate." That must have seemed very much like passing the ball back to the IODE. A sum far short of the goal was raised. Whether this was due to donor fatigue, weaker efforts than usual by local women or simply the inexperience of the special committee must remain open to speculation.

There was nothing weak about the efforts of the female organization involved in the second event. In many respects, the meeting in February 1919 harkened back to the miners' revolt of June 1915. Thomas Uphill was in the chair arguing the case for equitable treatment of foreign-born residents. He had the full support of the union leadership. Facing them was an angry crowd demanding otherwise. But this was not a meeting of the Gladstone local union. The chair occupied by Uphill was the mayoral chair of Fernie to which he had been returned once again by acclamation a month earlier.

Despite bitterly cold weather, the angry crowd—described as the largest to attend a city council meeting for years—had been motivated to attend by a report in the *Free Press* that Uphill had dismissively rejected a request from Vancouver city council to support the deportation of all undesirable aliens, regardless of whether they had been interned during the war.

It was not unusual for the civic government to receive requests for support in political matters from councils of other communities. The request from Nanaimo to protest the release of interned miners in 1916, for example, and another from Toronto in 1918 seeking support for a proposed referendum to abolish the Canadian Senate were both quietly filed with no apparent public complaint. This occasion was different. The resolution from Vancouver was part of a nationwide agitation calling for deportation of "dangerous foreigners." Spearheaded by the GWVA, the demand was being supported by politicians, newspapers and civic governments in terms every bit as strident as were their calls for internment in May 1915. Fernie's newly dominant patriotic organization, the GWVA, attended the council meeting in strength with its women's auxiliary to demand that their community join the chorus by adopting the position outlined by Vancouver and endorsed by communities right across the province. Just a few weeks earlier, the Fernie branch of the GWVA had unanimously voted to support deporting enemy aliens and met with CNPCC officials to press that demand. Members of the women's auxiliary publicly deplored the action of the mayor and council for not immediately endorsing the patriotic stance taken by Vancouver and called on them to "adopt an attitude more in accordance with public sentiment."[246]

Also in attendance was Harry Martin, who proclaimed the union would never agree to the Vancouver resolution; Eliza Moffatt, IODE stalwart and president of the GWVA women's auxiliary, retorted that she was not aware the Gladstone local union ran the civic government. Nine returned soldiers—members of the GWVA as well as the UMWA—stood to indicate support for deportation. Again echoing June 1915, another miner said he would not work beside an Austrian or a German. The division apparently remained between an executive defending the civil rights of enemy aliens and at least a portion of the membership willing to deny them those rights. Uphill argued that only those who "by action or speech had proven themselves undesirable" should be deported. After much debate, Uphill's more temperate stance was endorsed by Fernie aldermen. Fundamentally, however, this was not like the miners' revolt of June 1915. The angry crowd at the city council meeting did not have voting power.

Evidently, the issue of how to deal with enemy aliens was still very much alive. Of course, this was true not only in Fernie. Returned soldiers often fanned the flames, and the violence they instigated against foreigners in Winnipeg in late January was only the most extreme example of the incidents reported. There were widespread demands for punitive measures against Canada's enemy-alien population in the months following the armistice, but those demands continued to be blunted by rapidly changing perceptions about precisely which aliens were supposed to threaten Canadian society. While the GWVA in Fernie was lobbying council to deport Germans and Austrians, their counterparts in Lethbridge were calling for the deportation of "all persons manifesting Bolshevik predilections." Generally, that was understood to describe Russians, Ukrainians and other ethnic groups originating in the profoundly destabilized regions of eastern Europe—some former foes and some former friends.

The armistice may have ended the fighting in western Europe, but it brought chaos to Germany and eastern Europe. Week after week, newspapers in early 1919 acquainted their Canadian readers with news of Bolshevik fortunes in the civil war, the Spartacist revolution in Germany and other socialist uprisings almost everywhere else. And in Britain, the United States, Australia and throughout Canada, strikes were widespread. Reports of developments from the Paris Peace Conference were often crowded off the front pages of newspapers by news of labour disruptions. The unrest in Canada was widely attributed to enemy aliens, and in February the federal government used the War Measures Act to grant judges new powers to intern them.

In this volatile political climate, District 18 opened its annual convention in Calgary in mid-February with a new president-elect. Receiving solid support from the Alberta locals, Phillip Christophers of Blairmore had overcome the big votes from Coal Creek and Michel for David Rees. Significantly, the convention began with an indication of the anger still felt towards the international UMWA for its lack of support during the strikes of 1916, 1917 and 1918. Delegates refused to distribute within District 18 copies of a newspaper just received from headquarters in Indianapolis.[247] They then proceeded to pass a resolution condemning the shooting of Albert "Ginger" Goodwin, called for the end of the ban on so-called seditious literature, and following the example of miners in the UK, voted to examine ways of forming a "working agreement" with railway workers. They also spent considerable time debating whether or not the allowable alcohol content of beer should be raised to 2.5 percent alcohol by weight.

The *District Ledger* and the printing plant in Fernie caused delegates much concern. The professional and business communities of Fernie were placing their advertisements only sparingly, and Lawson's weekly appeals encouraging every miner in the district to subscribe were having little effect. The printing plant was seen as a white elephant, and both its sale and its transfer to Calgary were advocated. Lawson insisted a physical move would be too expensive, but agreed that the plant should indeed be sold and the money-losing newspaper published through arrangement with a printer in Calgary. The question was left unresolved and placed in the hands of the executive. The days remaining to the *District Ledger* were clearly numbered.[248]

Matters of western alienation were raised frequently at the convention. The anger that was giving rise to the United Farmers of Alberta and the Progressives federally was felt deeply in labour organizations throughout western Canada. They were also bitter at the dismissive treatment their concerns surrounding conscription and social reform consistently received from the more established conservative unions that dominated the national Trades and Labour Congress. At the suggestion of David Rees, western union leaders made plans for their own Western Labour Conference in Calgary in March. The agenda quickly took on a radical appearance, with resolutions on industrial unionism and the possibility of a general strike to be considered. The District 18 executive and convention delegates seemed broadly supportive, but outgoing international board member and Fernie resident David Rees was already expressing reservations about the emerging agenda. In mining circles and within the broader community, these first hints of the turmoil that was to come received surprisingly little attention.

William Wilson: Increasingly powerful within the Crow's Nest Pass Coal Company, he was also in his third year as president of the Western Coal Operators' Association. Glenbow Archives NA-4964-1.

In contrast, veterans' concerns were at the centre of public discourse. The Fernie District Committee for National Reconstruction formed in January and made jobs for veterans a priority. The Gladstone local union agreed, and, recalling William Wilson's promise of 1914, urged that all returning soldiers should be able to return to the jobs they left. The *Ledger* supported that view, but Wallace saw that endorsement as simply a ploy to curry favour with veterans and insisted "the local organ of the Bolsheviki" would fail in the attempt. On behalf of the Red Cross, members of the IODE sustained their efforts for soldiers not yet returned from Europe, and were also supporting the Red Cross initiative on behalf of refugees and residents of France and Belgium whose lives had been disrupted by four years of war. The GWVA moved their club rooms to the lower floor of the Napanee Hotel, the original location in the 41 Market Company block having become too small to accommodate a rapidly growing membership. Also housing the Victory Loan office and the rooms devoted to the work of the IODE and Red Cross, the Napanee had become the patriotic centre of the community.

Emerging as a significant political force, the local GWVA and its new president, Gerald Moffatt, refused to accept the compromise position arrived at by city council pertaining to Vancouver's call for the deportation of all enemy aliens. They circulated a petition in support of Vancouver's resolution and organized a meeting intended to force city council to reconsider the matter. Attended by members from each of the GWVA, the Committee for National Reconstruction and city council, the meeting was another indication of how divisive the question of enemy aliens remained. As indicated by warring newspaper columns, the GWVA petition and the moderate resolution adopted by city council, there was no community consensus. A strongly worded resolution from Sherwood Herchmer found favour with the meeting, but Joseph Rudnicki wanted Poles, Czechs and Slovaks exempted. Suggestions that Ukrainians and Russians should also be regarded as enemy aliens further complicated the issue. The gathering rejected Mayor Uphill's motion to deport only those "who by word or action have shown themselves to be undesirable." Instead Vancouver's resolution was fundamentally endorsed. Unhappy with the decision, Committee for National Reconstruction member Harry Martin wrote to the minister of justice asking for several clarifications of government policy and an opinion on whether or not Russians could be classed as enemy aliens. The confusion and conflicting viewpoints enabled Uphill and his council to avoid revisiting the issue.[249]

Collectively, Russians and Ukrainians were garnering attention in the region for another reason. At the midpoint of the war, William Wilson had speculated that the Austrians and Russians would "all rush back" to their homelands when the conflict was concluded. It proved to be an astute prediction, although Wilson could not have known that the optimism many of the migrant workers shared for the Russian Revolution would enhance their desire for a return migration. Perplexed that the continuing chaos in eastern Europe meant little news (if any) was reaching them from their homes and families in Belarus and eastern Ukraine, as many as a hundred Russians—almost all of whom had been employed at the coke ovens or in the lumber industry—left Fernie in mid-February intending to return home via Vancouver.[250]

The *Ledger* reported that a letter received from Russia by one local resident painted a favourable picture of the new Bolshevik state. The main reasons for the Russian exodus, however, were perhaps more practical. The men had arrived in the months preceding the war and typically would have intended to return within two to three years. The war had prevented that, but the war was over. Pacific shipping routes were said to be the most reliable route from Canada to Russia, and employment conditions in the Elk Valley were worsening rapidly. The Russian migrant workers were known (and widely criticized) locally for their excessive frugality, so many of them possessed the financial resources required to leave the region.

Russian-born migrant workers were not the only ones seeking a return to their homelands. The prospect of an independent Ukraine was becoming less certain as Poland at the Paris Peace Conference forcefully claimed the Austrian provinces of Galicia and Bukovyna. Approximately four dozen Austrian-born Ukrainians, whose number included those recently fined for possession of Marxist literature, approached *Ledger* editor Peter Lawson for assistance in arranging their return. On their behalf, Lawson wrote to the Secretary of State in Ottawa advising him that the men were willing to vacate their jobs in favour of returned soldiers if their passage home could be arranged. The reply he received stated that, unfortunately, making such arrangements would simply be too complicated.[251] Nevertheless, even reportedly without the savings of their Russian-born counterparts, Austrian-born Ukrainians were also leaving the region.

The matter of return migration was intimately connected to unemployment concerns. The coke-oven jobs being abandoned were not those preferred by veterans, but job opportunities of any variety were scarce. The Michel local union issued a "stay away" notice in January—as did Hillcrest in February—because of "too many miners." Although it seems all returned soldiers who wanted to return to jobs at Coal Creek were indeed being accommodated, the CNPCC reported "a great falling off in both coal and coke orders" and cut back production sharply in early February. The mines were operating only two days per week.[252] The economic situation in Fernie in the months following the war had become distressingly similar to what it had been in the months preceding the war.

The same components were all present: serious unemployment, reduced hours for those who were employed, a glut of coal on the market and a downturn in the lumber industry. The *Ledger* noted the departure of Russians and Ukrainians had no effect on the availability of jobs and editorialized that an "unemployment spectre" was hanging over Fernie. The job openings at the coke ovens quickly proved to be a mirage. Due to the sharp post-war drop in demand, the CNPCC shut down the coke operation completely and indefinitely on April 4.[253] Membership in the Gladstone local union, steadily eroding since before and during the war years, had fallen by nearly a hundred from a year earlier to just 641 by April 1919.[254]

At the same time, there were further indications that a more modern Fernie was beginning to emerge. A serious initiative was undertaken to exploit Fernie's geographic isolation and scenic beauty to advantage. The attempt to invigorate the board of trade the previous year seems to have faltered, but an initiative by Fernie photographer Joseph Spalding to advertise the district as a tourist destination promised more lasting results. Rail service to Fernie was excellent, but attracting tourists required good roads. Sherwood Herchmer, elected as a director of the Good Roads Association of British Columbia the previous September, was vocal on that score, but promoting tourism required a broader effort. Spalding outlined the potential benefits in a letter to the *Free Press*, and a dramatic increase in membership to the board of trade soon resulted. Within just a few weeks, members of the board of trade, the Rod and Gun Club and the district automobile association co-operated to establish the Fernie Tourist Association. And with the coke ovens out of production, the whole initiative took place in an atmosphere notably more favourable to tourism.[255]

The new golf course was attracting enthusiastic attention—initially from the local curlers—and baseball and football (soccer) leagues were formed in the spring. The city of Fernie and local merchants announced that, with some exceptions, their employees were to be granted an eight-hour day in accordance with new provincial legislation. But most indications of progress had to do with the growing popularity of the automobile. Emilio Picariello garnered much admiration in Fernie in February for his purchase of a Mc-Laughlin Six Special (and, at the same time, the dubious distinction of being fined in Alberta for illegal possession of alcohol). At Blairmore in early April, with delegates from the Fernie district automobile association participating, the Crow's Nest Pass National Highway Association was formed. Resolutions were passed urging that the proposed all-Canadian trans-continental highway be routed through the Crowsnest. Calls were renewed to have British Columbia (and not only East Kootenay) drive on the right-hand side of the road. Unfortunately, not all indications of modernity were as positive. The first fatality caused by an automobile within Fernie city limits occurred in April when a young boy in the Annex was killed by a car suspected of exceeding the speed limit.

Numerous changes occurred in the realm of policing. Former city police chief Albert Brown died unexpectedly in Fernie in April; current city police chief George Welsby, whose wife had been killed by the Spanish flu, resigned in May and moved to New Jersey to join his brother in a business venture. After an unsuccessful search for a suitable veteran to fill the position, Joseph Boardman—with nine years' experience as a popular provincial police constable at Coal Creek—was appointed.[256] Residents bade him a fond farewell with a grand social on June 3. Provincial police inspector Owen, receiving good wishes and high praise for his integrity from Lawson at the *Ledger*, was transferred to Vancouver. His replacement as East Kootenay provincial police supervisor, Joseph Fernie, nephew of the city's founder William Fernie, was expected to arrive from Kamloops at the end of July.[257]

Perhaps most significantly in regard to policing, a detachment of the Royal North West Mounted Police (RNWMP) was located in Fernie in April. Composed primarily of veterans and responsible for enforcing federal laws, the RNWMP were being deployed in several locations in British Columbia for the first time. This deployment was very likely a response to the secret report prepared for the RNWMP which identified the Crowsnest Pass as one of three main locations of Bolshevik activity in western Canada. The federal government, increasingly concerned at the spread of revolutionary politics, also expected the force to "infiltrate the radical movement."[258] Yet Lawson at the *Ledger* was effusive in welcoming the force to Fernie, insisting that their primary role would be to enforce federal laws against the smuggling of liquor. He specifically discounted rumours that they were there in anticipation of strike trouble. Nevertheless, he offered no explanation of why two officers were to be stationed in Coal Creek if their main purpose was to keep an eye on smuggling routes.

As most Canadian military personnel had returned or were about to return from Europe, the Canadian Patriotic Fund was concluding its welfare efforts for families of soldiers on active service. After March 31, donations were no longer sought or accepted, and the national organization turned to an accounting of its activities during the war years. Its final report states that, between the establishment of the local branch in September 1914 and the period ending March 1919, approximately 250 families in the Fernie district received support. Disbursements totalled over $100,000, while local contributions amounted to $77,000. Following the withdrawal of the Gladstone local union from the mandatory deduction scheme, district collections covered only 40 percent of payments. In addition to supporting dependents of soldiers, donations from local contributors were also distributed through the APF to Canadian and British Red Cross societies, the Navy League of Canada, the YMCA's Red Triangle Fund, the Army Hut Fund of the Knights of Columbus and to Belgian, Polish and Serb relief funds. The final report does not mention disbursements to the Tobacco Fund, but, more oddly, fails to make any reference to the Mount Fernie IODE.[259]

GAMBLING ON A DREAM

Those concerned about the possibility of revolution in western Canada could point to a growing body of evidence that their concerns were justified. The Western Labour Conference in mid-March drew a great deal of attention by proving to be even more radical in its pronouncements than anticipated. Subject to ratification by their respective unions, delegates voted overwhelmingly to end their affiliations with international unions and to form one all-encompassing Canadian organization. That new organization was to be structured as an industrial union—one that would unite workers of various skills and in various industries into a single union. Conference delegates also expressed sympathy with the Bolsheviks in Russia and the Spartacists in Germany and called for an end to Allied military intervention in Russia, going so far as to threaten to strike if troops were not withdrawn by the first of June. Plans were made to reconvene in June to consider how to proceed if their respective unions voted in favour of a new organization, which already was commonly being referred to as the One Big Union (OBU). David Rees, who had been instrumental in organizing the conference, was increasingly alarmed at the direction it was taking. He left the gathering on its first day of proceedings.[260]

The issues that were soon to convulse Fernie and the whole of the Elk Valley and Crowsnest were not new. All of the elements of the approaching and perhaps inevitable strike had been part of the turmoil in District 18 during the years 1909 and 1911.[261] These included the impulse to form an independent regional miners' union, the practical reasons for remaining with the international UMWA, a job action by fire bosses, the argument between socialist and non-socialist miners about the merits of various approaches to reform and revolution, the censure of the mainstream press, a prevailing economic recession, the ambivalent attitudes to foreign-born workers and the involvement or non-involvement by federal and provincial governments. But because of the events and experience of the war years, these elements combined in 1919 to produce a profoundly different outcome compared to that of a decade earlier.

The collective agreement between the Western Coal Operators' Association and District 18 expired at the end of March, but both Commissioner Armstrong and the Coal Operators agreed to a union request to extend its term until after the signing of the Peace Treaty in Paris, expected in a few weeks' time. The extension also gave Phillip Christophers and District 18 executive members time to consult the international union in Indianapolis on points of contention and on unresolved policy matters.

Upon returning from those consultations, Christophers showed little enthusiasm for the international union's declared bargaining priorities. The most important of those priorities was the prospect of a six-hour day, a proposal that was being debated by miners in the United Kingdom, Nova Scotia and throughout the American districts of the UMWA in the months following the war. Christophers was concerned that the recent lifting of the embargo on the importation of American coal was discouraging Canadian production and speculated that the international's push for a six-hour day would make coalfields in District 18 less competitive. In early April, he dismissed the matter entirely from District 18's bargaining position. However, the decision brought the union no closer to signing a new agreement. The Coal Operators believed Christophers's hesitation was entirely due to a reluctance to act before he knew of the rank and file's decision about the proposed formation of the One Big Union.

The district executive was indeed moving quickly on that matter. On March 29 it had voted at a special meeting to "fall in line with the OBU."[262] Executive members visited locals to present the case for the OBU and to gauge support. Peter Lawson added his voice to the initiative. He travelled to

Blairmore to speak enthusiastically in favour of industrial unionism (overenthusiastically, according to the *Lethbridge Herald*), and Christophers addressed a large crowd at the Grand Theatre in Fernie on April 4. Urging his listeners to seriously consider breaking with the UMWA, Christophers nevertheless warned them that such a course of action would be difficult. The report of his speech in the *Ledger* indicates his listeners that evening were little disposed to heed that note of caution.

Just as negotiations with the Coal Operators were expected to resume, members of District 18 UMWA were asked to respond to two questions by secret ballot. The vote on both questions throughout the entire district was overwhelmingly affirmative. At Fernie, 533 miners answered yes when asked, "Are you in favor of severing your affiliation with your present international craft union and becoming part of the One Big Industrial Organization of all workers?" Barely two dozen were opposed. Similarly, the vote at the Michel local union was 322 to 12.[263] By almost the same margins, members of both local unions supported a possible general strike to establish a six-hour working day. The vote on that second question—already dismissed as a local issue by Christophers—had no local consequences, but the overwhelming support for the prospect of forming a single industrial union sent political shock waves throughout the Elk Valley. Those shock waves were also being felt elsewhere in the province as hard-rock miners in West Kootenay and lumbermen at the coast were also voting to abandon their international unions in favour of the OBU.

Superficially, it appeared that the miners of Fernie, Coal Creek and Michel had swung suddenly and almost unanimously behind a set of revolutionary principles. That many favoured those principles is undeniable. The dismal results achieved by the region's Socialist candidates in the elections of 1916 and 1917 disguised the enduring strength of socialist opinion and the broad range of radical political views that had long been espoused in the mining communities of the Elk Valley. Those views were attracting a newly sympathetic audience due to the example of the Russian Revolution.

The miners who so recently had supported Conservative and Liberal candidates cannot have abandoned their recent and more mainstream political preferences so quickly and so collectively. What they had entirely abandoned was the desire to retain their association with the international union. What united the members of the Gladstone local union was a profound optimism that better times were achievable through the OBU. With no apparent division along lines of job categorization or ethnicity, socialist miners may have voted to press for dramatic social change, but non-socialist miners had cast their ballots along with them not primarily in response to the siren call of international revolution, but in defence of workplace concerns that their own international union seemed always inclined to dismiss.[264]

Consistently unresponsive to local issues in the Crowsnest, the Indianapolis-based UMWA was seen as little more than an impediment to resolution of those issues—another eastern-based organization dismissive of western concerns. The One Big Union, even with no policies or organizational structure yet in place, seemed to offer a way out of the international union and a strengthening of local bargaining power at the same time. Urging caution, David Rees—favoured overwhelmingly by Gladstone miners during the executive election in January—was almost universally ignored by those same miners in April.

A voice urging caution: David Rees consistently argued that the promise of the OBU was leading miners into a blind alley. Fernie Musem and Archives DL-PF-1909-0270.

Also disillusioned with the UMWA, the former international board member nevertheless insisted that the escape offered by the OBU would prove to be not only a blind alley, but also one that would weaken union strength.

Adding to the confusion of unresolved negotiations and new union horizons was provincial legislation in British Columbia requiring an eight-hour-day. Underground miners had long achieved that standard, but many categories of mine employment above ground entailed nine-, ten- or even eleven-hour shifts. When it was realized that the reduction in hours meant a significant reduction in wages for CNPCC employees working the longest shifts, the Gladstone local union asked provincial authorities if the new regulations were intended to result in such a reduction and was told they were not. Nevertheless, Commissioner Armstrong issued Order 124, which confirmed that certain job categories, while benefitting from the reduction of working hours would, by the same token, also suffer a wage reduction of approximately 15 percent. The District 18 executive endorsed the Gladstone objections, had ballots printed at the *Ledger* office, and recommending rejection, polled members district-wide on whether or not to refuse to work under Order 124. The results were not overwhelming—even the Gladstone local union voted only two to one in favour of a refusal—but a substantial majority overall did vote to defy Order 124.[265]

Of course, miners on the Alberta side of the border were not subject to provincial legislation from British Columbia, but in order to prevent neighbouring coal companies from gaining an advantage over the CNPCC, Armstrong applied the order throughout District 18. Few, if any, wage reductions resulted for outside workers in Alberta. Loss of wages due to the British Columbia legislation may have affected only two dozen men, the majority of them working at Coal Creek.[266] The vote to defy Order 124 by the Alberta local unions was fundamentally one of support for their British Columbia counterparts. District 18 in May 1919, therefore, found itself in very much the same situation it had been in the previous September: threatening a general strike on an issue that negatively impacted only members in British Columbia. Whereas the single-shift issue had pertained only to Coal Creek, the wage reductions under Order 124 would take effect as well at Michel and Corbin. Thomas Biggs, as district president in 1918, had realized how problematic a strike on such a localized basis could be and did not follow up on his threat to call one. Just eight months later, when Phillip Christophers received Armstrong's refusal to investigate the matter or to cancel Order 124, he proclaimed a general strike to begin at noon on May 24.

What had changed? The confidence of the District 18 executive in the political promise of the OBU must have been the determining factor. Otherwise the prospects of a successful strike were appallingly weak. The union had no funds available to provide even minimal relief to its striking members and knew it could expect no assistance from the international union for what was yet another unsanctioned walkout. That the federal government was eager to conclude its wartime intervention in the mines was evident. The Coal Operators' eagerness for a confrontation with the union uncomplicated by government interference was equally well known. Orders for coal declined significantly as they always did with the arrival of warmer weather, and the demand for coke had also dropped sharply as the metals industry cut production at the end of the war. Consequently, most mines in District 18 were operating on only a half-time basis. Because of that, miners were unlikely to possess personal savings to sustain them through a long strike.

Circumstances such as these indicate that any union in a position of such profound weakness would be ill-advised to call a general strike, but the overwhelmingly affirmative vote in the OBU referendum—district-wide only 256 of the nearly 6,000 miners who voted were not in favour of joining the OBU—convinced the executive that the miners' solidarity would trump all other factors.[267] The ostensible issue of wage reductions for some workers functioned only as a pretext for a confrontation Christophers believed would result in a dramatically stronger bargaining position for the miners of District 18. Because the point at issue was relatively minor, he may also have believed a quick resolution was likely. But it is difficult to resist the conclusion that Christophers also fundamentally wanted a work stoppage in sympathy with the Winnipeg general strike, which had begun just a week earlier.

The *Free Press* reported critically on the events leading up to the miners' strike, but refrained from commenting editorially on them. The *District Ledger*, on the other hand, quickly placed itself firmly in the camp of those supporting the OBU. Lawson provided generous space to both David Rees and new international board member Robert Livett, both of whom were warning miners that their hopes surrounding the formation of a new breakaway union would prove to be only illusions. Nevertheless, Lawson's editorials and reportage made it abundantly clear he disagreed with them. He was sharply critical of the few members of the Gladstone local union who had voted against the resolution to become part of the new union, and he devoted column and advertising space to solicit much-needed donations—one dollar each from one thousand readers for what was called the "$1,000 Victory Bond for the One Big Union"—for the fledgling organization. Basically, after the Western Labour Conference in March, the *District Ledger* was an organ of the OBU, not of the UMWA; at the *Free Press*, every article on the subject expressed its editor's adamant opposition.

Depending on one's perspective, the emergence of the OBU held out the promise of a better world, the threat of chaos in labour relations, or both. The first two weeks of the strike provided Lawson with considerable grounds for optimism and Wallace with reason for despair. Christophers declared the strike would be conducted on "One Big Union principles," although he did not elaborate on what that might mean in practice. The fire bosses at Coal Creek, who by their contracts were expected to keep the mines safe during labour stoppages, refused to do the work of striking miners and resigned. (In contrast, the pit bosses—also responsible for mine safety—declared they would continue working because they had not been asked to do the work of strikers.)

On orders from their union in Vancouver, workers at the power plant went on strike on May 28. Fernie was plunged into darkness. The general strike in Winnipeg was being supported by sympathetic walkouts in Calgary, Vancouver and Lethbridge. More than a hundred thousand workers across western Canada were on strike as part of a labour revolt that stretched from coast to coast. The OBU—still just an idea preparing for its founding convention in Calgary in early June—was declared responsible for the Winnipeg strike by the minister of labour in Ottawa two days before the lights went out in Fernie. Blame for the upheaval was placed firmly on the shoulders of an organization that did not yet exist.[268]

The Gladstone local union's first strike bulletin promised co-operation with city police to preserve order and to cause minimum inconvenience to the public, but the shutdown of the power plant caused much disruption. Wallace was forced to print the May 30 issue of the *Free Press* in Cranbrook. Mayor Uphill met with strike leaders and secured an agreement that was outlined in the second strike bulletin. After two nights without power, the plant resumed operations at 5:00 p.m. on May 30. However, there was to be no power supplied after 7:00 a.m. daily. As a condition of the agreement, the miners had required a guarantee from city police that "all hotel bars and other places be closed tight against the sale of intoxicants." The city posted a bulletin outlining the terms agreed upon, and the strike committee posted its own notice, earnestly requesting all striking workers to comply.[269]

The insistence on making alcohol unavailable indicates the union was seriously concerned to prevent any disturbance fueled by alcohol, but it also reveals that prohibition meant little in Fernie. Alcohol was available to anyone with a thirst for it. Inspector Owen had recognized this and, in early May—well before the strike began—received approval from the attorney general to conduct an undercover sting operation. Two constables from West Kootenay began operating in Fernie as hopeful purchasers of alcohol on May 26. By the end of the week, with hotelkeepers beginning to get suspicious, the undercover agents had successfully purchased illegal alcohol at a grocery store and at eight of Fernie's ten operating hotels. Nine individuals were arrested, including the proprietors of the King's and the Central hotels.[270] The striking miners' insistence on no booze, therefore, came a day after the wave of arrests had scandalized the community. With a strike just beginning, a power cut, a successful undercover police operation and the Elk River again close to the flood levels of 1916, the last week of May probably provided more excitement than most would have wished for.

It was not a week that pleased John Wallace. He had to print his newspaper in Cranbrook, and his dislike of prohibition and its absurdities was well known. He numbered hotel owners amongst his friends. Whether due to a bad mood or to a genuinely reactionary political outlook, he urged the men of the local GWVA to follow the example of their peers in Lethbridge, where force was used to keep the power plant in operation. Little more than an incitement to vigilante action, it was an intemperate statement even by Wallace's standards. That no such action was undertaken is undoubtedly due to the fact that, as the majority of Fernie's returned soldiers had been miners, so too were most of Fernie's GWVA members. A good many of them had returned from the war to work in the mines. They too were on strike.

If the last week of May distressed him, Wallace found little comfort but much cause for outrage in the first week of June. In a special mid-week two-page issue, the *Ledger* published an extensive article alleging that the CNPCC was on the verge of closing the mines at Coal Creek and opening production at Sparwood, where costs would be much lower. The apparent reason for such a change was that the company's major shareholder, the Great Northern Railway—identified in the article as the "Great Northern octopus"—considered costs of production too high at Coal Creek. At the same time, Christophers cabled Premier Oliver in Victoria to echo the allegation and to make other complaints about the CNPCC.

The article caused uproar in Fernie; the cable caused consternation in Victoria. A petition was sent to Premier Oliver from the city's property owners demanding an investigation. In turn, Oliver sought an explanation from the CNPCC.[271] William Wilson had just been elected as a vice-president by company shareholders, so his words were accorded even greater weight than usual. His rather vague admission that the company could indeed mine at Sparwood someday allowed the uproar to continue for another week.[272] Wallace at the *Free Press* noted that, unless the mines were utterly ruined by the strike, there was "little fear of Fernie becoming a second Hosmer." Lawson simply dismissed the *Free Press* as the "official organ" of the CNPCC.

For all its bluster and sensationalism, the *District Ledger* again faced the prospect of suspending publication. Advertising by the Fernie business community fell considerably after May, and only approximately 25 percent of union members were subscribers. The size of the weekly publication was reduced to four pages in mid-June, and Lawson appealed to union locals each week, encouraging them to increase circulation by placing the question of subscriptions on their meeting agendas. He told them, "It is a part of your share in the big struggle that is now convulsing the whole world." The decision to revive the *Ledger* the previous year had been taken on the clear understanding that the newspaper was to be self-supporting. District 18 had been willing to subsidize the costs of production only temporarily and, with membership dues suspended during the strike, was no longer able to do so. It is likely the life of the *Ledger* was extended by several weeks because it was a necessary means of communicating with men on strike and because its editorial stance was in perfect accord with the OBU sympathies of the executive. But it would not be long before economic considerations would trump political ones.

The month of June provided little optimism for those hoping for a quick settlement of the strike. Octopus or not, the Great Northern was the parent company of the CNPCC, and its decision to fire miners who had just found temporary work on the rail line to Elko closed one avenue of economic relief used in previous work stoppages. Although employment was available in lumber mills to the south, the economic downturn sharply narrowed that option as well. But apart from the sensationalist allegations of the *District Ledger*, the local situation was overshadowed by events in Calgary and Winnipeg. The founding convention of the OBU in Calgary produced a constitution that was sent for consideration to all participating union locals, including of course, those in District 18 of the UMWA. Both critics and supporters of the new union would soon find the document left unanswered as many questions of policy and organization as it answered. The general strike in Winnipeg finally ended in arrests and bloodshed on June 21 when the RNWMP charged a crowd of protesters. Wallace found no kind words for Uphill in the agreement that provided power to Fernie only part of the time and criticized him harshly for not acting more forcefully, but with strikes ending in Vancouver and elsewhere, power was fully restored on the morning of June 24.

In a criticism that residents and newspaper editors alike in Fernie found increasingly tiresome, the *Mining and Engineering Record* of Vancouver claimed the situation "was entirely due to the narrow, selfish, ignorant policies of a few agitators, mainly foreigners, in the Crow's Nest Pass."[273] Certainly the ethnic makeup of the union leadership in District 18 had changed dramatically since the early months of the war. By early 1919, Italians and eastern Europeans had been elected as secretaries in roughly a quarter of the district's forty local unions—more than double the number of locals in 1914, but now with only three in British Columbia—and Lawson noted with approval that the annual convention had been "a real melting pot." Nevertheless, English-speaking miners still dominated local union executives, and district officers were all English-speaking. Earlier in the year, members of the GWVA in Fernie had received no encouragement at all from officials of the CNPCC when they pressed for the deportation of foreigner-born miners. Lawson sarcastically suggested that the CNPCC would probably prefer to consider the possibility of deporting the local English, Scottish and Welsh strike leaders. Those leaders, in turn, had their own observations on ethnicity. During a visit to Lethbridge in June, Harry Martin noted that the strike-breakers there—brought in to do the work of striking fire bosses—were all English-speaking.[274]

The miners pleaded with both the federal and provincial governments to intervene. In response, MP Saul Bonnell advised the president of the Gladstone local union that the federal government had no jurisdiction over working conditions in mines operated by the Crow's Nest Pass Coal Company. He said that "was entirely in the hands of the provincial government at Victoria."[275] Technically, the power to intervene in the operation of the mines exercised by Commissioner Armstrong was in place until the peace was signed, but it was apparent there was no intention to exercise that power. And after initial indications from the provincial government that it might intervene, no action followed. Mines minister Sloan promised to visit Fernie but did not, and there was no reply from Premier Oliver to the union's request for a commission of inquiry. The Coal Operators were at last in the position that William Wilson had particularly desired for over two years. They were able to deal with the miners of District 18 without interference from governments. It was not an opportunity they intended to squander.

. The disarray in the ranks of the miners caused by the proposed abandonment of the UMWA affiliation enabled the Coal Operators to prolong the strike, knowing that their striking employees—whether motivated by the prospect of an autonomous union, the possibility of social revolution or a combination of both—were becoming financially desperate. When the miners' bargaining committee made serious overtures at the end of June and again in early July, the Coal Operators refused to talk until it was established that they would be dealing with officials of the UMWA and not of the OBU. The adversary of past disputes had become—perhaps not surprisingly—an ally in the present one. The international union was anxious to discipline the independently minded executive of District 18, and the Coal Operators knew that very well. Even as Christophers insisted District 18 was still part of the international organization, the Coal Operators showed no inclination to negotiate. Although victory was clearly theirs, a complete surrender was required. It was also apparent that any intervention by the federal government this time would favour the mine owners. As part of a nationwide crackdown following the suppression of the Winnipeg general strike, District 18 headquarters in Calgary were raided by the RNWMP.[276]

The Coal Operators were no doubt pleased when the process of surrender began with the same group of men who had initiated the war. Fernie's ethnic fault lines appear to have played a role. Dominic Nicoletti had formerly been a bartender—an occupation to which he would soon return—but for the moment he was an employee of the CNPCC. He privately advised a senior company official that, following procedures outlined by the union constitution, Italian miners anxious to return to work were petitioning the Gladstone local union executive to call a special meeting for July 8. The purpose of the meeting would be to sanction the involvement of UMWA representatives in negotiating an end to the strike. The company official wrote to William Wilson that Nicoletti was confident "the Italians would have the support of other foreign nationalities" and that their return to work would be immediate.[277]

The petition was apparently successful, and support for its objectives clearly crossed ethnic lines. Just two days later than originally planned, what the *Free Press* described as a well-attended "insurgent meeting" of the Gladstone local union resulted in motions to return to work under the old agreement and to have negotiations for a new agreement conducted by the UMWA. The meeting was acrimonious and the motions supported by large majorities, but far from reflecting a new affection for the UMWA, the positions adopted speak of desperate men seeking a practical solution. The only intention stated by Nicoletti that was not achieved was an immediate return to work, allowing the *Ledger* to report but briefly on the failure of an attempt to persuade Italian miners at Coal Creek to break ranks with the union. Beyond that, the *Ledger* provided its readers with no information about the meeting. The *Free Press* quietly added that Harry Martin was to resign—without specifying whether from employment or from his union position—for reasons of ill health.

Officially, the Michel local union was the only one to follow the lead of the Gladstone miners, but District 18 officials quickly declared their members were prepared to return to work under Order 124. Still Wilson and the Coal Operators were not satisfied. The strike—better described as a lockout by this time—continued. Just as the miners' overwhelmingly favourable vote to join the OBU should not be interpreted as support for revolutionary principles, neither was the Coal Operators' intransigence a principled stance to confront those principles. They were fundamentally intent on teaching a lesson in industrial power to what they regarded as an unreliable and aggressive workforce. The original issue—reduction in wages for some outside employees of the CNPCC—was rarely mentioned. It had been completely replaced by the question of whether or not the miners of District 18 could freely choose their union affiliation. Both the Coal Operators and the international UMWA insisted they could not. On that stance, the confrontation continued.

In the midst of all this, the war of words between the *Free Press* and the *Ledger* had spilled into the law courts. Wallace's personal attacks on union men sometimes led him to petty and insensitive remarks. When the wife of one active union member died, he somehow found it necessary to comment the widower was "an aggressive member of the Gladstone local." But his weekly barrage of criticism of District 18 affairs and the political orientation of the *District Ledger* did not go uncontested. Lawson often responded in tones of a schoolmaster tutoring a reluctant pupil, and letter-writers urged Wallace to show a little more understanding for men who had to work for a living. If the admonitions concerned Wallace, they did not restrain him. Finally, the situation came to a head. Following the March 7 issue of the *Free Press*— containing the usual quota of remarks critical of union positions, renewed allegations of the *Ledger* receiving "pap" from MLA Alexander Fisher and a swipe at its editor's business acumen—Lawson lost patience.

In his next edition, he included an angry anonymous letter alleging Wallace was in the pay of the CNPCC and suggesting it was time to run him out of town. Relying on information from a former Fernie alderman, he published his own short article alongside the letter hinting darkly that Wallace had pilfered money donated for patriotic purposes. He promised to reveal details if Wallace didn't keep his nose out of the affairs of the Gladstone local union. Wallace immediately sued for libel. A couple of weeks later in apparent retaliation, Christophers and the executive of District 18 sued Wallace for $5,000 in damages for slanderous remarks he allegedly made about Christophers. The lawsuits were very much of a tit-for-tat nature; one opposed the claim of misappropriation of funds by Christophers when he was a union leader at Morrissey in 1903; the other opposed the claim that Wallace had failed to account for funds collected for the proposed purchase of the machine gun after that offer was turned down by military authorities in 1915. The *Ledger* editor announced that he looked forward with great anticipation to reporting on the legal decisions.

However, when the cases were heard in British Columbia Supreme Court in Fernie in mid-June, it was the *Free Press* editor who gleefully advised readers of the outcomes. In court, Wallace denied having made the alleged statement about Christophers, and it took a jury very little time to conclude that a slander could not be proven to have occurred. And in the Lawson suit, the former Fernie alderman upon whose information Lawson had based his published allegations refused to appear in court. Before the libel case could be heard, MLA Alexander Fisher was able to arrange a settlement which required District 18 and Lawson to pay damages of $250 as well as all court costs. In addition, Lawson agreed to print a public apology to Wallace in the *District Ledger*. There was no doubt whatsoever about who had won the contest on the legal front.[278]

The court battles may have been concluded, but the newspaper wars continued, each editor putting his own spin on the legal outcomes and continuing to spar on other matters. Wallace, unhappy with Lawson's weak public apology, actually returned to court to demand a more fulsome statement. But none of all this seemed too significant as news arrived from Paris at the end of the month. On June 28, five years to the day following the assassination of the Archduke and his wife in Sarajevo, German delegates had reluctantly signed the Treaty of Versailles.

Fernie's war was over.

PEACE DAY

But the strike was not. For the fourth year in a row, miners at Coal Creek were at the heart of a significant dispute. Sometimes pitted against their own local union, sometimes against only the Crow's Nest Pass Coal Company and sometimes against the Western Coal Operators' Association, these disputes were always complex, but none more so than that of 1919. March had brought the Western Labour Conference and contract negotiations; April more contract negotiations, the prospect of District 18 breaking with the UMWA and new labour legislation in British Columbia. Separately, each issue was complicated. Taken together, they created confusing cross-currents that quickly swept the miners and the broader communities of Fernie and Coal Creek into completely uncharted waters. District 18 was playing a part—a very significant part indeed—in the unprecedented uprising of labour that swept across especially western Canada in the summer of 1919.[279] The OBU strike was equally as controversial and pivotal in the wartime history of Fernie as the internment of 1915.

The mines at Coal Creek were still silent, but community life otherwise followed familiar patterns. July brought the annual celebration of Dominion Day. This time, the GWVA organized the sports events and the IODE provided the catering, but as an indication of changing times, a patriotic organization was not to be the designated beneficiary of any profits. These were to be devoted to improved playgrounds or perhaps even a swimming pool for the children of Fernie, who turned out in their hundreds to take part in the parade. After an absence of several years, a travelling circus placed Fernie on its circuit. Sanger's Greater European Show promised great spectacle, but according to one observer from Coal Creek, provided only "a couple of small tents, two white horses and a monkey." Another serious forest fire on Mount Fernie and Mount Proctor in mid-July caused considerable damage and destroyed at least two camps operated by the Elk Lumber Company.

The court cases resulting from the undercover police operation attracted much attention when the accused appeared before police magistrate Whimster in early July. By then, the proprietors of the Waldorf and Northern hotels had been added to the list of those charged under the British Columbia Prohibition Act. Whimster sentenced all who came before him to six months in the jail at Nelson, but, by failing to provide the option of a fine, he also created grounds for appeal. Each of the accused was released on $2,500 bail while the appeals were processed. They and their community would have to wait a little longer to see if the convictions would be sustained.[280] And in Vancouver, another undercover police operation resulted in a charge against a Russian national for disseminating seditious literature to miners in the Crowsnest Pass. The consequence of that operation, too, would not be known until fall.[281]

The highlight of July 1919, however, proved to be an event barely contemplated in June. After delays and weeks of indecision, the Peace Committee established by the British government finally decided that July 19 would be designated Peace Day throughout the British Empire. Just as Canada had followed Britain into the war, so too did the Canadian government endorse that Saturday in July to celebrate its conclusion. From coast to coast, communities hurriedly scrambled to establish programs that would do justice to the occasion. In Fernie, despite having only two weeks to prepare, the District Committee for National Reconstruction met on July 4 to begin planning for what it intended to be "the biggest celebration" ever held in the city.

Eleven subcommittees were soon at work. In a community so profoundly divided over the ongoing strike, there must have been some awkward situations, perhaps few more so than when Wallace and Lawson found themselves brought together as members of the advertising committee. A number of Italian residents were involved in various aspects of organization, but if committee membership alone is an accurate gauge, it was fundamentally the British community that was preparing to celebrate.[282] Several young women were nominated for the role of Victory Queen, a program of sports and games was announced, and residents and businesses were requested to decorate their homes and storefronts. Invitations to attend were issued as far west as Cranbrook, as far east as Blairmore and as far south as Eureka, Montana. Two dozen men were set to improving the city park grounds and race track, and it was announced that all profits from the day's program would be donated to the Soldiers' Memorial Fund.[283] To mark the occasion, the *Free Press* published a list of military engagements that had involved local volunteers and published the names of Coal Creek and Fernie men killed. The number of the war dead continued to grow, most notably with the addition of the names of three Italian reservists and seven Russian volunteers. The list still purportedly identified only men from Fernie and Coal Creek but did include a few known to have come from smaller communities to the south, while the Russians were all former residents of Hosmer.[284]

The spectacle of Peace Day. A queen is crowned, a war is ended. Fernie Museum and Archives 6086.

The Peace Day parade began at the grounds of the Central School at ten o'clock. The new Fernie detachment of the RNWMP led the procession. Accompanied by the Fernie Pipers and the newly formed Fernie Bugle Band, as many as two hundred veterans in full uniform followed.[285] The float representing Britannia and the entry celebrating the new state of Czechoslovakia were judged to be the best, with the Italian Society's float—designed by Dominic Nicoletti as a caricature of the Big Four discussions in Paris—receiving an honourable mention. Buildings and store windows all along Victoria Avenue were decorated; spectators cheered the decorated floats, automobiles and bicycles that were interspersed at intervals by the Salvation Army Band, the Italian Band and the Coal Creek Colliery Band. At the heart of the procession was Jessie Richardson, who, by virtue of having lost two brothers to the war, had easily outpolled her rivals for the title of Victory Queen.

The final destination was the Victory Arch, erected on Victoria Avenue specially for the occasion. Described as a masterpiece by the *Free Press*, the arch was inscribed with "Glorious Victory" on one supporting column and "An Honorable Peace" on the other. It also listed the names of all Fernie and Coal Creek men who had lost their lives and the battle locations in which British and Empire forces had engaged. Pressed on all sides by an excited crowd, Mayor Uphill crowned Queen Jessie beneath the arch and presented

At the Victory Arch: First Nation participation added significantly to the pageantry of Peace Day. Fernie Museum and Archives 6093.

184 — Fernie at War

her with a small box of precious stones. Following speeches by Mayor Uphill and MLA Fisher, the crowd moved on to the city park. Sports events included a scoreless draw in football between Fernie and Coal Creek and a convincing victory by a team of loggers from Waldo in the final baseball game. Generating the most excitement were the half-mile and mile horse races, both won by Indigenous competitors. Many tried their luck at games of skill that included "pasting the Kaiser" and kept the near-beer booth busy all day before attending the evening dances that were organized at two separate halls to end the celebration. Apart from the near-beer booth, catering was provided by the Rebekahs and the women's auxiliary to the GWVA, thereby giving the Mount Fernie IODE a well-deserved rest.

The event was declared the biggest gala day ever held in Fernie, although there were disappointments. Cranbrook organized its own celebration (earning that community another rebuke from Wallace), as did the several Crowsnest communities at Blairmore, where Emilio Picariello was one of the sponsors. With $2,500 in prize money awarded to a lesser number of participants than expected, the financial benefit to the Soldiers' Memorial Fund was not as significant as hoped. Nevertheless, the people who took part in the Peace Day celebrations were all looking forward to better days. Peace had been assured at Versailles—the horrors of the trenches, the death and maiming of local men in battle, the disputes about loyalty and patriotism all now safely assigned to yesterday—and less stressful times could be anticipated. And a community that was no stranger to labour disputes knew that strikes, too, had their conclusions.

At the end of a journey, it is not out of place to think again of its beginning and to reflect upon the course it has taken. No one could have imagined that fully five years would pass between the event that triggered the war and the signing of the first of the treaties to officially end it. And no one could have foreseen how difficult those years would be for the small communities of Fernie and Coal Creek. The battlefields and the mines had demanded a terrible price. In the recurrent demonstrations of ethnic and class divisions, there was much to forgive and much that the communities might prefer to forget. For those celebrating Peace Day, the Great War had become the past. The story that unfolded between June 1914 and July 1919 in the Elk Valley and in Europe could be remembered and imagined and perceived as the presumed solid ground of history. Only the uncertain terrain of the future—providing no such comfort, no such certainty—lay ahead.

AFTERWORD

Throughout recorded history, warriors have always received the applause of their civilian populations, workers have always sought to improve their living and working conditions and foreigners—typically subject to suspicions and fears—have always become particularly vulnerable during periods of conflict. Seen from that perspective, the tensions and forces at work in the Elk Valley during the years of the First World War were by no means unique. They can cynically be dismissed as unremarkable and their consequences as perhaps even predictable. Yet, from these common and ubiquitous elements emerged a wartime experience that was genuinely exceptional in very many respects.

Readers who followed this narrative to its conclusion may well remain unconvinced that Fernie can legitimately claim to have had the most remarkable history of any small city in Canada during the First World War. They are, of course, wise to reserve judgement. That is a subjective question as well as one of comparison, and, without the necessary comparisons being made, it remains unanswerable. Because so much of the community's wartime experience was determined by its coal-based economy, the claim must also fail that it might represent a microcosm of the history of communities of comparable size in Canada during the war years.

Fernie was a geographically isolated community a century ago, but it did not experience the war years in isolation. Like all towns and cities, it was subject to regional, provincial, national and international influences; events beyond the Elk Valley had a profound impact on local outlooks and actions. The military activity and the labour unrest did not spring from purely local conditions. Negative perceptions of foreigners held by the majority of the English-speaking residents of Fernie were entirely in step with views held by their peers across the country. The most dramatic events of the period—the internment of 1915 and the OBU strike of 1919—serve as reminders of the intertwined themes that underpinned everything in Fernie and Coal Creek between 1914 and 1919. Those themes, of course, were loyalty, labour and ethnicity. It was their combination—a seldom comfortable and often toxic combination—that produced such a distinct period in local history.

It goes without saying that just as the future could not be predicted in 1914, neither was it foreseeable at war's end. And regrettably, July 1919 is an artificial and unsatisfactory date at which to conclude this narrative; so many of the themes considered here simply do not end with the celebrations on Peace Day. However tempting it may be to continue, a book devoted specifically to examining Fernie during the years of the First World War cannot legitimately go beyond the summer of 1919. The bizarre suspicion that Uphill was smuggling alcohol, the emergence of the champion women's ice hockey team, the collapse of the Home Bank, the steady decline of the coal industry and the equally steady reduction in population numbers, the attempts to bridge ethnic divisions—all these and more are topics for a study of Fernie during the interwar years. I can only hope that the several abrupt thematic endings required here will suggest future lines of inquiry to curious researchers.

But perhaps a few words about the three major storylines left unresolved at the end of this narrative will be forgiven. Two of them—the issue of immigration from societies seen as foreign by established Canadian communities and the issue of government regulation or non-regulation of intoxicants—are stories still unfolding a century after the time period covered here. Of course, the same can be said about the third storyline, that of labour and capital and their interaction. Although the particular matter of the OBU is now seen as a closed chapter, it was a chapter with a long way to go after July 1919. The *District Ledger* ceased publication with its edition of August 1, 1919, defiantly declaring the issue had been "Published by District No. 1, Mining Department One Big Union." The combined efforts of the Coal Operators, the international UMWA and the federal government were soon successful in defeating the strike, but ironically, they also strengthened the political radicalism of the rank and file miners. The OBU in Fernie was far from finished, but the domination of District 18 by the Gladstone local union was. With district headquarters removed to Calgary, the *Ledger* no longer publishing and the union executive dominated by Alberta locals, the miners (and the communities of Fernie and Coal Creek with them) lost the regional influence they had sustained since 1903.

While the nation would soon emerge from the post-war depression, the coal industry and the local economy would not. Few could have understood at the time that the war years were an economic watershed for Fernie and that the prosperity enjoyed from late 1915 to late 1918 would prove to be an anomaly. The pre-war belief that Fernie was destined to become a major industrial centre found few adherents after 1919. In retrospect, the removal of the boast that Fernie was the Pittsburgh of Canada from the front page of the *Free Press* in 1915 proved prophetic. The scope and nature of the community's destiny for decades to come would be much more limited.

Perhaps a few notes about some of the major figures would also not be entirely out of place. The remarkable career in provincial politics of Thomas Uphill is now sadly little known. Uphill was first elected to the Legislature in 1920, and his record as the longest continuously serving MLA in British Columbia history still stands. William Bowser led the Conservative Party until his defeat in the election of 1924; a small community on Vancouver Island was named after him in 1918. Defeated by Uphill in the election of 1920, Alexander Fisher was named to the Supreme Court of British Columbia in 1929. By the end of 1919, the Premier Mine, located near Stewart and the border with Alaska, had made millionaires of William Wilson and fellow investors Amos Trites and Roland Wood. All three moved to Vancouver in the 1920s. Wilson was elected president of the CNPCC in 1920, and relinquished his duties as general manager to his son in 1926. Trites acquired a property near Manning Park in 1930 that was the site of a Japanese internment camp during World War Two.

Saul Bonnell returned to medical practice in Fernie after his defeat in the election of 1921 and—if I may be permitted a personal note—attended to the birth of my mother in 1922. Both Bonnell and Sherwood Herchmer tried unsuccessfully to unseat Uphill in the 1920s. Joseph Mackay was appointed administrator of mines for the state of Montana soon after war's end. John Wallace continued as editor and publisher of the *Fernie Free Press* until 1947. Former *District Ledger* and *Fernie Mail* editor Frank Newnham worked as a printer in Calgary for many years; former *District Ledger* editor Peter Lawson is rumoured to have been murdered in the United States in the 1920s. Albert "Ginger" Goodwin had a short section of the Inland Island Highway near Cumberland named after him in 1996; the road signs were controversially removed in 2001. The tragic story of Emilio Picariello has somehow acquired almost legendary status. Like so much relating to prohibition, his fate has become a morality play from which sharply differing conclusions continue to be drawn.

For the other significant individuals and collective groups in the history of Fernie during the war years, few traces remain in either memory or documents. The exceptional efforts of the Mount Fernie chapter of the IODE on behalf of the Canadian Red Cross and the more concentrated response of residents combatting the Spanish influenza are largely forgotten. Information about the individual and collective experiences of Fernie's returned soldiers

Fernie Cenotaph: At the end of the day... Columbia Basin Image Bank 0470.0049.

may now be irretrievable, but given the exceptionally high number of enlistments, a serious and sustained community effort may yet be able to gather wartime and post-war details about a good number of these men.

Where documents do survive, stories remain untold. The complicated intertwining history of the UMWA, the OBU and the Gladstone local union has not yet been examined, nor has the closely connected business history of the Crow's Nest Pass Coal Company. And of Thomas Biggs and Harry Martin, Frank Newnham and John Wallace, and others who were prominent during the war years? Only in imagination can we see Wallace talking with his next-door neighbour Saul Bonnell on Walmsley Street or gazing across Victoria Avenue from the *Free Press* office at the Miners' Union Building, where perhaps Thomas Uphill is discussing union affairs with Harry Martin or David Rees. And isn't that Lieutenant Colonel Mackay having a quick word with William Wilson, who is walking from his home on Prior Street to the coal company building on Pellatt Avenue? The Fernie Museum would surely welcome any information that might help convert imagination to historical reality.

Where they overlap, local history and local memory provide a curious blend of fact and fiction. The war dead from Fernie and Coal Creek have their memorial. Its official unveiling on May 24, 1923 in front of the courthouse—on the same grounds where the internees of June 1915 were first assembled—was accompanied by a display of patriotism that equalled any the war years had produced. Framed against the background of Trinity Mountain, the lone bareheaded soldier conveys a sense of beauty that is almost classical. The selection committee—either unaware of the sculptor's German origins or perhaps unconcerned about it—chose well.

Unlike the aggressive figures atop war memorials in Victoria and else-where, Emanuel Hahn's granite statue in Fernie conveys a sense of genu-ine sorrow at the loss of the ninety-three men whose names are recorded beneath it. The letters that spell those names are beginning to fail after the passage of nearly a century, and, like memorials across the country, the nom-inal roll records primarily the sacrifice of men of British origin. The names of the Russians from Hosmer found in the published lists of the fallen in July 1919 are not included. Nor are the names of Italian, French and Belgian reservists—also then residents of Fernie and Coal Creek—who left to die fighting with their European military units.

Nearly a century afterwards, the internees of 1915, too, have collective-ly received their commemorative plaque, placed appropriately at the former site of Fernie's long demolished skating rink near the foot of the Howland Avenue hill. As a group and individually, their voices are still largely absent from the historical record. Because a reliable list of those initially impris-oned—almost all residents of Fernie, Coal Creek, Michel and Natal—is still not found, many of their names seem increasingly likely to be lost to history.

It is perhaps a mark of how different the perspective of today's Fernie is compared to that prevailing during the First World War that the centenary of the 1917 mine disaster at Coal Creek went unremarked. However, the men killed in the explosion are acknowledged by a pillow marker at the Hill-crest Cemetery, and the British Columbia Labour Heritage Centre recently located a memorial plaque at the splendid Miners' Walk in front of Fernie City Hall.

Local author Gordon Sombrowski recalls that when he first saw the community of Fernie amidst the mountains, he was overwhelmed by its beauty. Historians are generally modest enough to recognize that few of their readers will be overwhelmed by depictions of history. In the pursuit of accuracy, historical narratives are sometimes compelled to include de-scription and analysis of interest only to the most avid reader. A chronolog-ical structure—as is presented here—can present additional challenges. But when all is said and done—as for me now it is—I can only hope that some readers will be able to agree that, regardless of the merits and deficiencies of this particular presentation or of any other, the history of Fernie possesses a fascination hard to equal and hard to ignore.

BIBLIOGRAPHY

AND A NOTE ON SOURCES LOST
AND FOUND

Any present-day attempt to decipher the history of a city—even of a
very small city during only a very brief period—must necessarily rely
on surviving records. The primary sources available to make that attempt for
Fernie during the years of the First World War are scattered widely. At the
British Columbia Archives in Victoria, I was permitted access to restricted
files of the British Columbia Provincial Police. These are particularly useful
in connection with matters pertaining to enemy aliens and prohibition. At
the Glenbow Archives in Calgary, records of the Western Canadian Coal
Operators' Association, the Crow's Nest Pass Coal Company and District
18 of the United Mine Workers of America all provide essential detail. The
Minutes of City of Fernie council meetings are useful, as are the photographs and miscellaneous holdings of the Fernie Museum. At the Library
and Archives Canada, records of the RCMP and the Department of Labour
and the surviving files of Internment Operations all contain significant information.

Secondary sources provide much detail to place Fernie's experience in
context, but very little specifically about Fernie itself. I have mentioned elsewhere that the history of the Elk Valley is left out of provincial histories of
British Columbia because it does not fit comfortably into the broad mainstream narratives. The mining history of District 18 is typically told from an
Alberta perspective which tends to ignore events and personalities west of
the Continental Divide. Unfortunately, it is also apparent that when historians of internment and ethnic relations do consider what happened in Fernie,
their explanations are confusing and often simply mistaken.

I have reluctantly depended heavily upon newspapers and particularly,
of course, those published in Fernie. I was very fortunate indeed to have the
ongoing record provided by the *Fernie Free Press*, but was also aware that its
content is selective and highly partisan. The same is certainly true of the

content of the *District Ledger*, published during the first year of the war and the last. Both newspapers had political agendas of which neither made any secret. While suspect for those agendas, the newspapers are rich in detail not found elsewhere. Issues of the *Fernie Free Press* of mid-July to mid-August 1915 are missing from the newspaper collection at the Legislative Library in Victoria and therefore are not included on the widely distributed microfilm copies taken from that collection. A great many pages of the *District Ledger* from August 1918 to February 1919 in available microfilm copies are effectively unreadable.

A comment on the absence of other source material may also be of interest. The lack of records from ethnically based organizations in the Elk Valley leaves a very considerable gap. The Minutes of the three annual conventions of District 18 held in Fernie in 1916, 1917 and 1918 are missing from the UMWA fonds at the Glenbow Archives. All others are available. Likewise, Minutes of the Gladstone local union held at the Glenbow do not include the years 1914 to 1919. None of the group photographs taken annually at District 18 conventions could be located. Records of the CNPCC relative to the internment of 1915 are not found. British Columbia Provincial Police records pertaining to the three weeks of provincial responsibility for the internment camp in June 1915 are not included in files held at the British Columbia Archives. Significant correspondence records of the British Columbia Department of the Attorney General were destroyed by fire in 1939 and more were then lost to a flood in the basement of the Legislature. Most Internment Operations files created during federal control of the camp while at Fernie and at Morrissey have been destroyed. No issues of the *Fernie Mail* of 1916 have been located. The Legislative Library has no record to confirm that copies were ever received there.

I regret the absence of such potentially rich material; I am grateful for the wealth of information that is available. Listed below are sources that have contributed to my understanding of the experience of Fernie and Coal Creek during the years of the First World War.

Newspapers

Blairmore Enterprise

British Columbia Federationist

British Columbian (New Westminster)

Calgary Daily Herald

Camp Worker (Vancouver)

Cranbrook Herald

Cumberland Islander

Daily Colonist (Victoria)

Daily News Advertiser (Vancouver)

District Ledger (Fernie)

Fernie Free Press

Ladysmith Chronicle

Lethbridge Daily Herald

Lethbridge Telegram

Morning Albertan (Calgary)

Morrissey Mention

Nanaimo Free Press

Vancouver Daily Province

Vancouver Sun

Vancouver World

Victoria Daily Times

Archival Sources

British Columbia Archives (BCA)

Provincial Police Force. GR-0445

Provincial Police Force. Superintendent. GR-0057

Provincial Police Force. Superintendent, Prohibition Files. GR-1425

Saanich Prison Farm Records. GR-0306

Premiers' Records. GR-0441

Military Service Tribunal No. 12. GR-2498

British Columbia. Sessional Papers.

Tribute to Tom Uphill. Cassette tape T3338.1

Glenbow Archives (GA)

Crowsnest Resources Limited Fonds. Crow's Nest Coal Company. M-1561

United Mine Workers of America. District 18 Fonds. M-2239

Coal Association of Canada Fonds. Western Coal Operators' Association. M-2210

Library and Archives Canada (LAC)

Department of Labour. Strikes and Lockouts. RG 27

Royal Canadian Mounted Police. RG 18

Privy Council Office. RG 2

Records of the Secretary of State. Internment Operations Branch. RG 6 H1

Soldiers of the First World War. RG 150

City of Fernie Archives (CFA)

Crow's Nest Pass Coal Company Fonds. Record of Personal Injuries. All Collieries, 1910–1916.

Minutes of Council Meetings.

Fernie Museum and Archives (FMA)

City of Fernie Police Records.

WEBSITES

Information about internment nationally and recent measures of redress: The Canadian First World War Internment Recognition Fund.

http://www.internmentcanada.ca/

Information about individual soldiers: The Canadian Great War Project.

www.canadiangreatwarproject.com

Nominal roll of the 54th Kootenay Battalion: http://54thbattalioncef.ca/

DOWNLOADABLE FILES

Nominal roll of the 225th Kootenay Battalion: http://www.mediafire.com/view/muiw84iiew62r4l/225th_Battalion.pdf

Nominal roll of the192nd Crow's Nest Pass Battalion: http://www.mediafire.com/view/n1nqwtmijqd/192nd_Battalion.pdf

BOOKS AND ARTICLES

Bercuson, David J. *Fools and Wise Men: The Rise and Fall of the One Big Union.* Toronto: McGraw-Hill Ryerson, 1978.

Bowen, Lynne. *Whoever Gives us Bread.* Vancouver: Douglas & McIntyre, 2011.

Buckley, Karen. *Danger, Death and Disaster in the Crowsnest Pass Mines 1902–1928.* Calgary: University of Calgary Press, 2004.

Campbell, Robert A. *Demon Rum or Easy Money: Government Control of Liquor in British Columbia from Prohibition to Privatization.* Ottawa: Carleton University Press, 1991.

Davies, Adriana A. *The Rise and Fall of Emilio Picariello.* Fernie, BC: Oolichan Books, 2015.

Dvorak, Grace. "Childhood Remembered: A Coal Creek Memoir." In *The Forgotten Side of the Border*, edited by Wayne Norton and Naomi Miller, 189–94. Kamloops, BC: Plateau Press, 1998.

Felske, Lorry W. "The Challenge above Ground: Surface Facilities at Crowsnest Pass Mines before the First World War." In *A World Apart: The Crowsnest Communities of Alberta and British Columbia*, edited by Wayne Norton and Tom Langford, 158–69. Kamloops, BC: Plateau Press: 2002.

Freese, Barbara. *Coal: A Human History.* New York: Penguin Books, 2004.

Hamilton, Douglas L. *Sobering Dilemma: A History of Prohibition in British Columbia.* Vancouver: Ronsdale Press, 2004.

Heron, Craig. *The Workers' Revolt in Canada, 1917–25.* Toronto: University of Toronto Press, 1998.

Hutcheson, Sydney. *Depression Stories.* Vancouver: New Star Books, 1976.

Jameson, Sheilagh S. *Chautauqua in Canada.* Calgary: Glenbow Museum, 1987.

Kealey, Gregory S. "1919: The Canadian Labour Revolt." *Labour/Le Travail* 12 (Spring 1984): 11–44.

Kordan, Bohdan S. *Enemy Aliens, Prisoners of War: Internment in Canada during the Great War.* Montreal and Kingston: McGill-Queen's University Press, 2004.

____. *No Free Man: Canada, the Great War, and the Enemy Alien Experience.* Montreal and Kingston: McGill-Queen's University Press, 2016.

Kukushkin, Vadim. *From Peasants to Labourers: Ukrainian and Belarusan Immigration from the Russian Empire to Canada.* Montreal and Kingston: McGill-Queen's University Press, 2007.

Luciuk, Lubomyr. *Canada's First National Internment Operations and the Ukrainian Canadians, 1914–1920.* Kingston: Kashtan Press, 2001.

Mayse, Susan. *Ginger: The Life and Death of Albert Goodwin.* Madeira Park, BC: Harbour Publishing, 1990.

McCormack, A. Ross. *Reformers, Rebels and Revolutionaries: The Western Canadian Radical Movement, 1896–1919.* Toronto: University of Toronto Press, 1991.

Moogk, Peter. "Uncovering the Enemy Within: British Columbians and the German Menace." *BC Studies* 182 (2014): 45–72.

Morgan, Wesley. "The One Big Union and the Crowsnest Pass." In *A World Apart: The Crowsnest Communities of Alberta and British Columbia,* edited by Wayne Norton and Tom Langford, 113–19. Kamloops, BC: Plateau Press, 2002.

Morris, Philip H. *The Canadian Patriotic Fund: A Record of its Activities from 1914 to 1919.* Ottawa: Canadian Patriotic Fund, c.1920.

Norris, John. "The Vancouver Island Coal Miners, 1912–1914: A Study of an Organizational Strike." *BC Studies* 45 (1980): 56–72.

Ramsey, Bruce. *The Noble Cause: The Story of the United Mine Workers in Western Canada.* Calgary: UMWA, 1990.

Robertson, Leslie A. *Imagining Difference: Legend, Curse, and Spectacle in a Canadian Mining Town.* Vancouver: UBC Press, 2005.

Roy, Patricia E. *Boundless Optimism: Richard McBride's British Columbia.* Vancouver: UBC Press, 2012.

Rutherdale, Robert. *Hometown Horizons: Local Responses to Canada's Great War.* Vancouver: UBC Press, 2004.

Schade, Daniel. "A Militia History of the Occupation of the Vancouver Island Coalfields, August 1913." *BC Studies* 182 (2014): 11–44.

Seager, Allen. "A Proletariat in Wild Rose Country: The Alberta Coal Miners, 1905–1945." PhD diss.: York University, 1982.

_____. "Socialists and Workers: The Western Canadian Coal Miners, 1900–21." *Labour/Le Travail* 16 (Fall 1985): 23–59.

Stonebanks, Roger. *Fighting for Dignity: The Ginger Goodwin Story.* St. John's: Canadian Committee on Labour History, 2004.

Swyripa, Frances, and John Herd Thompson. *Loyalties in Conflict: Ukrainians in Canada during the Great War.* Edmonton: Canadian Institute of Ukrainian Studies, 1983.

Vance, Jonathan F. *Death So Noble.* Vancouver: UBC Press, 1987.

ENDNOTES

A COMMUNITY GOES TO WAR

1 Although part of Ktunaxa traditional territory, the Elk Valley contained no permanent settlement. It was a site of seasonal hunting, primarily by the Tobacco Plains First Nation located near the border with Montana.

2 The *Free Press* had not yet caught up with the modern spelling of Pittsburgh. The American city added the terminal h in 1911.

3 The Slovenian-language articles were identified by the *District Ledger* as "Slavonian." The use of Italian, Polish and Slovenian strongly suggests that these languages were calculated to reach the largest non-English-speaking components of the UMWA membership in District 18.

4 *Fernie Free Press*, July 31, 1914, 4. If the reference to the Japanese sounds like a slur disguised as a compliment, it was. Anti-Asian sentiments found frequent expression in both local newspapers, and the Crow's Nest Pass Coal Company excluded Asians from employment as required by its collective agreement with District 18 of the UMWA.

5 *District Ledger*, August 8, 1914, 4; August 15, 1914, 4.

6 See their advertisements in the *Fernie Free Press*, August 21, 1914, 8.

7 The contingent included several volunteers from Hosmer and the small communities to the south of Fernie. Men from Michel and Natal would have boarded the eastbound train at Michel.

8 Both newspapers reported the departure of a dozen French reservists on September 1 and of one more on September 2. However, the *Free Press* later identified the dozen as Belgian. *The Ledger* noted the departure of four more Belgian reservists in October. See *Fernie Free Press*, September 4, 1914, 1, and May 19, 1916, 3; *District Ledger* September 5, 1914, 1, and October 17, 1914, 1.

9 The wording here is slightly adjusted for modern usage and clarity but not content. The original text is found in *Opportunities in British Columbia* (Toronto: Heaton's Provincial Booklet Series, 1915), 29.

10 *District Ledger*, September 19, 1914, 4. The band made the point that it was "composed entirely of English-speaking men" when it first formed. See *District Ledger*, November 29, 1913, 6.

11 *Fernie Free Press*, September 25, 1914, 1.

12 The term "enemy alien" typically replaced "alien enemy" in popular usage and therefore is used hereinafter.

13 The full texts of the proclamation and the public notice are found in Frances Swyripa and John Herd Thompson, *Loyalties in Conflict: Ukrainians in Canada during the Great War* (Edmonton: Canadian Institute of Ukrainian Studies, 1983), 171–74; the full text of the War Measures Act is found at http://www.cfr.org/canada/canadian-war-measures-act/p24846.

14 *District Ledger*, October 17, 1914, 1.

15 Welsby to Colin Campbell, October 6, 1914, British Columbia Archives (hereinafter BCA), Provincial Police Force, Superintendent, 1912–1922, GR-0057, box 21, file 13; *Fernie Free Press*, October 2, 1914, 1. Following the Vancouver Island coal strike of 1912–14, disrespect for the militia found frequent expression in mining communities.

16 *British Columbia Federationist*, October 16, 1914, 3.

17 BCA, Provincial Police Force, Superintendent, 1912–1922, GR-0057, box 22, file 14; *District Ledger*, October 10, 1914, 1. For assessments of Canada's internment operation during the First World War, see Bohdan S. Kordan, *No Free Man: Canada, the Great War, and the Enemy Alien Experience* (Montreal and Kingston: McGill-Queen's University Press, 2016), and *Enemy Aliens, Prisoners of War: Internment in Canada During the Great War* (Montreal and Kingston: McGill-Queen's University Press, 2004).

18 Technically, each man was arrested and then paroled after signing his undertaking. Sherwood to Colin Campbell, August 27, 1914, BCA, Provincial Police Force, Superintendent, 1912–1922, GR-0057, box 13, file 1.

19 Allen Seager, "Socialists and Workers: The Western Canadian Coal Miners, 1900–21," *Labour/Le Travail* 16 (Fall 1985): 56 (Appendix 1, Table 2).

20 The former CNPCC administration building now serves as Fernie City Hall, while the splendid courthouse still conveys that sense of grandeur.

21 Plans for a genuine workingmen's club at the Miners' Union Building were scuttled when the superintendent of provincial police in December 1909—almost certainly in response to the lobbying of local hotel owners—refused to renew the liquor licence initially issued in August for the Workingmen's Club and Institute of Fernie. A reading room was being supplied, a gymnasium worked on and beer tokens had been issued when the refusal was issued. BCA, Provincial Police Force, GR-0095, Clubs Regulation Act, Vol. 1, Correspondence, 1909–10, files 4/1 and 4/2.

22 See "Report of the Socialist Party of Canada, Fernie Branch 17 for 1915," *District Ledger*, July 25, 1915, 2. Branch 17 moved from its storefront in the Miners' Union Building to more spacious premises on Pellatt Avenue in March 1914. The address is nowhere stated, but was probably the former Roller Rink near the *Ledger* office.

23 Vadim Kukushkin, *From Peasants to Labourers: Ukrainian and Belarusan Immigration from the Russian Empire to Canada* (Montreal and Kingston: McGill-Queen's University Press, 2007), 54, 94–98.

24 Lynne Bowen, *Whoever Gives us Bread* (Vancouver: Douglas & McIntyre, 2011), 162–75.

25 Of the several immigrant communities making Fernie their home during the war years, the Chinese is the least mentioned in the historical record. The *Free Press* did report on occasional legal matters and did record contributions from Chinese individuals to fundraisers, sometimes identifying a donor by name and sometimes as simply "a Chinaman."

26 *District Ledger*, May 2, 1914, 4; May 9, 1914, 6. *Jeffries Southeast Kootenay Directory, 1914* contains remarkably few eastern European surnames at Michel and Natal and virtually none at Coal Creek, but making judgements about national origin based solely on surnames is fraught with obvious peril. For example, in 1916 one volunteer from Fernie with an apparent British surname was Russian by birth. And again, are individuals with apparent French surnames of French-Canadian, French, Belgian, Swiss or even Italian origin? A much deeper analysis than that undertaken here would be required to determine the national origins of residents of the Elk Valley during the years of the First World War.

27 *District Ledger*, September 5, 1914, 1; *Fernie Free Press*, September 18, 1914, 6. Some of these are likely the Russian nationals who did sign up with either the 54th Kootenay Battalion in 1915 or the 225th East Kootenay Battalion in 1916. See Chapters 2 and 3.

28 Eighteenth Annual Report of the Crow's Nest Pass Coal Company (1914), 5, Glenbow Archives (hereinafter GA), Crowsnest Resources Limited Fonds, Crow's Nest Coal Company, Series 3, Annual Reports, M-1561, file 21.

29 Mayor John Gates to Premier Richard McBride, December 16, 1914, BCA, Premier, GR-0441, Series V, box 166, file 2.

30 *Fernie Free Press*, November 6, 1914, 4. Often pronounced "hussif," the housewife elsewhere was called a ditty-bag, originally a term for a small pouch containing a sailor's needle, thread, thimble and other domestic items.

31 Three of the volunteers were back in Fernie by the end of September, having been declared medically unfit at Valcartier. See *District Ledger*, September 26, 1914, 1. Most commonly rejections were due to vision or hearing impairment, bad teeth or flat feet.

32 Minutes of meeting, November 9, 1914, GA, United Mine Workers of America, District 18 Fonds, Series 3, Minutes of the Executive Board, M-2239, vol. 2, Minutes 1910–1919, 157.

33 *District Ledger*, October 17, 1914, 4; December 5, 1914, 4.

34 *Fernie Free Press*, December 18, 1914, 5.

35 See John Norris, "The Vancouver Island Coal Miners, 1912–1914: A Study of an Organizational Strike," *BC Studies* 45 (1980): 56–72; Roger Stonebanks, *Fighting for Dignity: The Ginger Goodwin Story* (St. John's: Canadian Committee on Labour History, 2004), 36–54; Daniel Schade, "A Militia History of the Occupation of the Vancouver Island Coalfields, August 1913," *BC Studies* 182 (2014): 11–44.

36 Welsby to Colin Campbell, November 18, 1914, BCA, Provincial Police Force, Clubs Regulation Act, GR-0095, box 2, file 5.

THE WAR COMES TO FERNIE

37 In addition to the business office of the Gladstone local union, the Miners' Union Building housed the Grand Theatre and provided street-level rental space for two businesses. The theatre operation was leased and its entertainment bookings managed by the lessee.

38 Uphill was at the beginning of his long political career. See Robert McDonald, "'Simply a Working Man': Tom Uphill of Fernie," in *A World Apart: The Crowsnest Communities of Alberta and British Columbia*, eds. Wayne Norton and Tom Langford, (Kamloops, BC: Plateau Press, 2002), 99–112.

39 *Nineteenth Annual Report of the Crow's Nest Pass Coal Company* (1915), Address to shareholders by William Wilson, 13, GA, Crowsnest Resources Limited Fonds. Crow's Nest Coal Company, Series 3, Annual Reports. M-1561, file 21.

40 *District Ledger*, May 15, 1915, 1; May 22, 1915, 1; May 29, 1915, 1.

41 Their number would have been higher, but several prospective volunteers were rejected after medical examinations performed in Fernie. Two more were declared unfit at the coast.

42 Their names are found in the *Fernie Free Press*, March 12, 1915, 1. Two were soon back in Fernie, having been discharged for refusing to be inoculated against typhus.

43 *District Ledger*, May 22, 1915, 1; *Victoria Daily Times*, May 13, 1915, 2; W.J. Bowser to Robert Borden, June 21, 1915. Premiers' Records, Series IX, GR-0441, vol. 398, 524–26.

44 The amount approved for distribution in the whole of District 18 was $7,500. Minutes of meeting, May 25, 1915, GA, United Mine Workers of America, District 18 Fonds, Series 3, Minutes of the Executive Board, M-2239, vol. 2, Minutes 1910–1919, 166–68.

45 *Annual Report of the Minister of Mines for 1915*, BCA, British Columbia, Sessional Papers 1916, K425–26.

46 The CNPCC figures, which may include clerical and salaried staff, are derived from a report sent by the official court reporter at Fernie to the Department of Labour. See Report by Fred G. Perry, June 28, 1915, Library and Archives Canada

(hereinafter LAC), Department of Labour, Strikes and Lockouts, RG 27, vol. 304. The other figures are from the *Vancouver Daily Province* of June 8, 1915, 1. The *Lethbridge Telegram* put the number of German and Austrian employees at precisely 152. The *Lethbridge Daily Herald* agreed with that figure, its Fernie correspondent stating there were 32 Germans and 120 Austrians. See *Lethbridge Telegram*, June 10, 1915, 1; *Lethbridge Daily Herald*, June 8, 1915, 1.

47 BCA, Provincial Police Force, Superintendent, 1912–1922, GR-0057, box 22, file 4.

48 *Fernie Free Press*, May 28, 1915, 3. Germans were widely regarded as crafty and subversive. See, for example, Dorothy Livesay's short story "Mrs. Spy" in *A Winnipeg Childhood* (Winnipeg: Peguis Publishers, 1973).

49 Bohdan S. Kordan, *No Free Man*, 96–99; Minutes of special meeting, May 20, 1915, City of North Vancouver, http://www.cnv.org/your-government/council-meetings/council-meeting-minutes/council-minutes-archive; *Nanaimo Free Press*, May 14, 1915, 2.

50 *Fernie Free Press*, April 28, 1915, 1. Later renowned for bootlegging and subsequently hanged for murder, Picariello was a legitimate businessman in Fernie during the war years. See Adriana A. Davies, *The Rise and Fall of Emilio Picariello* (Fernie, BC: Oolichan Books, 2015), 19–22.

51 *Lethbridge Daily Herald*, June 8, 1915, 1.

52 The union leadership was "firmly committed to a no strike policy" for the duration of the recently signed collective agreement. See Allen Seager, "A Proletariat in Wild Rose Country: The Alberta Coal Miners, 1905–1945," (PhD diss., York University, 1982), 278–80.

53 The delegated men were Thomas Uphill, Thomas Biggs, William Phillips, Harry Martin, Nick Micisco and Sam Heany. *Lethbridge Daily Herald*, June 9, 1915, 1. Phillips would be killed in France in 1917. See Chapter 4.

54 J.D. McNiven to Deputy Minister of Labour, June 23, 1915, LAC, Royal Canadian Mounted Police, RG 18, vol. 490, file 433–1915. The wording was reported differently in the *Lethbridge Daily Herald*, June 9, 1915, 1. The *Herald* had it as: "Resolved, that the men as Britishers, and others who are friendly, are willing and will work, but not under present conditions, that is, not with alien enemies."

55 Patricia E. Roy, *Boundless Optimism: Richard McBride's British Columbia*, (Vancouver: UBC Press, 2012), 270.

56 *Ladysmith Chronicle*, May 26, 1915, 1; *Victoria Daily Colonist*, May 26, 1915, 6.

57 Reports of Constable George Allen, May and June 1915; Report of Constable Alex Mustart, May 1915, BCA, Provincial Police Force, GR-0445, box 24, file 4. On May 27, an explosion at the Western Fuel Company mine in Nanaimo claimed the lives of twenty-two men. Judging by the names of the deceased, it is quite possible that at least a couple of them escaped internment on May 28 by being killed on May 27. See the *Victoria Daily Colonist*, May 27, 1915, 1.

58 Prison records nearly agree with the figures cited in newspapers: fifty-one prisoners under military guard were received at Saanich on May 28. BCA, Saanich
Prison Farm Records, GR-0306, vol. 1, 550.

59 *Nanaimo Free Press*, May 28, 1915, 1, and June 1, 1915, 1.

60 *Cumberland Islander*, June 5, 1915, 8; Report of Robert Mills, June 1915, BCA,
Provincial Police Force, GR-0445, box 21, file 7.

61 Report of Joseph Boardman, June 1915, BCA, Provincial Police Force, GR-0445,
box 21, file 2; Report of John English, June 1915, BCA, Provincial Police Force,
GR-0445, box 23, file 13.

62 J.D. McNiven to Deputy Minister of Labour, June 23, 1915, LAC, Royal Canadian Mounted Police, RG 18, vol. 490, file 433-1915.

63 *Fernie Free Press*, August 20, 1915, 1.

64 BCA, Provincial Police Force, GR-0445, box 21, file 13; W.J. Bowser to Robert
Borden, June 16, 1915. Premiers' Records, Series IX, GR-0441, vol. 398, 514.
The curling rink located adjacent to the skating rink was not part of this arrange-
ment.

65 BCA, Provincial Police Force, GR-0445, box 21, file 2; *Fernie Free Press*, June 11,
1915, 1.

66 BCA, Provincial Police Force, GR-0445, box 21, file 5; *Lethbridge Daily Herald*, June
14, 1915, 1 and 3.

67 BCA, Provincial Police Force, GR-0445, box 23, file 13; box 24, file 6; *Cranbrook
Herald*, June 17, 1915, 4.

68 The czar had decreed in April that Russian nationals could join Allied armies,
but enlisting in Canadian forces was made legitimate only on June 5. See Kukushkin, *From Peasants to Labourers*, 132. In the successful recruitment drive for the 54th
Kootenay Battalion in May and June 1915, more than a dozen eastern European
names appear in the lists of recruits. See *Fernie Free Press*, June 4, 1915, 1, and July
9, 1915, 4. They seem to have joined as a group during the week ending June 4.
Theirs are the only eastern European surnames listed with the approximately 350
British names of local men then in active service. Five of those names appear on
lists of men of the 54th who saw service overseas, and all five identify their next
of kin as residing in Grodno province, then a territory in western Russia. They
were therefore probably Belarusans or perhaps Poles or eastern Ukrainians, but of
course were categorized at the time as Russian nationals.

69 *Vancouver Sun*, June 12, 1915, 4.

70 *Vancouver World*, June 10, 1915, 6; *Daily News Advertiser* (Vancouver), June 9, 1915,
4. Throughout June, while the newspapers focussed upon the patriotic motivation of the miners, Bowser continued to address the problem presented by
the province's "over-abundance of labourers." He wrote to railway officials and
prairie politicians attempting to secure special rates for labourers wanting to

seek employment in Saskatchewan and Alberta. BCA. Premier. GR-0441, box 166, file 3.

71 Minutes of meeting, September 13, 1915, GA, Crowsnest Resources Limited Fonds, Crow's Nest Coal Company, Series 1, Minutes, Directors' Meetings, M-1561, vol. 9, Minute Book, 262.

72 BCA, Provincial Police Force, Superintendent, 1912–1922, GR-0057, box 22, file 2 and file 14; Provincial Police Force, GR-0445, box 21, file 5 and file 10; *Cranbrook Herald,* June 24, 1915, 4.

73 *Fernie Free Press,* June 11, 1915, 1; *Lethbridge Daily Herald,* June 15, 1915, 1; *District Ledger,* June 19, 1915, 1; July 10, 1915, 1; *Victoria Daily Times,* June 19, 1915, 7; J.D. McNiven to Deputy Minister of Labour, June 23, 1915, LAC, Royal Canadian Mounted Police, RG 18, vol. 490, file 433-1915.

74 W.J. Bowser to Robert Borden, June 16, 1915; W.J. Bowser to G.H. Barnard, June 14, 1915. BCA, Premiers' Records, Series IX, GR-0441, vol. 398, 504–7, 514.

75 *Nanaimo Free Press,* June 18, 1915, 2; *Lethbridge Daily Herald,* June 17, 1915, 1. The surnames were also spelled in newspaper reports as Janasten and Bovroski. The name Martin Brobovski is found in CNPCC personnel records. Employee Records, GA, Crowsnest Resources Limited Fonds, Crow's Nest Coal Company, Series 9, M-1561, file 282. Stephan Janastin was a lamp man at Coal Creek. Crow's Nest Pass Coal Company Fonds, Record of Personal Injuries – All Collieries, 1910–1916, City of Fernie Archives.

76 It can only be speculatively stated, but the rifles used by the guards may have been those confiscated by Welsby from enemy aliens the previous year. Monthly reports by regional provincial police officers list only pistols in their possession, while five confiscated rifles were held by Welsby. See Welsby to Colin Campbell, December 23, 1914, BCA, Provincial Police Force, Superintendent, 1912–1922, GR-0057, box 25, file 6.

77 *District Ledger,* June 19, 1915, 1; *Lethbridge Daily Herald,* June 21, 1915, 4.

78 LAC, RG 2, Privy Council Office, Series A-1-a. The full text of the order-in-council is found in Frances Swyripa and John Herd Thompson, *Loyalties in Conflict,* 177–78. Appearing for Macredy, Vancouver lawyer Clarence Darling attended all court dates in Victoria. See *District Ledger,* July 24, 1915, 4 and *Victoria Daily Times,* June 28, 1915, 12.

79 That the absence of governmental response permitted a quick resolution of the Hillcrest strike is made clear by the reports submitted by J.D. McNiven to the Deputy Minister of Labour. LAC, Royal Canadian Mounted Police, RG 18, vol. 490, file 433-1915.

80 Report by Fred G. Perry, June 28, 1915, LAC, Department of Labour, Strikes and Lockouts, RG 27, vol. 304.

81 *Fernie Free Press,* July 16, 1915, 1; July 30, 1915, 3; August 6, 1915, 3.

82 Mackay to Otter, May 23, 1916, LAC, Records of the Secretary of State, Internment Operations Branch, RG 6 H1, vol. 754, file 3219.

83 J.D. McNiven to Deputy Minister of Labour, June 29, 1915, LAC, Royal Canadian Mounted Police, RG 18, vol. 490, file 433-1915.

84 *District Ledger*, July 3, 1915, 1. This suggests the number of internees on June 29, the date of the handover of responsibility to Internment Operations, was approximately 330 (inclusive of the Czechs and others released on June 30). The present author has been unable to locate either a roster of prisoners held by provincial police or of those transferred to federal custody. The names of some men held at the skating rink are found in Bohdan S. Kordan, *Enemy Aliens, Prisoners of War*, Appendix, Prisoners' Rolls: Morrissey, 190–95. They are also found in Lubomyr Luciuk, *Roll Call: Lest we Forget*, (Kingston: Kashtan Press, 1999), and found at http://www.uccla.ca/Roll_Call_2000.pdf. The names of the few German prisoners are not included. Those with identification numbers under approximately 330 were in custody at the time of transfer to Internment Operations.

85 Bohdan S. Kordan, *No Free Man*, 132–33.

86 *Fernie Free Press*, July 9, 1915, 3; September 24, 1915, 3.

87 *British Columbia Federationist*, June 25, 1915, 2; *District Ledger*, July 10, 1915, 1.

88 *Fernie Free Press*, July 16, 1915, 1; July 30, 1915, 1; August 13, 1915, 1.

89 The figure provided is for the month of May 1915. See Philip H. Morris, *The Canadian Patriotic Fund: A Record of its Activities from 1914 to 1919* (Ottawa: Canadian Patriotic Fund, c.1920), 32.

90 *Lethbridge Daily Herald*, August 5, 1915, 1 and 4.

91 *Lethbridge Daily Herald*, August 20, 1915, 1 and 5. The Italian reservists' names are found in the *Free Press*, August 20, 1915, 1 and September 10, 1915, 1.

92 *Fernie Free Press*, July 16, 1915, 1. Back in Victoria, Ridgeway Wilson was soon supervising the final touches to the building for which he is most remembered, the Bay Street Armoury, which opened in November 1915.

93 List of Credit Balances due Escaped Prisoners of War, November 19, 1920, LAC, Records of the Secretary of State, Internment Operations Branch, RG 6 H1, vol. 819, file 1995.

94 GA, Crowsnest Resources Limited Fonds, Crow's Nest Coal Company, Series 9, Employee Records, M-1561, file 325, January to November 1915.

95 In October the Coal Creek mines worked 17.5 days. *Annual Report of the Minister of Mines for 1915*, BCA, British Columbia, Sessional Papers 1916, K 425.

96 *Nineteenth Annual Report of the Crow's Nest Pass Coal Company (1915)*, 9, GA, Crowsnest Resources Limited Fonds, Crow's Nest Coal Company, Series 3, Annual Reports, M-1561, file 21.

97 Included in that figure were costs of approximately $2,400 incurred by the provincial police. BCA, Provincial Police Force, GR-0057, box 22, file 2.

98 *Auditor General's Report 1915–1916: Internment Operations,* Canada, Sessional Paper No. 1 (1917), ZZ-19–20.

99 BCA, Provincial Police Force, Superintendent, 1912–1922, GR-0057, box 22, file 3.

100 *Fernie Free Press,* December 24, 1915, 1.

101 The national organization reported these percentages were applied to incomes under and over $100 on a monthly basis. See Morris, *The Canadian Patriotic Fund,* 102.

102 *Fernie Free Press,* October 29, 1915, 1.

103 *Cranbrook Herald,* November 25, 1915, 3; Peter Moogk, "Uncovering the Enemy Within: British Columbians and the German Menace," *BC Studies* 182 (2014: 59.

POLITICS AND PROHIBITION

104 Lorry W. Felske, "The Challenge above Ground: Surface Facilities at Crowsnest Pass Mines before the First World War," in *A World Apart: The Crowsnest Communities of Alberta and British Columbia,* eds. Wayne Norton and Tom Langford, (Kamloops, BC: Plateau Press, 2002), 161.

105 *Daily News Advertiser* (Vancouver), June 27, 1915, 9.

106 *Blairmore Enterprise,* March 3, 1916, 1.

107 *Fernie Free Press,* March 3, 1916, 1; Sandra Sauer Ratch, "'Do Your Little Bit': The 143rd Battalion Canadian Expeditionary Force, 'BC Bantams,'" *BC Studies* 182 (2014): 151–76.

108 Herchmer to Bowser, May 15, 1916; Bowser to Herchmer, May 20, 1916, BCA, Premiers' Papers, GR-0441, box 173, file 1.

109 Minutes of meeting, September 11, 1916, GA, Crowsnest Resources Limited Fonds, Crow's Nest Coal Company, Series 1, Minutes, Directors' Meetings, M-1561, vol. 9, Minute Book, 287.

110 James Mason to Otter, May 12, 1916; Elias Rogers to Otter, May 12, 1916, LAC, Records of the Secretary of State, Internment Operations Branch, RG 6 H1, vol. 754, file 3219.

111 Captain Shaw to Otter, June 7 and 8, 1916, LAC, Records of the Secretary of State, Internment Operations Branch, RG 6 H1, vol. 754, file 3219.

112 See *Lethbridge Daily Herald,* June 3, 1916, 1.

113 Otter to A. McNeil, May 22, 1916, LAC, Records of the Secretary of State, Internment Operations Branch, RG 6 H1, vol. 754, file 3219.

114 Circular issued July 24, 1916 by A.P. Sherwood, BCA, Provincial Police Force, Superintendent, 1912–1922, GR-0057, box 7, file 4.

115 Minutes of meeting, September 11, 1916, GA, Crowsnest Resources Limited Fonds, Crow's Nest Coal Company, Series 1, Minutes, Directors' Meetings, M-1561, vol. 9, Minute Book, 292.

116 Memorandum July 31, 1916, LAC, Records of the Secretary of State, Internment Operations Branch, RG 6, H 1, vol. 754, file 3219; BCA, Provincial Police Force, Superintendent 1912–1922, GR-0057, box 17, file 3.

117 *Nanaimo Free Press*, September 12, 1916, 1; September 26, 1916, 1; *Fernie Free Press*, September 22, 1916, 1.

118 Minutes of meeting, January 8, 1917, GA, Coal Association of Canada Fonds, Series 2, Minutes, Western Coal Operators' Association, Minute Book 1916–17, M-2210, File 3. The document states nine hundred had enlisted from "one colliery." That could mean from Coal Creek alone, but could also be a combination of figures for both the Coal Creek and Michel mines.

119 Minutes of meeting, September 11, 1916, GA, Crowsnest Resources Limited Fonds, Crow's Nest Coal Company, Series 1, Minutes, Directors' Meetings, M-1561, vol. 9, Minute Book, 288.

120 *Morrissey Mention*, September 16, 1916, 2. The editorial by editor Private Randolph Stuart could not have been published without the approval of Major Shaw, the internment camp commander.

121 Stonebanks, *Fighting for Dignity*, 25–29; *District Ledger*, March 14, 1914, 1.

122 Susan Mayse, *Ginger: The Life and Death of Albert Goodwin* (Madeira Park, BC: Harbour Publishing, 1990), 89; *Fernie Free Press*, February 25, 1916, 1.

123 Goodwin to Bowser, March 6, 1916; Bowser to Goodwin March 13, 1916, BCA, Premier, GR-0441, box 171, file 3.

124 A complete list of Fernie Conservative Association members is found in *Fernie Free Press*, July 14, 1916, 1.

125 *Fernie Free Press*, June 2, 1916, 1 and 6.

126 The *Vancouver Daily Province* indicated Uphill's election bid was endorsed by the UMWA, and, in an interview with CBC Radio in 1963, former Coal Creek miner Bill Hunter stated "the union" asked Uphill to run as a Conservative (BCA, Accession No: T3338.1, "Tribute to Tom Uphill" cassette tape). However, this support was of an informal nature; neither Uphill nor local Conservatives ever claimed his candidacy was endorsed by the union.

127 *Fernie Free Press*, June 30, 1916, 2.

128 Minutes of meeting, February 27, 1916, GA, United Mine Workers of America, District 18 Fond, Series 3, Minutes of the Executive Board, M-2239, vol. 2, Minutes 1910–1919, 180.

129 *Fernie Free Press*, September 8, 1916, 2; June 7, 1918, 4.

130 BCA, Accession No: T3338.1, "Tribute to Tom Uphill" cassette tape.

131 *Fernie Free Press*, September 22, 1916, 1. Final results from each local community for the election and for both plebiscites are found here.

132 Night letters, March 19–21, 1916, BCA, Premier, GR-0441, Series VI, box 169, file 2.

133 Norman Knowles, "'A Manly, Commonsense Religion': Revivalism and the Kootenay Campaign of 1909 in the Crowsnest Pass," in *A World Apart: The Crowsnest Communities of Alberta and British Columbia*, eds. Wayne Norton and Tom Langford, (Kamloops, BC: Plateau Press, 2002), 9.

134 Douglas L. Hamilton, *Sobering Dilemma: A History of Prohibition in British Columbia* (Vancouver: Ronsdale Press, 2004), 111.

135 *Fernie Free Press*, October 27, 1916, 5.

136 *Fernie Free Press*, November 3, 1916, 2. The printing press at the *Ledger* office did not immediately fall silent with the last issue of the *Fernie Mail*. Through an arrangement with either Newnham or District 18, the *Morrissey Mention*, the fundraising newspaper of the 107th Kootenay Regiment in charge of the Morrissey internment camp, was printed there from mid-September until its final edition of January 6, 1917.

137 *Blairmore Enterprise*, September 15, 1916, 4 and 8. Provincial prohibition legislation was constitutionally unable to ban cross-border sales of liquor. In early November, the Pollock Wine Company ceased its Blairmore advertising.

138 Minutes of Council Meeting, September 21, 1916, City of Fernie Archives.

139 *Fernie Free Press*, July 21, 1916, 1. The Presbyterians voted ninety-one to nil, and the Methodists eighty to five.

140 Welsby to Colin Campbell, December 5, 1916, BCA, Provincial Police Force, Superintendent, 1912–1922, GR-0057, box 11, file 16. The names of donors and the amounts donated are found here.

141 Morris, *The Canadian Patriotic Fund*, 23.

142 Full figures for disbursements to families in the Fernie district for 1916 are found in *Fernie Free Press*, January 26, 1917, 1. The shortfall was not unique to the Fernie district. Over the course of the war, both British Columbia and Alberta relied heavily on surplus funds raised by the Canadian Patriotic Fund in Ontario and Quebec.

143 *Fernie Free Press*, February 25, 1916, 1. Wallace gave full credit for the turnaround to William Wilson for taking command when inexperienced and incompetent officials had brought the company to "the verge of ruin." See *Fernie Free Press*, March 3, 1916, 2.

144 *Lethbridge Daily Herald*, August 5, 1916, 1.

145 Minutes of meeting, November 16, 1916, GA, Coal Association of Canada Fonds, Series 2, Minutes, Western Coal Operators' Association, Minute Book 1916–17, M-2210, File 3.

146 Minutes of meeting, July 29, 1916, GA, Coal Association of Canada Fonds, Series 2, Minutes, Western Coal Operators' Association, Minute Book 1916–17, M-2210, File 3.

147 *Annual Report of the Minister of Mines for 1916*, BCA, British Columbia, Sessional Papers 1917, K 412. The names of those killed are found in the *Calgary Daily Herald*, August 9, 1916, 1.

148 *Fernie Free Press*, November 10, 1916, 1.

149 Minutes of meeting, November 16, 1916, GA, Coal Association of Canada Fonds, Series 2, Minutes, Western Coal Operators' Association, Minute Book 1916–17, M-2210, file 3; *Lethbridge Daily Herald*, November 17, 1916, 1.

150 Minutes of meeting, December 14, 1916, GA, Crowsnest Resources Limited Fonds, Crow's Nest Coal Company, Series 1, Minutes, Directors' Meetings, M-1561, vol. 9, Minute Book, 301.

151 Minutes of meeting, December 8, 1916, GA, Coal Association of Canada Fonds, Series 2, Minutes, Western Coal Operators' Association, Minute Book 1916–17, M-2210, File 3.

152 *Fernie Free Press*, December 22, 1916, 1.

LABOUR, LOYALTY AND MORAL REFORM

153 Report of Constable Charles Kerr, February 1917, BCA, Provincial Police Force, GR-0445, box 37, file 4.

154 *Cranbrook Herald*, March 22, 1917, 2; *Fernie Free Press*, March 23, 1917, 1; March 30, 1917, 2.

155 City of Fernie Police Records, Fernie Museum and Archives.

156 Minutes of Council Meeting, April 5, 1917, City of Fernie Archives; *Fernie Free Press*, April 6, 1917, 1.

157 Davies, *The Rise and Fall of Emilio Picariello*, 20; *Fernie Free Press*, March 2, 1917, 5.

158 *Fernie Free Press*, February 16, 1917, 2–4. The Red Cross committee at Coal Creek was inactive after the middle of 1916.

159 *Fernie Free Press*, January 19, 1917, 5. Mackay was apparently not content with that assessment. After another examination in April, Medical Officer Douglas Corsan declared him fit to serve with the Canadian Overseas Expeditionary Force. LAC, Soldiers of the First World War, RG 150, Accession 1992–93/166, box 4930–35.

160 *District Ledger*, February 28, 1919, 7. The date of his death is unrecorded. See http://www.canadiangreatwarproject.com/searches/soldierDetail.asp?ID=147776.

161 *Auditor General's Report 1916–1917: Internment Operations,* Canada, Sessional Paper No. 1 (1918), ZZ—29–30. The Trites-Wood Company also provided clothing to the camp at Mara Lake and, rather bizarrely, ninety-five dollars' worth of sundry small supplies to the Amherst internment camp in Nova Scotia. See Sessional Paper No. 1 (1918), ZZ—14 and 28.

162 Memorandum for Attorney-General by Deputy Attorney-General, February 7, 1917, BCA, Provincial Police Force, Superintendent, 1912–1922, GR-0057, box 22, file 1.

163 Allen Seager, "A Proletariat in Wild Rose Country: The Alberta Coal Miners, 1905–1945," (PhD diss., York University, 1982), 286–87.

164 Minutes of meetings, January 8 and January 12, 1917, GA, Coal Association of Canada Fonds, Series 2, Minutes, Western Coal Operators' Association, Minute Book 1916–17, M-2210, file 3. The full text of the letter to Crothers was made public and is found in *Fernie Free Press,* January 26, 1917, 1 and 6.

165 *Calgary Herald,* January 6, 1917, 1. His remarks were consistent with long-held views on war and the working class. See Bruce Ramsey, *The Noble Cause* (Calgary: UMWA, 1990), 105.

166 Welsby to Colin Campbell, January 19, 1917, BCA, Provincial Police Force, Superintendent, 1912–1922, GR-0057, box 2, file 9.

167 Minutes of meeting, February 3, 1917, GA, Coal Association of Canada Fonds, Series 2, Minutes, Western Coal Operators' Association, Minute Book 1916–17, M-2210, file 3. See also *Lethbridge Herald,* February 4, 1917, 1 and 6.

168 Minutes of meeting, February 9, 1917, GA, Coal Association of Canada Fonds, Series 2, Minutes, Western Coal Operators' Association, Minute Book 1916–17, M-2210, file 3; *Fernie Free Press,* February 9, 1917, 1.

169 Sydney Hutcheson, *Depression Stories* (Vancouver: New Star Books, 1976), 14.

170 Address to shareholders by Elias Rogers, April 13, 1917. *Twentieth Annual Report of the Crow's Nest Pass Coal Company (1916),* 9, GA, Crowsnest Resources Limited Fonds, Crow's Nest Coal Company, Series 3, Annual Reports, M-1561, file 21.

171 H.A. Wilkes to Attorney General, April 5, 1917, BCA, Provincial Police Force, Superintendent 1912–1922, GR-0057, box 28, file 4.

172 Welsby to Colin Campbell, April 7, 1917, BCA, Provincial Police Force, Superintendent 1912–1922, GR-0057, box 28, file 4. The names of those killed are found here and in *Fernie Free Press,* April 13, 1917, 1.

173 For an analysis of community responses to mine disasters, see Karen Buckley, *Danger, Death and Disaster in the Crowsnest Pass Mines 1902–1928* (Calgary: University of Calgary Press, 2004), 96–113.

174 *Fernie Free Press,* April 27, 1917, 1, 4 and 8.

175 *Calgary Herald,* May 7, 1917, 1; *Fernie Free Press,* May 11, 1917, 1; *Morning Albertan* (Calgary), May 16, 1917, 1.

176 *Calgary Herald*, May 26, 1917, 11; *Morning Albertan* (Calgary), May 28, 1917, 1.

177 *Fernie Free Press*, June 1, 1917, 1.

178 Reports of Chief Constable George Welsby, May and June 1917, BCA, Provincial Police Force, GR-0445, box 37, file 12.

179 *Fernie Free Press*, June 22, 1917, 1.

180 As commissioner, Armstrong would receive a salary of $3,600 annually and $15 per diem. *Auditor General's Report 1918–1919: Labour Department*, Canada, Sessional Paper No. 1 (1920), ZZ—38.

181 W.H. McNeill to H.P. Hill, July 6, 1917, GA, Coal Association of Canada Fonds, Series 6, General Business, Western Coal Operators' Association, W.H. Armstrong, Director of Coal Operations, 1917–1921, M-2210, file 80.

182 Report by Fred G. Perry, July 1917, LAC, Department of Labour, Strikes and Lockouts, RG 27, vol. 305. Perry was the official court reporter in Fernie and, by mid-1917, was also serving as secretary to Armstrong in the Commission on Cost of Living in District 18.

183 Sheilagh S. Jameson, *Chautauqua in Canada* (Calgary: Glenbow Museum, 1987), 24–32.

184 *Fernie Free Press*, September 21, 1917, 1.

185 Morris, *The Canadian Patriotic Fund*, 26, 96–97.

186 *Fernie Free Press*, May 12, 1917, 1; October 12, 1917, 1; November 9, 1917, 3.

187 *Fernie Free Press*, June 8, 1917, 5.

188 Report of Chief Constable George Welsby, October 1917, BCA, Provincial Police Force, GR-0445, box 37, file 12; Minutes of Council Meeting, October 11, 1917, City of Fernie Archives.

189 Douglas L. Hamilton, *Sobering Dilemma: A History of Prohibition in British Columbia* (Vancouver: Ronsdale Press, 2004), 112. Robert A. Campbell, *Demon Rum or Easy Money: Government Control of Liquor in British Columbia from Prohibition to Privatization* (Ottawa: Carleton University Press, 1991), 22–23.

190 *Fernie Free Press*, August 31, 1917, 1.

191 Report of Chief Constable George Welsby, September 1917, BCA, Provincial Police Force, GR-0445, box 37, file 12.

192 *Fernie Free Press*, October 12, 1917, 1; December 14, 1917, 1. Perhaps coincidentally, for financial or political reasons or perhaps somehow in anticipation of prohibition, the Gladstone local union resumed active management of the Grand Theatre in July. Only speculation is possible as union records from the war years have not been located. Miner Frank Brindley is named as manager of the Grand for 1918 and Harry Martin for 1919 in *Wrigley's British Columbia Directories*.

193 Thomas Uphill would later characterize such brews as simply "spoiling good water."

194 *Fernie Free Press*, November 30, 1917, 6.

195 *Fernie Free Press*, November 23, 1917, 1. Wallace couldn't help but note at the end of the drive that Cranbrook District raised only $206,150. See *Fernie Free Press*, December 14, 1917, 5.

196 *Lethbridge Herald*, November 15, 1917, 1.

197 *British Columbia Federationist*, November 9, 1917, 9.

198 *Fernie Free Press*, December 7, 1917, 5.

199 *Lethbridge Herald*, December 14, 1917, 1.

200 *Fernie Free Press*, March 8, 1918, 1. Soldiers voting in Europe could only mark their ballots for Government or for Opposition. It was left to election officials to decide how and where to distribute the Opposition vote.

201 Address to shareholders by Elias Rogers, April 13, 1917. *Twentieth Annual Report of the Crow's Nest Pass Coal Company (1916)*, 13, GA, Crowsnest Resources Limited Fonds, Crow's Nest Coal Company, Series 3, Annual Reports, M-1561, file 21.

202 Report of Chief Constable George Welsby, December 1917, BCA, Provincial Police Force, GR-0445, box 37, file 12.

OLD PROBLEMS, NEW POLITICS

203 *Fernie Free Press*, March 22, 1918, 1.

204 One individual caught during the push to enforce liquor laws was Mike Bobrovski, who was fined $100 for bootlegging. He may well have been the same Martin Bobrovski in whose name the legal challenge to internment was initiated in 1915. See *Fernie Free Press*, February 22, 1918, 1.

205 *District Ledger*, April 4, 1919, 1.

206 Biggs to Armstrong, February 27, 1918, cited in *Lethbridge Daily Herald*, March 1, 1918, 1.

207 Minutes of meeting, December 11, 1917, GA, United Mine Workers of America, District 18 Fonds, Series 3, Minutes of the Executive Board, M-2239, vol. 2, Minutes 1910–1919, 240; *Lethbridge Daily Herald*, February 27, 1918, 1.

208 *Blairmore Enterprise*, January 25, 1918, 8; February 1, 1918, 5.

209 Report of Acting Chief Constable Owen, April 1918, BCA, Provincial Police Force, GR-0445, box 44, file 18; Report of Constable Boardman, April 1918, GR-0445, box 44, file 4; Report of Constable Gorman, April 1918, GR-0445, box 44, file 15.

210 Report of Inspector and Acting Chief Constable W. Owen, May 1918, BCA, Provincial Police Force, GR-0445, box 44, file 18; *Lethbridge Daily Herald*, May 25,

1918, 1. In October, adding insult to injury, Fernie City Council insisted Brown hand over five dollars in dog licence fees allegedly collected before his dismissal. See Minutes of Council Meeting, October 10, 1918, City of Fernie Archives.

211 BCA, Provincial Police Force, Superintendent 1912–1922, GR-0057, box 7, file 7.

212 *Fernie Free Press*, March 22, 1918, 1. It is not clear if the local union at Michel–Natal followed the example of the Gladstone local union.

213 Seventh Annual Report of Mount Fernie Chapter IODE, *Fernie Free Press*, February 14, 1919, 1.

214 Minute Book of the Clerk of the Court of Appeal, 14, BCA, Military Service Tribunal No. 12, GR-2498, file 1.

215 *Fernie Free Press*, April 19, 1918, 5; April 26, 1918, 5.

216 *Fernie Free Press*, July 12, 1918, 1; August 2, 1918, 1; November 22, 1918, 1.

217 *Fernie Free Press*, July 19, 1918, 5.

218 Stonebanks, *Fighting for Dignity*, 28–29. The full story of Albert "Ginger" Goodwin, his opposition to the war and the controversy still surrounding his death is found here.

219 *Lethbridge Daily Herald*, August 13, 1918, 1. The membership figure was stated by Harry Martin in a letter to minister of lands Thomas "Duff" Pattullo. See *Fernie Free Press*, August 2, 1918, 4.

220 Wilson had travelled to Stewart to assess mining properties adjacent to one he owned with Trites, Wood and A.K. Neill of Spokane. Impressed by what he saw, he advised acquisition. The staggering quantities of gold and silver subsequently extracted quickly made the Premier Mine world-famous.

221 Address to shareholders by Elias Rogers, *Twenty-second Annual Report of the Crow's Nest Pass Coal Company (1918)*, 8, GA, Crowsnest Resources Limited Fonds, Crow's Nest Coal Company, Series 3, Annual Reports, M-1561, file 21.

222 *Victoria Daily Times*, September 21, 1918, 13.

223 Report by Fred G. Perry, October 1918, LAC, Department of Labour, Strikes and Lockouts, RG 27, vol. 307.

224 *Victoria Daily Times*, September 26, 1918, 9.

225 *District Ledger*, October 3, 1918, 4.

226 Minutes of meeting, October 30, 1918, GA, United Mine Workers of America, District 18 Fonds, Series 3, Minutes of the Executive Board, M-2239, vol. 2, Minutes 1910–1919, 267; *Fernie Free Press*, October 25, 1918, 5. After being in effect for just one month, the ban was lifted a few days after the armistice was signed.

227 *Lethbridge Daily Herald*, December 12, 1918, 1.

228 *Fernie Free Press*, September 27, 1918, 4.

229 W. J. Claridge to Major Jukes, September 13, 1918; W. Owen to William Mc-Mynn, September 23, 1918, BCA, Provincial Police Force, Superintendent 1912–1922, GR-0057, box 12, file 5.

230 The full text of the orders-in-council and the regulations accompanying them are found in Frances Swyripa and John Herd Thompson, *Loyalties in Conflict*, 190–96.

231 *District Ledger*, October 24, 1918, 1.

232 *Fernie Free Press*, August 23, 1918, 2.

233 *District Ledger*, October 24, 1918, 4.

234 City of Fernie Police Records, December 1918, Fernie Museum and Archives; *Fernie Free Press*, December 13, 1918, 5.

235 Report of Inspector W. Owen, October 1918, BCA, Provincial Police Force, GR-0445, box 44, file 18; *Fernie Free Press*, October 25, 1918, 1.

236 *Fernie Free Press*, November 8, 1918, 1 and 6. The use of these languages in this context strongly suggests that Italians and Poles were Fernie's largest non-English-speaking communities in 1918.

237 *Fernie Free Press*, November 15, 1918, 1. Interestingly, mention of both the Italian Band and the Coal Creek Colliery Band is absent from reports of social events in the *Free Press* in 1918.

238 *Twenty-third Report of the Board of Health*, British Columbia, Sessional Papers 1920, vol. 1, B46.

239 *Auditor General's Report 1917–1918: Internment Operations*, Canada, Sessional Paper No. 1 (1919), ZZ—21–23: *Auditor General's Report 1918–1919: Internment Operations*, Canada, Sessional Paper No. 1 (1920), ZZ—22–23.

240 *District Ledger*, November 21, 1918, 1.

241 Reports of Inspector W. Owen, June to December 1918, BCA, Provincial Police Force, GR-0445, box 44, file 18; City of Fernie Police Records 1918, Fernie Museum and Archives.

242 Report of Constable Boardman, October 1918, BCA, Provincial Police Force, GR-0445, box 44, file 4; Report of Constable Gorman, October 1918, and Reports of Inspector W. Owen, October and November 1918, BCA, Provincial Police Force, GR-0445, box 44, file 15.

243 *Lethbridge Daily Herald*, January 10, 1919, 7.

244 *Auditor General's Report 1916–1917: Internment Operations*, Canada, Sessional Paper No. 1 (1918), ZZ—29; *Auditor General's Report 1918–1919: Internment Operations*, Canada, Sessional Paper No. 1 (1920), ZZ—22.

A Community at Peace?

245 S.S Taylor to E.K. Stewart, December 31, 1918, cited in *Fernie Free Press*, January 10, 1919, 4.

246 Minutes of Council Meeting, February 27, 1919, City of Fernie Archives.

247 David J. Bercuson, *Fools and Wise Men: The Rise and Fall of the One Big Union* (Toronto: McGraw-Hill Ryerson, 1978), 79.

248 The convention was reported on extensively by the *Lethbridge Daily Herald*, February 17–27, 1919.

249 *District Ledger*, March 7, 1919, 1 and 5; March 14, 1919, 5. *Fernie Free Press*, March 14, 1919, 1.

250 The *Ledger* placed the number at fifty; the *Free Press* at over a hundred.

251 P.F. Lawson to Secretary of State, February 10, 1919; Under-secretary of State to Lawson, February 18, 1919. See *District Ledger*, February 28, 1919, 1. The names of the individuals requesting assistance are also found here.

252 *Calgary Daily Herald*, February 21, 1919, 8; Address to shareholders by Elias Rogers, *Twenty-second Annual Report of the Crow's Nest Pass Coal Company (1918)*, 9, GA, Crowsnest Resources Limited Fonds, Crow's Nest Coal Company, Series 3, Annual Reports, M-1561, file 21.

253 *Report of the Minister of Mines 1919*, BCA, British Columbia, Sessional Papers 1920, N349.

254 Allen Seager, "Socialists and Workers: The Western Canadian Coal Miners, 1900–21," *Labour/Le Travail* 16 (Fall 1985): 57, Appendix 2.

255 Michael Pennock, "Joseph Frederick Spalding: Photographer—Tourist—Visionary," in Wayne Norton and Tom Langford (eds.): *A World Apart: The Crowsnest Communities of Alberta and British Columbia*, (Kamloops, BC: Plateau Press, 2002), 83–84; *District Ledger*, July 11, 1919, 4.

256 *Fernie Free Press*, May 23, 1919, 1. Boardman's appointment was delayed until the provincial police promised his replacement in Coal Creek would be a returned serviceman.

257 Joseph Fernie is remembered in Kamloops as the officer responsible for capturing the Bill Miner gang. See Peter Grauer, *Interred With Their Bones: Bill Miner in Canada* (Kamloops, BC: Partners in Publishing, 2006).

258 Bercuson, *Fools and Wise Men*, 92–93; A. Ross McCormack, *Reformers, Rebels and Revolutionaries: The Western Canadian Radical Movement, 1896–1919* (Toronto: University of Toronto Press, 1991, 162.

259 Morris, *The Canadian Patriotic Fund*, 93, 96, 102.

260 Bercuson, *Fools and Wise Men*, 84.

261 Allen Seager, "A Proletariat in Wild Rose Country: The Alberta Coal Miners, 1905–1945," (PhD diss., York University, 1982), 235–57.

262 Bercuson, *Fools and Wise Men*, 136.

263 *Camp Worker*, May 17, 1919, 5.

264 The revolutionary impulse is often given greater emphasis. See, for example, Wesley Morgan, "The One Big Union and the Crowsnest Pass," in *A World Apart: The Crowsnest Communities of Alberta and British Columbia*, eds. Wayne Norton and Tom Langford, (Kamloops, BC: Plateau Press, 2002), 113–19.

265 *Lethbridge Herald*, May 17, 1919, 1; *District Ledger*, May 23, 1919, 1; *Fernie Free Press*, May 23, 1919, 1 and 3. The Gladstone local union voted 385 to 187 against accepting Order 124.

266 Armstrong put the number of those affected at twenty-five; Christophers at approximately two hundred. *Fernie Free Press*, May 23, 1919, 4.

267 Allen Seager, "Socialists and Workers: The Western Canadian Coal Miners, 1900–21," *Labour/Le Travail* 16 (Fall 1985): 27.

268 Gregory S. Kealey, "1919: The Canadian Labour Revolt," *Labour/Le Travail* 12 (Spring 1984): 11–44.

269 *Lethbridge Daily Herald*, May 31, 1919, 1.

270 Report of Inspector Owen, May 1919, BCA, Provincial Police Force, GR-0445, box 51, file 17.

271 John Oliver to W.R. Wilson, June 12, 1919, Glenbow Archives, Crowsnest Resources Limited Fonds, Series 7, M-1561, file 183, Strike of 1918–1919.

272 Elected to the Board of Directors in May 1919, Wilson would become president of the CNPCC just one year later upon the death of Elias Rogers.

273 Cited in *Fernie Free Press*, July 11, 1919, 4.

274 *District Ledger*, June 20, 1919, 4; *District Ledger*, July 18, 1919, 4.

275 Saul Bonnell to Sam Whitehouse, cited in *District Ledger* June 20, 1919, 1.

276 *District Ledger*, July 6, 1919, 1. An old safe from the Ledger office, recently taken to District headquarters in Calgary, attracted much attention during the raid.

277 R.M. Young to William Wilson, July 5, 1919, Glenbow Archives, Crowsnest Resources Limited Fonds, Series 7, M-1561, file 183, Strike of 1918–1919.

278 *Fernie Free Press*, June 20, 1919, 1, 4 and 8; *District Ledger*, June 20, 1919, 1 and 4.

279 Craig Heron, *The Workers' Revolt in Canada, 1917–25* (Toronto: University of Toronto Press, 1998); Gregory S. Kealey, "1919: The Canadian Labour Revolt," *Labour/Le Travail* 12 (Spring 1984): 11–44.

280 The convictions were not sustained. On Whimster's technicality, Judge George Thompson would overturn them all in September. See Deputy Inspector W.

Owen to Superintendent William McMynn, August 1, 1919, BCA, Provincial Police Force, Superintendent, Prohibition Files, GR-1425, box 4, file 23.

281 Kukushkin, *From Peasants to Labourers*, 183.

282 Committee members are all named in the *Fernie Free Press*, July 11, 1919, 1.

283 The community would have to wait five years to unveil its memorial. Like so many others—in communities large and small across Canada—it proclaimed that death in battle was noble and not in vain. For a splendid comparative study of Canadian war memorials, see Jonathan F. Vance, *Death So Noble* (Vancouver: UBC Press, 1987).

284 *Fernie Free Press*, July 18, 1919, 5.

285 Unable to agree even on a detail such as this, the *Ledger* reported one hundred veterans were in the parade, while the *Free Press* recorded the participation of two hundred.

ACKNOWLEDGEMENTS

T his attempt to glimpse life in Fernie a century ago was built upon the generosity and goodwill of many people.

At the very beginning of the process, when I was wondering if sources would prove sufficient, Access Copyright awarded a travel research grant that allowed me to visit archives in Calgary and Fernie. That provided the necessary jumpstart to the project. Without the realization gained from those visits that there was indeed a story to be told—a story even more dynamic than the one I hoped and believed was there—I would not have undertaken to begin this book.

Having undertaken it, there were times when I seemed to find a dozen questions a day with which I needed help. Not for the first time during my forays into Fernie's history, I must particularly thank John Kinnear and Mike Pennock for their profound knowledge of the local past and their willingness to share it. Joe Pozzi proved equally knowledgeable about military matters and equally willing to help. The narrative here would be much weaker without the combined patience and guidance of these three individuals.

At Fernie City Hall, Mary Giuliano and Sheryl Zral willingly allowed access to City records, as did Ron Ulrich to collections held by the Fernie Museum. At the Glenbow Archives in Calgary, Doug Cass was both helpful and encouraging; at the British Columbia Archives, through a series of privacy requests and almost daily visits over two years, every archivist at every turn gave friendly assistance and advice. During various stages of research, assistance was provided by Tim Percival, Tom Langford and Will Langford. Cory Dvorak explored many avenues of enquiry, helping to discover which held promise and which were only blind alleys. Sincere thanks also go to Gwyneth Harkin, Daniel Ste-Marie, Rein Stamm, Robert Campbell, Sarah Beaulieu, Bohdan Kordan, Richard Mackie, Allen Seager, Gregory Evans, Ronald Greene, Brett Uphill, Shirley Haukaas, Jim McIndoe, Frank Mrazik, Phil Greenwood and Shanna Baslee.

I frequently asked colleagues to read the manuscript. These requests were usually premature. Again I am indebted to John Kinnear, Joseph Pozzi, Mike Pennock, and to R.A.J. McDonald and Tom Langford for suggestions and criticisms that made me aware of how much work remained to be done. I am grateful to Vici Johnstone for taking a chance on this book and for all the assistance and advice provided by Caitlin Press in bringing the project to life. Thanks are due particularly to Susan Mayse for the breadth and depth of her editorial suggestions and to Stephen Hume for depicting so splendidly the fleeting optimism that prevailed during the early months of the war.

Finally I want to thank my grandparents, Thomas and Ellen Reid, who had the courage to immigrate to Canada and the good fortune to live in Fernie.

INDEX

W